THE VISCOUS

Fig. 1. Hieronymus Bosch, *Ship of Fools* (1490–1500)

First published in 2020 by punctum books, Earth, Milky Way.
https://punctumbooks.com

ISBN-13: 978-1-950192-86-1 (print)
ISBN-13: 978-1-950192-87-8 (ePDF)

DOI: 10.21983/P3.0292.1.00

LCCN: 2020938074
Library of Congress Cataloging Data is available from the Library of Congress

Book design: Vincent W.J. van Gerven Oei
Cover image: Ania Mokrzycka, *Touching Lamella*, 2015

HIC SVNT MONSTRA

Freddie
Mason

The Viscous

Slime
Stickiness
Fondling
Mixtures

p.

Contents

Acknowledgments

Everyone has something to say about the viscous. More often than not, the writing contained here found its inspiration in the spontaneous, profound, mostly involuntary, observations made by the numerous friends, teachers, relatives, and acquaintances I engaged in conversation with over the issue of sliminess. These invisible guidances, pretty much impossible to reference, are the bedrock for the semi-solid growths herein. I'd like to thank, in no particular order: Christopher Morris, Brian Dillon, Steven Connor, Oscar Hudson, Francesca Alderuccio, India Harvey, Yasmine Seal, Jeremy Millar, Tomas Weber, Matt Phillips, Xavier Buxton, Nadja Voorham, Elizabeth Atkinson, Isabelle Held, Nathanial Kochen, Lise Thiollier, Biu Rainey, Philippa Scoones, Georgia Mason, Toby Buxton, Hatty Nestor, Merlin Sheldrake, John Dewitt, Leila Arenou, Julieta Garcia-Vazquez, Tom Graham, Aliya Ram, Oona Brown, Chantal Faust, Ella Fleck, Bryony James, Camille Yvert, Royal Aghamirzada, Yvo Fitzherbert, Butuney Hagverdiyev, Rebecca Maybury, Catherine Malabou, Esther Leslie, Alexander Hawthorne, Oscar Oldershaw, Laura Dee Milnes, Frances Morgan, Victoria Kaldan, Sarah Kelly, Tamu Nkiwane, Rebecca Salvadori, George Fitzherbert. A special thank you goes to Jazbo Gross, a true psychologist of semi-states and to Petra Casale for whom nothing will ever be gooey enough. Thank you also to Eileen A. Fradenburg Joy and Vincent W.J. van Gerven Oei for bringing this work to the light of day.

In memory of M.M., who, thank god, would not have approved

Introduction

Galaxies

In June 2018, the news from astronomers we had all been waiting for hit the press. It was not the huge subterranean lake of water they found on Mars. That, in any case, was found a month later in July. It was not the conditions for the possibility for extra-terrestrial life this water offered. No, it was something much more subtly transformative, a seemingly negligible alteration in the cosmological layout of things that was, like all of the most important upheavals, curiously astounding and then almost immediately unremarkable. Here is that landmark moment, using all the typographic emphases at my disposal to facilitate full absorption:

OUTER SPACE IS FULL OF GREASE.[1]

"Yeah, so?" a friend of mine said when I excitedly messaged her the headline. "It's massive, the universe, I'm not surprised, I'm

---

1 This discovery was widely reported in the mainstream press. The official article is, however, B. Güway et al., "Aliphatic Hydrocarbon Content of Interstellar Dust," *Monthly Notices of the Royal Astronomical Society* 479, no. 4 (October 1, 2018): 4336–44.

sure there's lots of stuff up there." True, the universe is massive: the 10 billion trillion trillion tonnes of gloop, enough for 40 trillion trillion trillion packs of butter, they claim to be dispersed until now imperceptibly through the voidish space really is just another day in those innumerable light years of the Milky Way. Future space ships traveling through interstellar space should expect to return lightly coated in hydrogen bound up with carbon in a grease-like form, a kind of naphthalene. I can almost see before me now the alien smear marks wiped off the surface of a large, smooth intergalactic phallus, squeezed out of a sponge into a plastic tub full of warm soapy water. Space grease: so what?

Like me, Hegel thought the stars were boring. They meant much less to him than a rash on a body, or an ant colony for that matter, which exhibits "intelligence and necessity." They are much less interesting than animality, even if that animality presents "nothing but jelly." The host of stars is an abstraction, this jelly is concrete, something we would be wrong to see as inferior to the heavens above. The passage from liquidity to sliminess was, for Hegel, a passage from the abstract to the concrete. The earth excretes the "abstractness of its fresh water," which hurries forth towards "concrete animation" in the sea. As the sea blooms in the summer months, it becomes turbid and slimy, yet full of a "multitude of vegetable points, threads and surfaces." This gelatinous slime takes on more determinate formations, "fusorial animalcula, transparent molusca," and contains a tendency to break out in "vast expanses of phosphorescent light." This momentary gelatinous existence cannot hold light, Hegel imagines, in the form of selfhood, so identity instead breaks out if itself as physical light, "densely crowded into galaxies."[2] An organic, jellied, submarine cosmos, *smelly yet glistening* — this is more real to Hegel than the stars.

In more recent times, it is extremely common, though somehow forgettably so, for us to imagine the starlight excreting

2   G.W.F. Hegel, *Philosophy of Nature Vol. III,* trans. and ed. M.J. Petry (London: Allen and Unwin, 2013), 36–38.

some goo-like substance. The popular imaginary of extra-ter-restrial encounter is almost always an encounter with a being of, if not total blobbiness, a corporeality of considerably intensified tremulousness.[3] With a few exceptions, opening a can of baked beans has more in common with how people tend, or tended, to imagine a meeting with the third kind than what scientists might be able to predict. The life forms on Earth chosen by the popular imagination as most likely to have come from the celes-tial are generally the jellied ones. This is perhaps because these creatures form bioluminescent aggregates that seem to mimic the cosmos. But also because jelly is a substance that while being most undoubtedly and cloyingly there, is something that speaks of the beyond, its texture is the texture of the "other." Which is, as much psychoanalysis teaches us, also the texture of our interior.

Stuff worming through the starlight is an intimation of the gruesome core of our supposedly most transcendent moments. In the 1955 horror B-movie The Blob, the kiss that initiates the film's love story is not seen on screen. Instead we have the cliché of the camera giving the lovers some privacy, turning its view gently towards the stars. The one shooting star we witness as a symbol of the kindling love, is also, as we find out soon, the coming to Earth of this viscous mass, the blob. What might we find in this monstrous starlight? The story is an old one — the struggle between spiritual love and carnal lust; what might feel like a celestial explosion of love in a man's heart is just his need to ejaculate. This we may know already. But now we have learnt that the cosmos is actually full of grease, does anything change? It is not monstrous, not transcendent, not recognizably intel-ligent, not "other," just ever so slightly buttery. Dare I ask — are things now more *real*?

It is not, either, unusual for us — as humans — to imagine the cosmos, or galaxy, as related in some way to emulsified

3   Mike Kelley writes about this is in "On the Aesthetics of Ufology," *Blastitude* 13 (August 13, 2002), http://www.blastitude.com/13/ETERNITY/ufology_kelley.htm.

dairy products. The Milky Way finds its mythological origin in Hermes suckling the infant Heracles at the breast of the sleeping Athena who, on awakening, pulls Heracles away, splattering milk through the heavens. In Hindu cosmology, the Ocean of Milk was the substance that separated directional space from non-directional space. Until, that is, one day the devas and the asuras straightened out a snake and used it to churn the ocean for a millennium until it curdled and released Amrita, the nectar of immortal life.[4] Milk is a substance of origins not only as, most likely, the first food to pass over our tongue, but also as something that can curdle, its body cracking open into differentiated being: cheese.

The grease in outer space belongs to a familiar realm, then: mythologies of emulsions, oozings of starlight. But these imaginaries are also strangely terminated by the revelations of a greasy universe. A viscous outer space becomes bathetically literal, rather than mythological. The awesome expanse of the void is normalized, brought into thrilling union with the interior walls of my oven. Grease in space? Exactly! "So what?" I realized — at long last, some information about the universe that isn't unutterably sublime, one that leaves me staring affectionately into my fridge, some imagery which *cannot* in any way be used to sell me broadband. It is this everydayness of the viscous, its normalizing powers that live simultaneously beside its presence as carnal horror, or its mythology, that I hope to persistently haunt this writing on its substance that follows.

Birds

For if we look for an origin to the viscous, it is in fact a trap, a trap specifically used for birds. Etymologically speaking, "viscous" comes from the Latin word *viscum* meaning "mistletoe," but also the sticky excretions produced by this plant that were extracted, then smeared onto branches as "birdlime." The birds

---

4   George M. Williams, *Handbook of Hindu Mythology* (Oxford: Oxford University Press, 2013), 53.

would land on the branch and find themselves stuck, before being yanked off and cooked. Would they break at the knees? I wonder if this is the reason we're meant to kiss underneath mistletoe at Christmas time, to inspire a particularly glutinous adhesion of the lips, the soul, the heart.

To ensnare you in things is the viscous way. The fact that you're struggling for freedom only ensnares you further is its irony. This entrapment through an enraging indifference, a maddening docility, is dramatized in the Bre'r Rabbit stories. The wolf, Bre'r Rabbit's nemesis, constructs a doll out of tar, dresses it in clothes and places it by the side of a road he knows Bre'r Rabbit will pass. When Bre'r Rabbit does indeed pass the baby, he greets the doll, but gets no response. Offended by the figure's apparent lack of manners, he greets him again, again being met with silence. Increasingly insulted to the apparent indifference to him, Bre'r Rabbit strikes the figure, getting stuck in its tar. As he strikes and struggles further, he is gradually consumed by the tar baby, left immobilized on the road side, before the wolf comes to gleefully bundle him up to cook.[5]

The bird caught in this *viscum* has been imagined by theologians like Saint Augustine as the predicament of mankind:

> Increase, O Lord, thy graces more and more upon me, that my soul may follow myself home to thee, wholly freed from the birdlime of concupiscence.[6]

For birdlime shares something with the results of his shame, Augustine's semen — stickiness: the quality of matter that binds

---

5   The story of the tar baby has deep significance for images of "blackness" in American and colonial race relations, something that goes beyond what is possible to discuss here. For insight into to this aspect of tar, see Marcus Woods's film made with Richard Misek, *High Tar Babies,* from 2001 (see Richard Misek, "High Tar Babies," *Vimeo,* September 10, 2013, https://vimeo.com/74189761). The film is accompanied by paintings, documented in Marcus Wood, *High Tar Babies: Race, Hatred, Slavery, Love* (London: Clinamen Press, 2001) .

6   Saint Augustine, *Confessions,* trans. William Watts (Cambridge: Harvard University Press, 1979), 153.

him to sin, which also reduces the bird's wings to useless flaps, no longer used to ascend. Wet dreams, Augustine wonders in this passage, might be considered a kind of rape, one caused by the soul's agglutination in the body. *Viscum* navigated into the Latin *viscus,* a word of ambiguous meaning, certainly involving the body, sometimes specifically the external parts of the genitalia, connective tissue between muscle and bone, the bladder, a kind of sausage, and sometimes all at the same time.[7]

To feel something *viscerally* is to feel it in the guts. To remove the organs, to empty something of meaning, is to *eviscerate*. And it is by some gut feeling that we are most likely satisfied with the fact that birdlime came to mean the *viscera,* and then onwards to *the viscous,* everything that is neither solid nor liquid, not one thing, but rather a quality of resistance and of flow, of stickiness and of slipperiness. *Because it is sticky* seems like justification enough. It spreads through likeness like magical thinking. The viscous is a bird trap, but also somewhere where we are prone to take flight into a myriad of different discrete worlds and objects, all in one way completely unrelated, yet in another all occupants of that one alluring aversion. To touch something sticky is to be sent out into an indeterminate network of other sticky things — dog's noses, the walls of caves, slugs, toothpaste, sugar syrup, sweaty palms. That is not to say that all these things are in anyway the same. No. One of the things I want to do with the viscous is to unfold its manifold articulations. And it is not, either, to say that we should allow these linkages to form thoughtlessly, without efforts to disassociate them. But *because they are sticky,* they associate, it seems, whether we like it or not. It is in this kind of web of association, at once deeply felt and wholly superficial, that the viscous traps us. It is something we are obliged to deal with when dealing with this matter.

7   Robert Renehan, "Viscum/Viscus," *Harvard Studies in Classical Philology* 84 (1980): 279–82, at 281.

The World

To be more involved with the world than we would like, or think we should be, is often the sensation theorized to be at the heart of the viscous encounter. It is an affront to an ethics, puts things out of whack, disturbs the sense we serenely construct of "things" on the one hand and "me" on the other. As Sartre famously theorizes in a passage of writing that forms an important basis for this book and which I will discuss at length in chapter one, to touch slime is to risk, it feels, *becoming* slime.[8] What is crucial, here, is the elongated sense of risk the viscous excites. At the core of this sensation is the fact that we never become slime, but continue feeling that we might. The slimy encounter locks us into a state of becoming, or rather the becoming of an un-becoming. We start to wonder that maybe there is no "world," just a monstrous congregation of different matters and textures, variously throbbing.

The Sartrean viscous is the site of a power struggle between the for-itself and the in-itself. During particular moments in our lives, the viscous can seem to take over. When we stop having ideas, during times of depression perhaps, the world can coalesce into singularity, become nothing but mass, density. But, as I will elaborate, this coalescence is, for Sartre, one also of intense excitement and adventure. It is simultaneously a vertiginous feeling, where rules feel as if they might be re-written. The task of his writing is to bring these two states of being into as close proximity as possible, without ever letting them merge.

Sartre's conception and description of the viscous has been immensely influential, and its effects can be traced through much subsequent writing on materiality. Bachelard responds to it first in *Earth and the Reveries of Will: An Essay on the Imagination of Matter,* where viscous matter is opened outwards not only as a threat, but as a site where different convictions and

8   Jean-Paul Sartre, *Being and Nothingness: A Phenomenological Essay on Ontology,* trans. Hazel E. Barnes (Washington: Washington Square Press, 1992), 610.

ideals might play out. The viscous can also be, for Bachelard, a moment of harmony, of deep satisfaction, an ideal coexistence of the soft and the hard. He, as opposed to Sartre, is more interested in the playful and oneiric states of mind that emerge out of the numerous practical applications of viscous semi-states, which he sees Sartre as having ignored in favor of this dreadful, needy, leechlike "feminine sucking."[9] And then there is also the explicit misogyny and fear of sex in Sartre's writing that Bachelard doesn't appear to share. In chapter one, I will attempt a reading of Sartre's blatant reduction of "femininity" to "slime" as also containing a way to escape such essentialism.

Sartre's writing on the sensation and processes where the distinction between the self and world might become confused, though not entirely erased, is at the heart of many contemporary discourses on issues such as ecology, technology and gender. In chapter two, "Sticky Words/Sticky Worlds," I will show how the dynamics of sliminess that Sartre identifies have become fundamental tools by which new philosophies of ecology are able to function. In chapter three, "Smear Screens and Fondled Things," Sartre's writing, as it is refracted through Bachelard, can offer useful starting points to thinking about media technology, specifically digital visual interfaces. And in chapter four, I hope to expose how the Sartrean viscous has been turned on its head, which is also, paradoxically, a realization of want it yearned for, in a contemporary work of gender theory, *Testo Junkie,* a work that takes the dizziness that Sartre feels and runs, finding in it an immense realm of volatile, subversive pharmacological possibility.

That is not to say, however, that the Sartrean viscous is in anyway the sole driving definition of what follows. For my writing on the viscous, I have used a multitude of different sources and domains for instruction, insight and guidance, often finding the most inspiration in places that are far removed from what we might call theory, art practices or literature. In chapter one, the Boston Molasses Disaster of 1919, a moment when a huge indus-

9   Ibid., 609.

trial molasses tank spontaneously burst, engulfing the people and buildings of its surroundings, constitutes our enigmatic entrance into a contemplation of what slime is when it meets the urban. The journalism of this moment seems to me a perfect introduction to the power of the viscous both in actuality and as an imaginative moment. Chapter two finds its origins in a trip I made to an asphalt lake in Baku, Azerbaijan, the "home" of petroleum oil. Chapter three is interested, primarily, in the digital, but found its opening into this region of experience and technology through the viral videos of teenagers playing with homemade slime on online platforms such as Instagram. Chapter four is a theorization of colloidal structures of matter — emulsions, gels, sols — that occurred to me as a possibility as I was making mayonnaise one day. These events — in the world, but always a troubling of what exactly that is — occurred at specific times and places and are the points from which I hoped and hope to take flight.

I want to approach these events as philosophical in themselves, as part of a perspective on philosophy that is slightly deviant. Although I use and discuss philosophers throughout what follows, I am not a philosopher and this is not a work of philosophy in any systematic or traditional sense. The viscous has an important philosophical tradition, and I am most interested in *how* the philosophers have felt it necessary to write about its stuff or idea, rather than solely the philosophical content of their work. I am interested in the kinds of expressive postures the viscous forces us to pull.

But the most important thought I've had while researching and writing the viscous is this: the viscous doesn't exist. It isn't a thing, nor is it anything. And if it is a thing, it is troubled, as I will discuss in just a moment. It is a quality of resistance and of flow, of stickiness and of slipperiness. But it is also many others: stretchiness, trembling, or its deeper version, shuddering. The list, as I see it, unfolds indefinitely. The viscous is an impossible state of matter, a fantasy, a fancy, one that extrudes itself from and attaches itself, at various moments, to reality. There is an unstable distinction between "slime" on the one hand, and the "viscous" on the other. Where the viscous doesn't exist as anything, "slime" does, but only slightly. Slime is the viscous edging into existence. Still a fantasy, still a fantastical matter, but unlike the viscous, it can be pointed to as an object in the world, in toy shops and in B-movies. But it is held in a state of retreat into the imaginary, stuff slipping into dream. Both the viscous and slime are dubious states of matter that dissolve eagerly into an operation of thought, a way of being and of feeling.

Beyond Flow

Brie is not shampoo. Just as wax is not chainsaw oil, *in the same way* that mayonnaise is not quicksand. But we might describe all these things, to a greater or lesser extent, as viscous. They occupy a common liminal space between solid and liquid, a space in which the manifold, sometimes contradictory, deviant material qualities of "the viscous" might be said to congregate. What makes the viscous so useful, so joyful, is that it is a site of abundance, it means far too much.

In grouping these substances together — brie, shampoo, oil, mayonnaise, quicksand — we are undertaking a particular study of matter, one that is attuned to the quality of its flow, the way it moves or creeps under pressure, whether spread across a surface or rubbed between the hands, dripped onto a table top, or used to lube up the mechanics of a machine. The study we are undertaking is what science calls rheology, a term coined by the American chemist Eugene Bingham in the 1920s. And something we learn from the science of rheology is something we all already, intuitively might know: that there is no such thing as pure flow. Or rather, there is no such thing as a linear continuum between solid things and liquid things, where substances get progressively more fluid until they reach an absolute state of fluidity, before puffing off into vapor. From within the fantasy trinity of solid–liquid–gas erupt all number of stickinesses, seizures, sudden stretchinesses, squirmings, slushinesses, shudderings, bouncings that overcome and engulf this tripartite system.

Scientists have managed, however, to produce a liquid that possess almost no viscosity at all. Helium liquefies when cooled to just above absolute zero, producing a liquid with little to no internal friction that exhibits bizarre and perhaps unexpected properties. It will drain out of a glass beaker, slipping its way through the microscopic holes in its structure. If placed in a special container, out of which it cannot drain, it will climb the walls, gushing out over the lip. This is a material intent on exceeding all containment. It has left the world of molecules and has begun obeying the laws of the quantum.[10]

Liquid helium to one side, the study of rheology has developed ways of modeling and understanding what we might call the deviance of viscous matter by dividing it into groups. We have viscoplastics, materials that accept and record form from outside influence, and we have viscoelastics, ones that accept influence, but try to hold their form, springing back to their former mode as soon as the force has stopped. We have linear and non-linear viscous materials. Linear viscous substances behave consistently regardless of how much force you impose on them. The sweet, non-toxic viscous fluid glycerol is an example of a linear substance. So is motor oil. Non-linear viscous substances change their state depending on the forces they encounter. When you pour oobleck (cornstarch mixed with water) slowly out of a container, it emerges gradually and flows out sleepily. Punch a tub of it or run across a whole lake of it, and the substance will repel you from its surface, holding your weight as you run. The same is true of a ball of bitumen. Leave it on a tabletop and it will "creep" into a puddle. Throw it against a wall and it will bounce back, exhibiting a resilience to changing form that puts most solids to shame. Matter that resists the exertions

---

10 Although the phenomenon of liquid helium has been well covered, I have in mind here a specific film made by scientist Alfred Leitner in 1963, *Liquid Helium II: The Superfluid* (see Brett Sylvester Matulis, "Liquid Helium III: The Superfluid," *Vimeo,* March 31, 2010, https://vimeo.com/10579813), a film that possesses significance for endurance athlete Christopher Bergland, as I will discuss in chapter two.

the world places on it are called thixotropic. Rheopectic matter relents, thinning out as force is applied, as ketchup does.[11]

But the models only go so far, the qualities of the viscous over-spilling its parameters into what is termed *texture,* the baroque interplay between a specific set of different seizures, slippages, raspings, etc. into something like a sensual singularity, the feel of a substance. Texture is the great excess.

The Heraclitean *panta rhei* uses the metaphor of the river. Water is, of course, the substance that is most commonly used as the metaphorical basis for notions of constant flux. But if we look into the physics of water it can become an almost monstrously sticky, gooey thing, with all number of clingy attributes. We have probably all experienced the way water seizes itself ever so slightly to the end of your finger when you press one down gently onto its surface. Or there is the way it is able to syphon its way over an object of any size as if it were the tentacle of come colossal squid. We see this sticky power, too, in its ability to stretch between the lips of two glasses pulled apart. The scientist Gerald H. Pollack has for some years (and not uncontroversially) been forwarding the theory that water has in fact a fourth phase, a gel phase, that modern science has almost entirely overlooked and which is responsible for many of the things that still mystify the science community about H_2O.[12] I am no scientist and have no research to counter or support Pollack's theories, but what I am interested in is how our imagination of materials can suddenly change, how what we might have always felt to be an undoubtedly fluid medium, might in fact (also) be sticky. And that its stickiness, its jellied state, is, it turns out, fundamental to its ability to support complex life. I am not in any way

11 I am not able to ever claim anything more than a superficial technical understanding of the immensely complex science of rheology. The definitions I use have mostly been derived from R.I. Tanner and K. Watts, *Rheology: An Historical Perspective* (London: Elsevier Science, 1998).

12 G.H. Pollack's books and articles on this subject are numerous, but most accessible to the reader, like me, from a non-technical background is *The Fourth Phase of Water: Beyond Solid, Liquid, Vapour* (Seattle: Ebner and Sons, 2013).

proposing science to have the answers to all our questions. It is, however a good place to start when disturbing the ideals of the material states whose textures and behaviors that hold so much power — and I mean this in a purely imaginative sense — over the ways we choose to live our lives: the metaphors we live by. This is something, of course, that greatly exceeds the scientific remit. *How* can water be sticky? What kinds of trouble does this idea cause?

Something else that rheology teaches us is that a substance's viscosity is never fully on display. All materials change their quality depending on how you interact with them; viscosity is a relational event. As I've said, thixotropic materials thin out as you spread them across a slice of toast, rheopectics seize up when you punch them. There is also that danger of breaking your back when jumping into water from a great height. Water, if you fall at it fast enough, becomes concrete. Slippery objects are also almost always sticky, fastening you securely to their surface, before moving you around crazily on it. The qualities that are expressed depend on how we move towards and within the substance. But that is not to say that it is all about different types of approach, it is not all relational. Viscosity is about the *disposition* of materials, the different ways materials are indeterminately disposed to act in and on the world. Rather than talk about material qualities, we should instead talk about their tendencies, tendencies to imperceptibly thicken until movement is no longer possible, or turn on a heel, reversing the rules of the game.

To help understand this notion of tendencies, we might want to turn to social theory that understands properties or outcomes as emerging through a complex of relations, rather than having their source in any one person, event, etc. Keller Easterling, in his book *Extrastatecraft: The Power of Infrastructure Space,* is similarly interested in the notion of disposition, from an infrastructural point of view. In the

fluid politics of extra-statecraft, disposition uncovers accidental, covert or stubborn forms of power — political chemistries and temperaments of aggression, submission or violence.[13]

The "fluid politics of extra-statecraft" are, for instance, the seamless cycles of novelty and innovation that keep buyers interested, but not disoriented. This might be things like planned obsolescence, which allows for the continual renewal of content without any fundamental change. In Easterling's conception, there is something that lives beyond, yet within, this flow, once it is seen from point of view of dispositions, a potential to seize up and snag. Thinking with the viscous is about unearthing and cherishing (not without suspicion) like forbidden jewels these hidden seizures.

Containers

The viscous puts pressure on our powers of description, our critical capacities, the ability we might see ourselves as having to research something and then write about it. It is about the creep of thinking. Its dispositions threaten any lovingly crafted network of knowledge with a collapse into mess. What mess is, how it occurs, is an on going concern of this writing. These questions have preoccupied me: is mess inevitable? If so, how can we accept the inevitability of mess without being useless? Is it possible to be messy and not totally useless? Or is mess, in fact, the outcome of being useful?[14]

It might be best, then, to view the four independent sections of writing that follow this introductory one, as something like containers, vats, cans, whose to potential to burst outwards is, I

13 Keller Easterling, *Extrastatecraft: The Power of Infrastructure Space* (London: Verso, 2014), 73.
14 Some key texts that have guided me in my inquiries into how to think with rather than against mess: John Law, *After Method: Mess in Social Theory* (New York: Taylor and Francis, 2004). A work of social and literary history which has also helped me conceptualize mess is David Trotter, *Cooking with Mud: Ideas of Mess in Nineteenth Century Art and Fiction* (Oxford: Oxford University Press, 2000).

hope, intensely present. But they are chapters and they remain so, composed most often through heterogeneous mixtures of material that try in different ways to become intimate with specific places, materials, thinkings, and feelings that possess an affinity with particular viscous dynamics of matter.

Dynamics are how tendencies manifest themselves. The viscous is a set of dynamics that are never all exhibited at once, but gather awkwardly under its sign. I do not hope to provide an exhaustive list of viscous dynamics, nor do I attempt to come up with a precise working definition of which dynamics are viscous and which are not. To do so would kill our understanding of this kind of matter dead. But something they all share is a discontinuity contained within their mobility. Their movements are clustered with resistance. They are complex, hesitant, doubtful. Their interactions are never perfect or fully complete. Bursting, for instance, which I will discuss in my first chapter, is comparable to an explosion, but integral to its dynamic are a variety of resistances of matter — the straining against pressure before the ultimate giving-way, or the matter we might find *lingering on* after a burst has taken place. Each of the four chapters has a specific viscous dynamic lurking as its core, whose outlines I will give some definition to now, definition that will inevitably become flipped, shaken and smeared along the way. That is, if they no longer feel right, or have been left to sit too long, acquiring that taste water acquires when its been un-drunk during the night.

The first is something I will term *indifference,* a condition addressed in chapter one. Viscous matter is, it feels, part-less, every bit of it is the same as every other bit. Viscous matter is, if we use an Aristotelian term, homoeomerous, a word which refers to substances whose identity stays the same however many times you divide them, the whole and part being "synonymous."[15] Water might be defined, for instance, to a certain extent as homoe-

15   Aristotle, "On Generation and Corruption," trans. H.H. Joachim, in *The Complete Works of Aristotle,* ed. Jonathan Barnes (Princeton: Princeton University Press, 1984), 512.

omerous: divide some water in two and you have two separate bits of water, the identity is consistent. The eye is anhomoeomerous: divide the eye and you get two halves of an eye, with different identities from eyes. The problems and exact details of Aristotle's conception of homoeomerous matter is the subject of philosophical debate. On what terms, for instance, do you define something's "wholeness"? But this is not something we will pursue at great length here. Rather, the notion of homoeomerous matter, not limited only to gooey things, helps us describe viscous matter. The viscous feels actively homoeomerous, a substance composed of sameness that wants, through some mysterious internal energy, to make everything around it the same as well. This non-differentiated interior is then expressed as an apparent indifference to whatever might surround it, driven by pure directionless want; its project is one of pure appropriation. This is the basis of the imaginary of the slime monster — it doesn't care what it eats as long as it keeps on eating, it will turn anything, somehow, into itself. But as I hope to expose in chapter one, from this state of indifference, we find a very particular drama of roaming specificity — reachings out into momentary specificity before plunging back into an indifferent whole.

Stickiness is also a fundamental viscous dynamic. It is a particular quality of adhesion that is internally undoing. Its enthusiasm for attachment continually undoes its attachments. Stickiness is persistently unpredictable, the bonds it forms, unlike loops, clasps and knots, necessarily finite and breakable. Attachment is more important to stickiness than the purposes or outcome of that attachment. A struggle of thinking with the viscous is not to try to repress or pacify its arbitrary adhesive tendencies, but to move with them, describe them, attune oneself to their indifference to meaning. This poses a huge challenge to the composition of this book — how to remain true to the bloody minded, insouciant, superficial, needy attributes of viscous matter, without becoming exactly that myself? And thereby producing something that is boring to read. The answer lies, I think, in the poise of the writing that accepts, even welcomes, these attributes, while never mistaking them for the whole of reality.

But this is, crucially, a mistake the viscous wants you to make. The viscous is, at times, the energy by which things, tiny details, creep outwards, consuming you, obsessing you, becoming the entirety of your world. In chapter two, I will trace different kinds of thinking, feeling and being that have involved, for better or for worse, in an attachment to stickiness.

Fondling is the third main activity and concept of this work. It stands for a kind of viscous encounter that is, in many ways, of a different category from the former two. When fondled, the viscous is softer, comforting, not threatening, not cloying, but doughy-eyed and cute. In the story of these semi-states, the fondled is an instance of the unruly powers of viscous matter tempered into submission. This is something Sartre doesn't seem to contemplate. What allegiances with other things have to be forged for this to happen? Of particular interest to this study is the phenomenon of Instagram slime: short clips of teenage hands fondling homemade slime on the internet. What can we learn about the status of digital technology from the emergence of this craze?

The last of the chapters concerns *mixtures,* the way in which most gloops are colloids, minute dispersions of two substances within each other that have to be worked, stirred, whipped-up into life. How the viscous might operate as a technology is a persistent interest of this book. In colloids, we find the viscous in its most technologized and technologizable state. It is the place where gooeyness might be designed. Through mixtures we find introduction to two other key dynamics, the dynamics of coagulation and coalescence. Colloids are, then, the tight maintenance of two substances in a state of inter-dispersal, always in the risk of an internal collapse into singularity, or the complete separation into difference. It is in colloids that we also find the viscous as a technology of mingling, of intimacy. If gloop is associated with obscurity, mess, blur, we have in colloids the viscous as also a substance that provides the very possibility of connection. This is, however, an unruly and fragile cohesion, one that lives off of its powers to fall apart, coagulate.

Life

The viscous is adhesive, it is excitable, yet it is slow, lingering. It has trouble getting to the point, but it loves the attention and will try to hold it for as long as it can. And it may have already become apparent, irritating even, that I often refer to this stuff as if it were a person with wants, intents, ambitions, confusions, moods, opinions, and so on. I justify this in two ways. First of all, this is something I've found that happens anyway in other attempts to work with or describe gooey matter. In senses that are phenomenological, biological, and technological, viscous matter often plays with our sense of aliveness. Rather than something I've invented, it is already part of its experience. As a means of getting closer to the material, rather than repress this impulse, I've chosen to follow and sometimes exaggerate it, involving myself in its allure.

But this is also an approach I've actively synthesized for myself, a kind of writing that allows for agency in material qualities to be not just metaphors for states of mind, but operators in and on the world. "Thing-power" has gathered momentum in recent years, thanks to the work of Bruno Latour and the various theories that have stemmed from actor–network theory.[16] My writing is not, however, about things, but a bundle of disparate qualities, that might and also might not be ascribed to particular objects. My question, then, is not so much about the generative power of things as they exist between people, but of material qualities as they exist between objects, people and things. I prefer to see this as an expanding of the power of metaphors, rather than a rejection of them.

All of this comes to pass as if we come to life in a universe where feelings and acts are all charged with something mate-

---

16 I'm thinking here primarily of the influential text by Jane Bennett, *Vibrant Matter: A Political Ecology of Things* (Durham: Duke University Press, 2010).

rial, have a substantial stuff, are really soft, dull, slimy, low, elevated etc.[17]

So says Sartre in the concluding pages of *Being and Nothingness*. His observation is a foundational notion of the "material imagination," a termed coined by his contemporary Gaston Bachelard, that holds there to be a certain continuity between the ways matter behaves and our imaginative processes.[18] This is not only limited to how we might imagine materials, but the materiality of the imagination itself, the way in which material transformations seem to condition how our thoughts "unfold," or don't. The "material imagination" has seen some exciting applications and refashionings by contemporary writers and theorists, notably Esther Leslie and Steven Connor, whose work has had major influence on my attempts at reading viscous materials. What we learn from these four writers is that the dynamics of matter, whether it bursts, trembles, sticks, shimmers or pulls is always as well an imaginative event.

Yesterday, I cleaned the window in the room where I've been working lately. I did a good job; the glass is completely free of marks and dust. Right now, I feel like I'm thinking quite clearly, managing to get the introduction written. The clean window and my managing to write suddenly find companionship. What's going on here exactly? We might assume that I've simply found a rather dull and extremely unimaginative way of describing my state of mind with the glass of the window in front of me. The slimier way to see things, however, is to consider the possibility that something much weirder is going on. Is there some material, non-human, link between the glass in the window and the feeling I have now? Is there some hidden slimy solidarity between being able to write and this glass over which we, as humans — even though we have constructed situations in which to

---

17 Sartre, *Being and Nothingness*, 605
18 Gaston Bachelard, *Earth and the Reveries of Will: An Essay On the Imagination of Matter,* trans. Kenneth Haltman (Dallas: The Dallas Institute Publications, 2002).

experience it — have no say? This is the implication of Sartre's speculation: my feeling somehow *charged* with the glass. Metaphors become momentary insights into a meshwork of material qualities that by day correspond to our will, but at night secretly migrate between bodies and brains, things and thoughts, creep across the border to get married.[19] Here, I am not so interested in whether or not this meshwork, these secret marriages or slimy solidarities actually exist, but rather what their feeling has made people do.

My work is on the viscous as it is both materially and imaginatively composed. But it is also about the tyranny of so-called "materiality," that is, the way in which this word, "materiality," has become something of a fetish, as if finding the material bases or "analogue" to something, some thought, were an end in itself. Or, there is the stranger tendency to try and find in materials ethical instruction on how to live. This is the idea that in the real properties of completely un-idealized matter we might find some "way of being" that is preferable to how we are now, whatever that might be. In this work, material states are, instead, always deeply ideological. The ways viscous matter is perceived, used, manipulated, twisted, engineered, felt, ignored, managed, and described are all traces of particular convictions, values, and worldviews. The dizziness of its repulsive allure can be at times, rather than a grounding in the materiality of "here and now," a state of mind that shuffles towards the utopian, as I will explore in chapter one. The viscous holds, for sure, a silent wonder.

But what do I mean, exactly, by "dynamics"? In using this word "dynamic," I am thinking in line with Daniel Sterns's use of the term as something that describes an activity in things that spreads itself between modalities. As he says in *Forms of Vitality*, experiences of bursting, pulsing, fading, are

19 This is an image used by Bruno Latour, *We Have Never Been Modern*, trans. Catherine Porter (Cambridge: Harvard University Press, 1993,) 6: "The tiny networks we have unfolded are torn apart like the Kurds by the Iranians, the Iraqis and the Turks; once night has fallen, they slip across the border to get married."

not sensations in the strict sense, as they have no modality. They are not direct cognitions in any usual sense. They are not acts as they have no goal state and specific means. They are the felt experience of force — in movement — with a temporal contour, and a sense of aliveness, of going somewhere.[20]

The story of this writing is a story from indifference to articulation. The viscous, while remaining viscous, shifts from being an amorphous blob threatening to ingest you to something of such delicate articulation that only appears indifferent. Everything and nothing changes. It poses, therefore, oblique questions to our conceptions of mechanization.

Technology

As I've said, the viscous has a troubled relationship with thingness. The mollusc, as Francis Ponge says, "is a thing — but almost a quality."[21] We might think of viscous objects as resisting thingness in their refusal to be neatly pocketed, used, bought sold, collected, arranged. These can all be considered the world-making attributes of things, things that connect us to the world, to our sense of ourselves, things we think through, the objects of our thought. Mucus, shit, and sludge, for instance, are not like this, they don't readily compose a world of activities and possibilities. They too easily make a mess, spread themselves maddeningly onto everything and reduce us to nothing but scrubbers. All powers of delicate articulation are denied as our hands, in a pot of some goo, acquire all the dexterity of cheeks.[22]

But as every exclamation of B-movie horror betrays — WHAT IS THAT...THAT *THING?!* — the slimy object is also the "thing" par excellence. As we've learnt from Bill Brown, things are objects whose objecthood has gone weird, gained access to our

20 Daniel Stern, *Forms of Vitality: Exploring Dynamic Experience in Psychology and the Arts* (Oxford: Oxford University Press, 2010), 8.
21 Francis Ponge, *Unfinished Ode to Mud,* trans. Beverley Bie Brahic (London: CB Editions, 2008), 19.
22 Bachelard, *Earth and the Reveries of Will,* 91.

35

souls, when their "flow within the circuits of production and distribution, consumption and exhibition has been arrested."[23] As Steven Connor observes, the weirdness of things comes into presence through us secreting part of ourselves into them, that part being, paradoxically, the capacity to be enigmatically "other." "Just like me in my otherness," is the paradox of the thing. Thingness comes to life when the object starts to resemble the subject

> not in sharing its particular powers or capacities, but in exhibiting the power of resistance or reserve, the power to withdraw or withhold itself from being known.[24]

The thing adheres to us while simultaneously withdrawing, just as a gooey toy might fasten itself to your finger, stretch outwards with it, to then suddenly relent, detach, recoiling back into its body. The slimy thing, then, performs its own thingness within its material behavior.

But it is this dubious status of the slimy object that may make it difficult to imagine as a kind of technology. Viscous technology might seem like squaring the circle, turning the very definition of the unarticulated, amorphous, negligible, messy matter into something with function, processes, repeatable maneuvers. But its substance as it squirms, shudders, and smears is a technologized state of matter, one that is becoming more and more so. As I will discuss in most depth in the last two chapters, viscous matter can be seen as containing extremely powerful kinds of articulation, the first (in the order I address them) being the liquid crystalline phase, a semi-solid state that, depending on its arrangement and the electrical currents passed through it, is able to represent the world in high definition images. As the physicist who first conducted rigorous analysis of the liquid

23 Bill Brown, "Thing Theory," *Critical Inquiry* 28, no. 1 (Autumn, 2001): 1–22, at 4.
24 Steven Connor, "Thinking Things," a talk given at the Textual Practice lecture, University of Sussex, October 14, 2009, http://www.stevenconnor.com/thinkingthings.

crystal, Otto Lehmann, in the early years of the 20th century, said:

It does not seem inconceivable that physics might succeed in learning from plants the secret of energy storage. In such a case it would be possible to replace the technology based on iron and steel and the steam engine. This new technology would use soft and half-fluid materials.[25]

Though not quite in the domains of energy storage, Lehmann's prediction was not far off the mark for the directions modern engineering and technology is taking us. The textures of our machines are changing. The conception of technology as composed of metallic materials, fueled by liquid ones, is coming to an end.

There have always been viscous substances. Its semi-state speaks of the "warm little pond," the primordial soup, from which it is generally accepted we emerged.[26] But with the large-scale extraction of petroleum from the earth, we have witnessed a proliferation in the variety of its forms. Stuff like Vaseline was made from the residue of petroleum distillation. The technologies of emulsions and gels produced new advancements in lubrication, explosives technology, lacquers, paints, emulsions, sols, gels, jellies, gums, plastics, and pastes. Gel cosmetics are a spectacle in themselves, frothing, fizzing as you rub them, secreting the nourishment of paradise gently through our skin, beckoning us to join them in their steamy eternity. Most recently we are confronted with semi-solid, gelled technologies and infrastructure. Slime mold, it turns out, can design better road networks than we can. The viscous is the frontline between the technological and the biological. Robotics is turning increas-

---

25 Otto Lehman, "Physics and Politics," quoted in David Dunmur and Tim Sluckin, *Soap, Science, and Flatscreen TVs: A History of Liquid Crystals* (Oxford: Oxford University Press, 2011), 58.

26 Darwin imagines the "warm little pond" in a letter to Joseph Hooker in 1871 in *The Correspondence of Charles Darwin,* vol. 19 (Cambridge: Cambridge University Press, 2012), 53.

ingly to silicone as its primary material, AI becoming soft like flesh. Articulation is being made through the channeling of air into rubber chambers, swelling like bubbles. Imagine a future where buildings will be grown like algae, constructed, potentially, of materials that can heal themselves, metabolize, breath. My screen as I write this is secretly squirming. I consider this all to be a change in our made environments into ones that increasingly include viscous states of matter as part of their technology. Importantly, the viscous isn't only the fuel, or the lubricant that allows the metallic parts to move smoothly, it isn't a facilitator of technological movement, but a technology in its own right. As we will see, the viscous has not only been channeled into a technologized state, but its dubiousnesses, its deviances, have been technologized as well.

My time frame for this work, then, is for the most part post-industrial. Time constraints like this, though, are always a performance of some kind; knowledges I employ have their origins in work and sensations that long precede the industrial and post-industrial periods. The viscous as something that reaches simultaneously into primordial depths and into the worlds of high technology requires a kind of approach to history that is willing to scramble erratically out of temporal continuity. That said, I want to expose how there seems to be a particular obligation in the contemporary moment (even if the viscous makes such a category difficult to sustain) to attune ourselves to non-solid, non-liquid, sometimes messy kinds of technology and knowledge. I would never suggest that this obligation is all encompassing, but it is there.

A Glass Eye

It may be surprising, perhaps disappointing, that I don't deal in any explicit or direct way here with the sensation of disgust. The viscous is, after all, the substance we might immediately associate with the abject, the repulsive, the gory, putrescence, shit. I have consciously avoided talking directly about disgust, because, first of all, a lot has already been written about it and

I felt my efforts would be more usefully placed elsewhere. But where instead? Just as I have chosen to see the viscous as a set of dynamics, disgust is similarly a kind of structure, or rather a collapse of structure that contains the potential for another kind of structure. Rather than disgust itself, I've become obsessed with the remarkable things the structure of disgust is able to transform into once the tendencies of repulsion or revulsion have subsided.

The most disgusted I have ever been was during a job I had before I started doing a PhD as a full-time personal assistant to a severely disabled woman. Antonia was the name of my boss. At the age of 7, she had been blown up by an unexploded Second World War bomb left in a stream in Sardinia, where she had grown up. In her fifties and living alone in London in a hotel in Bermondsey, she lives her life without arms and without eyes, relying on constant help from assistants like me that she selects herself via adverts on Gumtree. On the side of her face they managed to reconstruct, she has an eye socket fashioned, I believe, from the skin of her bicep that contains a glass eye. Her other eye is perpetually closed, containing, I think, pieces of eye, but the exact physiognomy is not clear to me. One of the tasks I would perform for her as her assistant would be to remove the glass eye from its socket with a specially designed miniature plunger, wash the eye and the socket with warm water, before inserting it back in. The procedure was not only terrifying, but also terrifyingly awkward. The eye refused to easily slot back in, you had to really ram it; I was ordered by Antonia not to be delicate: "There's nothing in there anyway! *Just get it in!*" There were all number of mysterious viscous semi-states involved, which I would flush out from the socket, and wipe from the surface of the eye.

Lear's "vile jelly," *Un Chien Andalou*'s razor blade to the cornea, Saint Lucia with her eyes on a plate, Bataille, Oedipus: eye enucleation is an archetypal horror. And the horror comes from the revelation of the eye's jelly, as opposed to the glassiness we might likely hope it to be. The jelly is the trembling vulnerability squirting out of what was supposedly the crystalline core of our subjectivity. But nevertheless, when Antonia first asked me to remove her eye with the plunger, I wretched, I panicked, I felt faint. I exhibited all the signs of total disgust. But I just about managed to do it. After a few times of removing and cleaning the eye, however, I no longer felt disgust. This is perhaps something we might expect: we get "used to things," however repulsive you found them at the beginning. It's what must happen to doctors when they learn how to cut into human flesh with a knife as if it were nothing in particular.

But I don't think this is what happened. It wasn't a tolerance that I found. I didn't just distance myself from the substances of the task or learn how to remove or repress my initial repulsion. I didn't mechanize the situation as I imagine doctors might do during the "clinical encounter." It wasn't a widening in the spectrum of what I was able to tolerate. I had the feeling of being just as sensitive and involved with the world as I had been when I wretched, but that the quality of this involvement had changed into something else. It became something I was good at doing. It became personal, part of the sense I had and have of myself. It became something I enjoyed. And this joy was deeply entwined with the sense that I had overcome something. The joy came, in part, through a sense of having pierced a barrier, defeating a resistance.[27]

We might often think of things bursting as disgusting, but it is rarer, I think, for us to think of disgust as something that can itself burst. And that, on the other side of its membranes, lie new structures of experience. I am not suggesting we try to entirely erase disgust, far from it. Disgust is just as much a complex part of life as anything else and *as disgust* has very important practical day-to-day applications. It of course saves us from doing things that might infect and potentially kill us. But it is also clear to see that this isn't only how disgust operates. Just as

27 Raymond Guess discusses a similar issue in *Public Goods, Private Goods* (New Jersey: Princeton University Press, 2001), 21: "It is part of the pleasure that a devotee of 'high' game or of strong cheeses experiences to overcome the ever so slight revulsion that could be caused by the smell."

I said of "the viscous" a moment ago, disgust spreads through likeness like magical thinking. It is intensely conscious not only of the threatening or poisonous *contents* of a particular disgusting object, but also that object's tactile attributes. Disgust is also an aversion to a particular *quality* of experience, one that quite often involves viscous dynamics. A major ambition of this work is to zoom in on these particular qualities of experience and engineer them out of their association with disgust. I want to find in them structures of being that can be experimented with, used and repurposed. For the most part, the attention of this book is placed in this region — the joy, the thinking, the writing, the making, the technology, the social possibility that emerge out of the structures that lie beyond disgust, leaving it behind, but involving its dynamics. This bursting does not constitute a numbing of sensation, nor an increase in what we are able to tolerate, but, I hope, something like the opposite, something more adventurous. These are our protagonists: indifference, stickiness, fondling, mixing. And it is to the aftermath of a huge, accidental burst that we will turn to now.

• • •

I do, here, hope to gesture towards certain ways in which we might attune ourselves to sliminess. But this is an attunement, it involves limits and necessarily some resistance.

This writing isn't completely slimy, slime isn't ever an answer.

While it recognizes the *want* of slime, it also resists this want.

These aren't the words the viscous always wanted me to write.

41

Fig. 1. The aftermath of the Molasses Disaster, *The Boston Globe.*

1

Of Slime and the City

PLACE: Boston, USA, 1919

Molasses, waist deep, covered the street and swirled and bubbled about the wreckage. Here and there struggled a form — whether it was an animal or human being was impossible to tell. Only an upheaval, a thrashing about in the sticky mass, showed where any life was. […] Horses died like so many flies on sticky paper. The more they struggled the deeper in the mess they were ensnared. Human beings — men and woman — suffered likewise.[1]

Flood

At 45 minutes past midday on January 15, 1919, a 25 foot high and 160 foot wide wave of molasses engulfed the city of Boston's waterfront. A tank that had been recently constructed near the harbor to contain the 23 million tonnes of industrial syrup had burst. The rivets that held the huge curved steel sheets pinged cartoonishly off before the sides gave way entirely, the dark gloop gushing out, carrying parts of the tank with it, tearing the world around it apart and plunging the streets and buildings of north Boston into sugary, viscous darkness. Where a tidal wave would have moved in one direction, this wave of molasses es-

1   *The Boston Globe,* January 16, 1919, 14

Fig. 2. The aftermath of the Molasses Disaster, *The Boston Globe.*

caped the tank in four directions, creating four walls of syrup that smashed through the wharf between it and the shore, the elevated railway to left of this picture (fig. 1) and the commercial and residential structures in the foreground and to the right.

Looking at this photo, you can make out the top of the tank at the top, center, just under the white building, nestled like the bald patch of a shy town planner amid the scattered strands and splinters of the debris. Figures are hopping about like birds, probably looking for bodies or survivors, prizing their feet free from the slick. One man is dressed in white — the angel of the syrup — the only figure with his back to the scene, heading determinedly home to bed to escape this madness.

One wave obliterated the North End Paving Yard buildings, the remains of which can be seen in the foreground, above the vehicles and crowd of onlookers. It pulled the Engine 31 firehouse from its foundations, destroyed a timber frame house occupied by the Clougherty family (whose remains and roof I think might be just by the railway), filled kitchens, cars, offices, workshops, sheds, freight cars, shops, and basements. It pulled electricity lines from their poles that fizzed and sputtered as they sank into the molasses. One of the steel sheets from the side of the tank surfed the wave and was propelled into and through one of the columns holding up the elevated railway, bringing the track down.

People in the area described hearing a deep rumbling accompanied by what they thought was machine-gun fire — the rivets whizzing and ricocheting off surfaces. The photographs taken during the rescue operations by journalists recall the images of post-World War II bombed out towns and cities, none of which of course yet existed. What had occurred, of course, were the slimescapes of the First World War trenches, where the fear, it is reported, was not so much of drowning in the mud but of turning into it. Twenty-one people drowned in the molasses flood, one child, the rest workers and laborers mostly of Italian and Irish descent.

The journalism following the event is full of surreal first-hand accounts of people being smothered and consumed by this thickness, of the dark wave approaching, of the stone cutter John Barry drowning in a dark basement filled with sweetness, of Giuseppe Iantosca searching desperately for his child he had sent looking for firewood at the base of the tank. There is Martin Clougherty's account, whose house was closest to the tank and completely destroyed. He had been asleep in bed at the moment of the explosion and was coming into consciousness as his bed gently overturned. He slid off the bed and began to sink, still half asleep, into a pool of molasses as it slowly filled up (what he thought was) his bedroom. It was only when the sweetness of the dark syrup touched his tongue that he came fully to consciousness and realized he was, along with the remains of his house, being swept down the street by a tide of brown ooze.

There are two books that cover the events of this disaster in detail. These are *Dark Tide: The Great Boston Molasses Flood of 1919* by American journalist Stephen Puleo and *The Great Molasses Flood: Boston 1919* by Deborah Kops. Through admirable archival research, both position the disaster in the legal and political situation of just-post-war America. The molasses was initially meant to be distilled into rum, but because of immanent prohibition was being held in the tank to be turned (ironically perhaps) into explosives instead. In the immediate aftermath of the disaster, the media and authorities were convinced that the tank had been blown up by Italian anarchists who were active in the area and were using bombs. In fact, although the causes for the tank's collapse have never been fully understood, it seems most likely that human error and negligence during the tanks construction combined with fermentation and overfilling led to its fracturing and eventual bursting. Puleo uses the molasses flood as a way to paint a picture of Boston at a particular historical moment — the anxieties, the perceived threats, the ethnic tensions, the paranoia, the impending gloom of prohibition. He is, or at least claims to be, exasperated by the perceived weirdness of the event as the reason that it is not taken seriously as a historical moment, the reaction that involves, "a raised eyebrow, maybe a restrained giggle, followed by the incredulous, 'What you're serious? It's really true?'"[2]

For me, these raised eyebrows and restrained giggles are part of, rather than hostile to, the history of this event. Or rather, there is a history that can be told that is the history of this collision — the viscous spewing out over the city — and its weirdness. It also seems to me that this event, each of its constituent parts, is a peculiarly modern one. And by modern I mean this: it requires the accumulation of matter in such quantities that it might suddenly erupt, overpowering the technologies made to contain it, and reduce the streets around it to what we might imagine as a pre-historical quagmire. It is a moment when an infrastructure can't appear to manage the abundance it produces. These images feel as if they unearth a set of dialectics: technologies of containment are simultaneously technologies of bursting. Technologies of control are simultaneously technologies of chaos.

2   Stephen Puleo, *Dark Tide: The Great Boston Molasses Flood of 1919* (Boston: Beacon Press, 2004), x.

Describing a Dream

The disaster — its flamboyance, its comedy, its suddenness, its fascination — has given me a spectacular and improbable excuse to interrogate how slime, its tendencies, and the city interrelate. I rewind and replay the event, from different angles and degrees of zoom by assembling moments, here, where slime collides again and again with the urban space in other times, places, and imaginations. Is this a possible way of doing history? A history that extracts particular sensual instances out from their context and rampantly connects them across thought plains, greased-up and eager for traffic. Maybe this is the kind of history the viscous demands, one that reaches out and grabs in the way we might when trying to remember a dream. Because a dream is, after all, what slime transforms a city into. The dream image of the city bursting and spewing, smearing and congealing, is one of singular excitation, of some other place where "business as usual" is treated with contempt. In Ursula Le Guin's novel *The Lathe of Heaven,* a novel where reality corresponds to a character's dreams, contains one of literature's most vividly gloopy cities, where the towering structures of bureaucracy turn into neglected food:

> The buildings of downtown Portland, the Capital of the World, the high, new, handsome cubes of stone and glass interspersed with measured doses of green, the fortresses of Government—Research and Development, Communications, Industry, Economic Planning, Environmental Control—were melting. They were getting soggy and shaky, like Jell-O left out in the sun. The corners had already run down the sides, leaving great creamy smears.[3]

I reach out, grab and assemble things that resemble it as an attempt to re-enact it, bring it into clearer focus, make myself

3   Ursula K. Le Guin, *The Lathe of Heaven* (New York: Diversion Books, 1999), 205.

Fig. 3. The Camden Town Hall Annex. Photo by the author.

more like it, even. What are we meant to do with the strange and impossible jealousy we might have for events like this? Not of the people who witnessed it, *but for the event itself?* Similarly, what are we meant to do with the desire to dig your fingertips into the joins of a building's architecture and tear it into pieces like an orange (as I imagine doing when I look at the former Camden Town Hall Annex on the Euston Road, now being developed into a luxury Crosstree Hotel)? Is the desire to eat a city or one its buildings just simply foolish, or is there something useful there to which we should be attentive, some type of knowing being made that is trying to overturn, to use Esther Leslie's phrase, the "settled world of day"?[4] I don't want to elevate the molasses disaster to some special historical position. I don't of course consider it as comparable to any of the real disastrous ruinations of the 20th century. One curious echo I've come across, though. It's reported that in the siege of Leningrad, the fires in the Badaevsky food warehouses produced rivers of molten sugar flowing across the city. As the sugar crystalized, it

4   Esther Leslie, *Derelicts: Thought Worms from the Wreckage* (London: Unkant Publishers, 2013), 2.

merged with the rubble and dust of the bombed-out buildings, which the city's inhabitants, starving to death, turned to eating.[5]

In many ways, my choice of this disaster is arbitrary. There are all number of other urban spewings-out to choose from, but I have persisted with it. I am drawn to it as a moment of accidental wildness (can wildness be anything but accidental?) within and involving the urban space, as if, somehow, the inorganic world was enacting a revenge for the supposed supremacy of so-called enlightenment thinking. Surely this isn't so. Or maybe it is. This is the question, then: what kinds of thinking does the molasses disaster propose?

This approach doesn't correspond to much, if any, recognized scholarly or academic methodology. But this is something that needs to be gotten to grips with if the viscous is to be allowed to flourish. The primary obsession of my research into this material state, the one to which I will return relentlessly, is the gelling of arbitrariness. It is the persistence of association even if no real justification for it can be found. Or, it is the continuance of association even if the justifications for it can be exposed as being wholly superficial, pop, as the associations I make here may often seem. The viscous, in this way, is anti-academic. It doesn't care too much about making ground or meaningful content. But it does care, in its own peculiar way, about something much harder to care about: those things that, though not explicitly meaningless, don't seem to give much at all, but mingle, stick with you, all the same.

I want to unearth the slimy parts to the city that are, perhaps, repressed, but essential to its functioning. But I also want to put slime next to the city, allow them to communicate in unexpected and unrealistic ways in order that we might learn more about what these things or places are independently and also how they might learn from each other, or, of course, have already done so.

5   Geoffrey Regan, *Military Anecdotes* (London: Guinness Publishing, 1992), 12. The bombing of the Badaevsky warehouses is covered in William Moskoff, *The Bread Of Affliction: The Food Supply in the USSR during World War II* (Cambridge University Press, 2002).

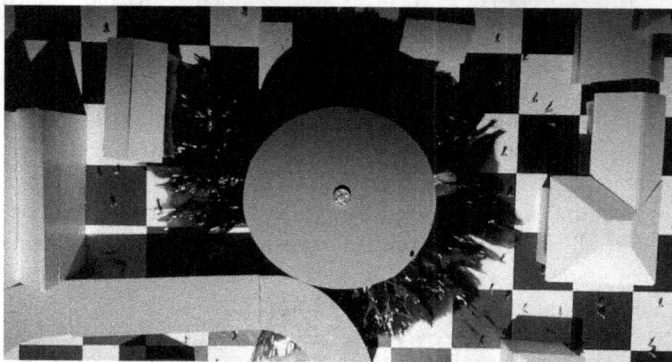

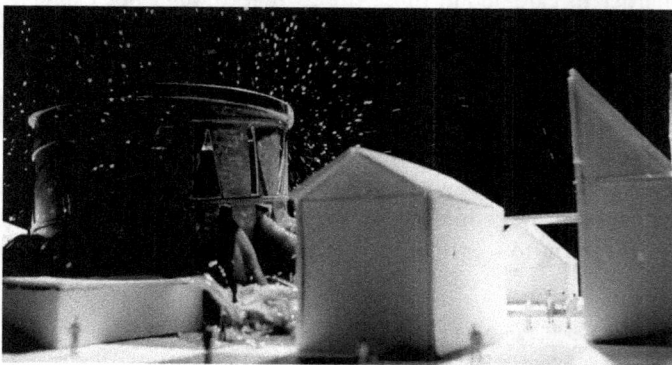

Figs. 4, 5, 6. Molasses Disaster Reenactment. Photo by the author.

Re-enactment

When researching the Molasses Disaster, I became obsessed with different ways I could synthesize its experience, ways, I suppose, of describing its dream. I applied for and received a small grant to build a scale model (about 1 m × 2 m) of the tank and its surrounding area of Boston in 1919. The tank I made was filled with sugar syrup and designed to burst on demand, flooding and destroying the buildings and elevated railway I'd lovingly replicated out of white foam board. This re-enactment was due to be performed at Somerset House in London as part of the (awkwardly named) Culture Capital Exchange Festival. The idea was to re-enact the disaster in the venue, film it in super slow-mo, then play back the slow motion version while I gave a 50-minute talk entitled "Of Slime and the City." It became apparent that this was impossible. It wasn't even permitted to eat in the wood-paneled cinema I was to present in, let alone blow-up re-appropriated ventilation shafts full of molasses. The Perspex walls with which I surrounded the model, which I'd promised to the organizers would keep the molasses safely within its confines, were not, I gradually realized, going to achieve anything. Instead, I resigned myself to filming the explosion from multiple different angles in slow-motion in an appropriate setting and play the result back in the venue, over my talk.

A skeleton crew and I set up five different cameras filming at 250 frames per second around my model. The ventilation shaft I'd cut up to act as the tank contained a large silver balloon against which the tip of a soldering iron was gently pressed, inserted through the metal, hidden under a shed adjacent to the tank. Once the balloon was filled with the syrup and the cameras filming, the soldering iron would be switched on, rupturing the balloon, sending the molasses gushing out over and ruining the little figures and buildings we'd assembled.

Molasses corrodes latex, it turns out, and before we'd turned the cameras on, the balloon ruptured of its own accord covering me and my companions head to foot in sticky, stinking, farm-grade molasses before we'd finished arranging a miniature version of Northern Boston in 1919. I collapsed in despair into a pool of syrup. My friends cleaned everything up, this was no small task, while I, managing to extract myself from a deep defeatist attitude, went to Lidl to buy the shop out of brown sauce. A few hours later we tried again, this time with a tank full of some disgusting concoction of brown sauce, treacle, brown paint, glue and any of the molasses we could recycle. We got the shot, though it was not nearly viscous enough. Appropriately, my attempt to re-enact the molasses disaster had been a disaster.

At Somerset House, the talk was received well. A woman in the Q&A at the end described a memory she had from her childhood of sneaking into her parents' larder at night to steal some chocolate. Not knowing where the light switch was, she rummaged around in the dark walk-in cupboard when suddenly there was a loud bang and she felt some substance slapping itself onto her face. A can of treacle had spontaneously exploded at precisely the moment of her sinful nighttime excursion. Haunted by this apparent desire of the world to expose and humiliate her, she'd come to my talk to get some answers. I didn't have any for her.

A City Bursts

Industrial disasters that involve foodstuffs can happen, though rarely do, in large sugar refineries, flour mills, and custard factories that are at risk of dust explosions, the rapid combustion of fine particles suspended in the air of a poorly ventilated factory spaces. The first of these was the Washburn "A" Mill in Minneapolis that exploded in May, 1878, killing 18 people which instigated an introduction of stricter regulations. The same thing happened in Banbury in Oxfordshire in 1981 when Bird's Custard factory (now an arts center) witnessed a smaller version of such an explosion. When the firefighters hosed the flames, the unburnt powder turned into custard and began "pouring down the streets."[6] These explosions are composed of a curious internal echo or prefiguring of themselves. The powder is ground down and dispersed invisibly throughout the space. Only when this dispersal is contained, when the particles are prevented from dispersing entirely, can a dispersal of a much larger and more spectacular kind take place, the sudden, explosive dispersal of the building itself.

The fact that most of our burstings, especially the food-related ones, are forbidden in public, certainly provides the molasses flood, and these other industrial food disasters, with some of its comic power. It is an absurdly amplified, industrialized, version of something that has at its core a symbol of human shame and vulnerability: the troubling of the boundaries between inside and outside that is the basis of the abject. In witnessing spectacles of bursting, there is an instant of hypnosis where we begin to momentarily forget the distinction we draw between ourselves and things. My stomach lurches mimetically, I begin to cross over with the world, sharing with these spectacles the contingency they express. Boston gets diarrhea, or we become a tank, thin-skinned and waiting to crack. In watching bubbles burst, in slamming your fist down on a jam doughnut, there is the structure of some great taboo having been broken. I find a structural continuity of the world with myself as a set of surfaces and apertures, but then I also feel a sublime detachment from it. I laugh at it — the bursting is ostentatiously not happening to me.

The spectacle of the burst, and the attention it demands, has been thrust into contemporary relevance by Peter Sloterdijk, whose epic trilogy on spherology opens with a mediation on the image of a child watching a bubble.

6   Robin McKie, "How to Set Young Minds on Fire," *The Guardian,* October 22, 2006, https://www.theguardian.com/uk/2006/oct/22/schools. education.

Fig. 7. Bubbles, mezzotint by G.H. Every, 1887, after Sir John Everett Millais.

> For the duration of the bubble's life the blower was outside himself, as if the little orb's survival depended on remaining encased in the attention that floated out with it.[7]

An intricate dialectic of internalization and externalization is at play in a moment of inter-encasement. The child leaves itself in the attention it gives to the floating object, as if he (not only his breath) were inside it, yet believes its survival depends on it being contained within his attention. The membrane of his consciousness and the membrane of the bubble are coterminous with one another. This solidarity with things takes place, Sloterdijk says, in a "field spread out through attentive involvement."

7 Peter Sloterdijk, *Bubbles: Microspherology,* trans. Wieland Hoban (Los Angeles: Semiotext(e), 2011), 17.

The joy of this activity is self-perpetuating, when the burst inevitably comes, it doesn't signify an end, but the possibility of renewal: again! This sense of your attention spreading is something I will discuss in more detail in just a moment.

But what are the differences and continuities between bursting and exploding? This distinction is, in fact, at the core of the confusion in the pages of the *Boston Globe* in its reporting of the disaster. Although the headline of newspaper that day dramatically announces "HUGE MOLASSES TANK EXPLODES," the actual accounts of the disaster in the following pages, describe a more unsettlingly muted progression of events. For onlooker Robert Burnett, there was

> no roar or explosion. I thought it was an elevated train until I heard a swish as if wind was rushing. It didn't rush. It just rolled, slowly, it seemed, like the side of a mountain falling into space.[8]

How is it possible for a disaster of such death toll to "swish"? There is an undeniable grace to the abstraction of Robert's description. The slow unfurling of the molasses seems to have given him a sense of geological time — a landscape descending into a void.

The sonic details of the first-hand descriptions of the event are characterized by a remarkable littleness and subtlety: pings, swishes, hisses, barely audible murmurings of something approaching — whimpers not bangs. These details are wound up with the determined attempts to find someone or some group to blame for the flood. Where the boom of an explosion would signify the presence of intention and the malignant project of the Italian communists and anarchists to wipe out the American way of life, these rustles and creaks, however, signify something much harder to accept and narrativize: the presence of simple

8   *Boston Globe,* January 16, 1919, 16

human error. An *accident*: an event, as Catherine Malabou says, that "eludes duration."[9]

Although it is not the case that explosions are only ever intended and bursts accidental, the complexity of what might be their cause is perhaps distinct. Where explosions spread rapidly from a single point of ignition, some charge, burstings spread from a single point of rupture. Bursting is tied to the presence of some initial breakage through its relation to "bust," a word with which it used to be interchangeable.[10] The dynamics of the burst are much cruder, much simpler, than that of the explosion. Bursts are explosions in their primordial form, no chemical reaction needs to take place, only a mere deficiency of matter in the face of a sheer excess of substance that causes the world simply to *let go*. In this way, the explosions in industrial refineries and mills feel like they work within the logic of the processes in question, an improbable yet logical outcome of grinding things down very small on a large scale. The bursting of the molasses tank, on the other hand, carries a sense of primordiality, one that is, importantly, only possible within modern industry's requirements for vats, tankers, silos and other structures of mass containment.

The history of how explosions have migrated between the imaginative, spectacular, bodily, and the militaristic is carefully surveyed by Steven Connor towards the end of his book *The Matter of Air*. Connor approaches explosions as an ontological structure that can transcend the distinction between the physic and physical, they are "a dangerous pleasure: always more than a physical event," that have been, among other things, "inflected by and given accent to desire."[11] He suggests that technologies of explosion were first developed by the Chinese in the ninth century, not as weapons of warfare, but as pyrotechnics: forms of entertainment. The spectacle of seeing something obliterated

9   Catherine Malabou, *The Ontology of the Accident: An Essay on Destructive Plasticity*, trans. Carolyn Shread (Cambridge: Polity Press, 2009), 54.
10 *OED*, s.v. "bust, n.3."
11 Steven Connor, *Matters of Air: Science and Art of the Ethereal* (London: Reaktion Books, 2010), 287.

in a sudden dispersal of light and sound both satisfies, reflects, and modifies our own rhythms of desire. This desire can be, in some cases, the analogue of the means by which life propagates itself across space through the dispersals of seeds, or it can be, in a related way, the desire for total self-obliteration. Conner shows how the vocabulary of explosives has been integrated into that of identity annihilating drug use: bombed, hit, blow your mind. He identifies the explosion as an event which destroys things to the point of almost nothing, an airborne dust. "This is," he suggests, "the ultimate reach of the death-drive, a death that not only brings life to an end, but also annuls the very time of its having existed."[12]

Something different is going on with the molasses flood, although part of its interest is in its promise of something similar. I want to position it as an event that contains dual forms of excitation that undercut one another. This "letting go" of matter as it slumps out over the city does not transform the bursting object into air, or dust, as Connor imagines, but lingers on, resists the immediacy from which it was born. In the spectacle of the molasses flood we have the close proximity of two contrasting kinds of excitation, one that comes from the dubious clamminess of the sugar syrup and the other from the desirous expulsions of the explosive. Time compacts and then suddenly elongates. In this crisis in the technologies of containment maybe we can find an analogue for the dynamics of modern economics, the familiar patterns of "boom and bust." Despite many claims of this pattern's culmination, the boom of economic excitation is only ever an incomplete explosion, the endless feasts they promise never arrive, the advances wind down, austerity tends to cling and linger. The explosion recoils into a gloopy downturn which, itself, contains the potential for an alternative excitation. But what exactly is this urban slime's "excitation"?

12 Ibid., 292.

Slow Beginnings

The dodgy pun I'm making with the title of this chapter is of course in reference to Terence Davis's complexly ambivalent urban cinematic eulogy *Of Time and the City,* where the "of" acts, it feels, as a signal of loss, as if the phrase, the title of the film, has itself fallen away from something larger, leaving us only with a straggled "pertaining to..." wandering aimlessly through the streets at dusk. The title seems to mourn already some loss of what might have preceded its beginning and in this way gathers its playfully portentous mood. This mood is perhaps an odd one when placed in conjunction with slime, a substance that "doesn't really care," as I've said, or at least is not prone to extensive reminiscence, not having much, in fairness, to reminisce about. But, then again, slime is for many a nostalgic state of matter. Especially for those who grew up in the 1980s and '90s, neon gunge was a must-have toy, one that seemed to disappear in the early 2000s only to return with force on Instagram and other platforms in recent years, transformed, for reasons I will discuss in chapter three.

But for sure — sliminess speaks of childhood, an imagined time when mess was not a problem to be dealt with, or somebody's fetish, but an actual tool for managing the relationship between "self" and "world." As Winnicot famously theorized, making a mess, smearing stuff on walls, rags, etc., is a crucial negotiation in infantile subject formation. Transitional objects, which often tend to be covered in mess, are neither the "world," nor are they "me." They act as a "resting place" in the "war waged by desire and need on reality."[13] The messy room gathers meaning through not being cleared away. The making of a mess, in this view of things, is not so much at odds with the making of meaning, but its necessary prerequisite, the thing that you must do to the world first before you are able to channel it into something that looks like "meaning."

13 D.W. Winnicot, *Playing and Reality* (London: Tavistock, 1971), discussed by David Trotter, *Cooking with Mud,* 5–6.

This punning on "slime" and "time" in my title is not particularly original, the joke is made by Iain Hamilton Grant in his essay "Being and Slime: The Mathematics of Protoplasm in Lorenz Oken's Physio-philosophy." And before Grant, the same joke is made by the character Ray Stantz (played by Dan Ackroyd) in *Ghostbusters II*. Imagining the newspaper headlines after the Psychomagnotheric slime has engulfed New York, Ray exclaims: "SLIME SQUARE!" This punning of "slime" and "time" implicates the one in the other just as, we might say, slime has been noticed to carry a timeframe within it. This "timeframe" for slime is slowness, it winds the world down, all of its maneuvers take place as matter in slow motion. For Sartre, slime is "fluidity in slow motion," a pace of alteration that reveals, yet also just is, its dubious, transgressive, aberrant nature. There is something both over and under eager about slime, it doesn't go quickly enough for us to want to have it. But, at the same time, whatever annoys us about it, it doesn't seem to do it enough — it is more irritating than demonic, a menace that can't really be bothered: "a lazy evil."

Slime is the substance of returns. If it slides us back nostalgically to a dream of our childhood, it is also imagined as belonging to another time altogether. Its slowness contains the sensual blueprint for the popular imaginary of "another time," a time that must somehow precede us, a dynamic totally oblivious to the crush and bustle of modern urban spaces. Slime and the city don't fit together. Their logics feel at odds with each other, we might say.

Where the invention of photography allowed people to freeze the world into snapshots, cinema has the capacity to slow the world down. For the early cinema theorist Jean Epstein, the effect of slow motion can return our bodies to the state of "smooth muscles moving through a dense medium in which thick currents always carry and shape this clear descendent of old marine fauna and maternal waters."[14] Cinematic slow-motion has the

14 Jean Epstein, *The Intelligence of a Machine,* trans. Christophe Wall-Romana (Minneapolis: Univocal Publishing, 2014), 29.

grace of a seemingly undisturbed gesture, removed from free-dom and will. It has the power, perhaps, of the uncanny, that is, the return of something primordial. The fascination of the body in slow-motion maybe comes from disinterring the memory we might all somehow, somewhere have inside us, in our flesh, in our brains, of being fish. There is also, of course, the analytical pleasure of being able to see the world anew and in a detail that isn't otherwise possible, like looking down a microscope. But, I do also feel when I watch footage in slow-motion, an obscure yearning for an impossible return, a less hostile, gloopier, mate-rial universe, for a world where I am not absolutely terrified of air travel.

But we must go further back than fish. It is the positioning of slime as the most basic and originary element of existence that Iain Hamilton Grant discusses in his essay on the 18th-cen-tury naturalist Lorenz Oken. The core philosophical problem of Oken's work, Grant suggests, is how something issues from nothing, how to get from zero to one. But, the question is not so much whether the "real ground of existence" might "= 0," but whether this 0 "stays the same," whether 0 always = 0, wheth-er, in other words, the 0 "*is slimy*."[15] Grant figures the Okenian solution to the problem of ontogenesis as a struggle between nothing and slime, which is in turn a meeting of biology and mathematics, a "mathematics endowed with substance."[16] For Oken, the study of life is mathematical, but this is a kind of slimy maths that trembles and shimmers. It involves "primal slime," or in German *Urschleim,* and that collects in manifestations of "slime points," *Schleimpunkte.* The viscous is not seen as at odds with quantities and their division, but allowed to pervade them, become part of their quality. Numbers are imagined as messy things and in this way generative. The zero oscillates gently,

15 Iain Hamilton Grant, "Being and Slime: The Mathematics of Protoplasm in Lorenz Oken's Physio-philosophy," in *Collapse IV: Concept Horror* (Falmouth: Urbanomic, 2009), 291.
16 Ibid., 292.

Oken imagines. This "wavering zero" is the generative core of being and slime.

But the complexity comes for Oken from the issue of primacy that is simultaneously invented and undercut by this slimy zero. What comes first: the slime or the zero? As Grant helps to show, slime has a contradictory function in Oken's philosophy.

> Man is the summit, the crown of nature's development must comprehend everything that has preceded him [while] man is a complex of everything that surrounds him, namely of element, mineral, plant and animal.[17]

Like honey lifted out of itself with a spoon, "mankind" rises above nature through its structures of knowledge and communication and, in so doing, bleeds confusingly back into its environment. The struggle of slimy thinking is not to linearize time or progression, but to think of things in parallel. The viscous loop Oken finds himself in is that the "summit" mankind has reached is also a plunging back into the complex of everything that surrounds him. This is mirrored in his extraordinary vision of o as displaying exactly this honey-like quality of emerging from itself, only to stay itself:

> [N]umbers have not issued forth from zero as if they had previously resided therein, but the zero has emerged out of itself [...], and then it was a finite zero, a number.[18]

Quantities do not extend themselves tenticularly out of o, but o churns away, emerging and collapsing, in a way that recalls Bachelard's description of vats of molten porcelain appearing to knead themselves.[19] But this is a crucial quality to viscous think-

17 Ibid., 304.
18 Ibid., 305.
19 Gaston Bachelard, *Earth and the Reveries of Will: An Essay On the Imagination of Matter,* trans. Kenneth Haltman (Dallas: The Dallas Institute Publications, 2002), 67.

ing and being — it plays with origins. It both invents and deletes them by stretching into the present the "having come before."

"The City" Churns

If bursting is the sudden expulsion of the inside, outwards, the rupturing of the bubble's membrane, the outline that is also everything that it is, isn't there a problem with this "the" before "city" in my title "Of Slime and the City"? The definite article before the abstracted concept of the urban space works, perhaps, in line with a tendency in some theory, especially the kind that operates effectively within art schools, of concretizing the abstract or the quality of some act or relation — "the cut," "the fragment," "the assemblage," "the inscription." In *Essayism,* Brian Dillon describes his frustration with New Materialist thinking that is devoid of any actual materials, a movement that endlessly proclaims its commitment to materials and their processes, but never actually arrives to talk about any. "Materiality without materials — what good are these to anyone except the intellectually immature and overreaching [...]?"[20] This is, arguably, the effect of this definite article. It allows us to "overreach," as Dillon would have it, eliding things that should probably be kept distinct. We keep ourselves safely and innocuously abstract, while pretending to be attentive to the peculiar, the specific. Is there something about cities that makes us want to give them this definite article? Have they tricked us into doing this to them? How does the "the" work differently between "the city" and "the fragment"? Is "the-ifying" the city like this as pointless or as misguided as proposing something like the *viscous*?

Thinking about the nature of "the" city has been epistemologically framed in this way since the urban sociology of the Chicago School, whose founders Ernest Burgess and Robert Park published their mission statement *The City* in 1925. As urbanologist Neil Brenner says, this terminology — the city — has evolved into a "basically self-evident presupposition," something

20 Brian Dillon, *Essayism* (London: Fitzcarraldo Editions, 2017), 80.

so "obvious that it did not require explanation or justification."[21] Urbanology is concerned with many different things, processes and debates, but beneath it all is a gaze placed exclusively on "city-like" "sociospatial units" whose qualities, possibilities, and problems arise from within a place that is distinct from zones that are definitively non-cities. All urban studies have been characterized by an entrenched "*methodological cityism*" which entails "an analytical privileging, isolation and […] naturalization of the city in studies of urban processes where the non-city may also be significant."[22] This is part of an emerging kind of urban sociology that looks to break the study out of its latent "cityism" to create a vision of the city "without an outside," one that absorbs the terrestrial, the subterranean, the atmospheric, the oceanic.

This isn't "the city" as the globalized space of flows, glistening rivers of car headlights in long-exposure photographs, but something slimier. Brenner, in trying to describe what he means by this absorptive urbanology, involves himself in a viscous vocabulary. Instead of the flows and streams between nodes, urban clusters are seen as "extended and thickened," he calls forth Jean Gottomann's notion of an "irregular colloidal mixture of rural and suburban landscapes," he imagines this space as a "kaleidoscopic churning" of terrain, the urban fabric becoming an "uneven" sort of "mesh." This slimy reconceptualization of the city does strange things to its "the." It doesn't deny it, doesn't discard its tendency towards specificity, nor does it throw us out into pure multiplicity; the city is still an iterable structure. Rather, we generate a kind of specificity that is absorptive. As "the city" starts to integrate things that were not formerly thought of as part of its body, words like "churning," "colloidal," and "thickened" are becoming the necessary terminology for this reinvention of its space.

21 Neil Brenner, ed., *Implosions/Explosions: Towards a Study of Planetary Urbanization* (Berlin: Jovis Verlag, 2014), 15.
22 Ibid.

But this is more than just a choice of words. For nothing turns the city and its transport network slimier than an experiment conducted by researchers at Hokkaido University in Japan in 2010. The scientists arranged pieces of oatmeal in a petri dish to form a map of the Japanese railway system, each piece of oatmeal being a station. They then introduced slime mold to the dish. As the organism fed on the oatmeal, it formed a network between each oatmeal station that almost exactly replicated the existing Japanese railway map. This slime mold experiment has been repeated by researchers at the University of West of England for road networks around the world and they've found that motorways in China, Belgium, and Canada have the most efficiently mapped motorway systems, while the ones in the US and Africa have the least. According to slime mold, the M6 should be rerouted through Newcastle.[23] Slime mold isn't slow, necessarily. It can, in fact, grow up to a centimeter an hour in optimal conditions, but it is an extremely simple, single-celled organism.

As a result of experiments like this, there has in recent years been an increased interest in the organizational and even imaginative powers of dispersed organisms like slime mold. The organism has been found to have a kind of memory, one that is external, spatial. As it moves in the search for nutrients, it leaves a thick mat of "non-living extracellular slime," consisting mostly of sulphated glucose polymers, which helps the organism(s) to remember where it's been and avoid covering the same area twice. As researchers at the Centre for Mathematical Biology at the University of Sydney have discovered, this avoidance of its own slime trail, appears to be a "choice": when all areas have been covered with its slime trail, the mold no longer avoids it and goes over the same ground. Its effectiveness at navigating

23 Shin Watanabe et al., "Traffic Optimization in Railroad Networks Using an Algorithm Mimicking an Amoeba-like Organism, *Physarum* Plasmodium," *Biosystems* 105, no. 3 (2011): 225–32. There is also the pop science article: David Parr, "Cities in Motion: How Slime Mould Can Redraw Our Rail and Road Maps," *The Guardian,* February 18, 2014, https://www.theguardian.com/cities/2014/feb/18/slime-mould-rail-road-transport-routes.

complex environments then greatly diminishes, however.[24] This kind of spatialized memory system is being developed by researchers for the purposes of robotics. Its powers of decision-making are also being harnessed by researchers developing new forms of experimental computing.

But it is not all logical. Researchers working elsewhere at the University of Sydney claim to have discovered behaviors of irrational decision making in *Physarum polycephalum*. Most fascinating is the discovery that slime mold is able to anticipate future events. When plasmodia are exposed to unfavorable conditions at constant intervals, they reduce their "locomotive speed in response to each episode." When they were then exposed to favorable conditions again, they "spontaneously" reduce their locomotive speed at a time when the next "unfavourable episode *would have occurred.*"[25] Slime has an understanding of the perfect continuous conditional.

Slime mold's power to make decisions troubles the very basis upon which our arguments about consciousness, in Western philosophy at least, are based. Kant considered the unity of consciousness, his "transcendental apperception," to be a necessary transcendental condition for the possibility of experience. But as Steven Shaviro has shown in his recent book *Discognition,* this (dis)unity of perception might simply be a question of "latency and bandwidth," or the pace at which signals are able to be transferred to different parts of a body. "If signals can't be transferred quickly enough through the brain (or equivalent) then unity cannot be maintained."[26] Consciousness as we know it becomes a result of the speed of electrical signal; the internal pulsations of nutrition in a slime mold are too slow for it to resemble the consciousness of an animal's brain, the speed of its synaptic firing. This means, though, that slime mold is able to

---

24 Chris R. Reid at al. "Slime Mold Uses an Externalized Spatial 'Memory' to Navigate in Complex Environments," *PNAS* 109, no. 43 (October 23, 2012): 17490–94.
25 Tetsu Saigusa et al., "Amoebae Anticipate Periodic Events," *Physical Review Letters* 100, no. 1 (January 2008).
26 Steven Shaviro, *Discognition* (London: Repeater Books, 2016), 213.

multitask more effectively, able to "probe multiple food sources simultaneously." The octopus, it has been speculated, may not have a unified consciousness because so many of its neurons are located "all along its eight arms and thousands of individual suckers."[27] Slime mold oozes about, actively probing and provoking its environment. It has a "dark phenomenology," experience without understanding or knowing it.

Both conceptually and literally, then, slime is a tool we can use to reimagine the urban space. Slime is something we can *bring in* to rethink things. It allows us to counter the projects of purification, in the Latourian sense, that have determined urban planning. Outside my fourth-story window in a terraced house in East London, I see a long stretch of land that backs onto the houses on my street, miserably divided up by flimsy pieces of wood, demarcating for each ground floor flat its plot of lawn, varyingly tended to. Trampolines creak maddeningly as law-abiding children count bits of gravel. There is surely space here to land light aircraft. What if this were a forest? Viewed through a period-feature sash window as I sit at my polymer-laminated Ikea plywood table. Is there enough space to let miniature bison loose? At least remove these pointless fences. There is one word that may direct us: *churn*.

This churned urbanism is finding exciting application by architectural practitioners and theorists trying to develop ways in which cities might be designed as living things. Rachel Armstrong from the Experimental Architecture Group based at Newcastle University, for instance, is working on ways in which living systems might be used to design structures that heal themselves. Using protocell technology, a new strand of synthetic biology that uses cocktails of chemicals that are "half alive," she hopes to *grow* a synthetic limestone base under Venice as a way of preventing the city from sinking any further into the mud. These simple metabolic systems are photophobic, turn away from the light and are drawn to the dark old wooden piles on which the city is currently built. They eat away at the wood and excrete a

27 Ibid.

limestone reef in its place. The city becomes food for things that are half alive, its structure: their waste excrescence.[28] This would be the use, interestingly, of a material that has already been used for millennia as a building material — limestone. The difference being, of course, that the stones were grown in the city, rather than quarried, heaved, cut and piled. Part of what I want to get closer to here is the kind of imaginative work and resistances that are involved in realizing this *churn*.

Stoned in Marseilles

I immersed myself in contemplation of the sidewalk before me, which, through a kind of unguent with which I covered it, could have been, precisely as these very stones, also the sidewalk of Paris. One often speaks of stones instead of bread. These stones were the bread of my imagination, which was suddenly seized by ravenous hunger to taste what is the same in all places and countries.[29]

So says Walter Benjamin, when extremely stoned in Marseille. He acts, in this state of reverie, not unlike a slime mold, his mind excreting some attentive substance that he smears onto things as his contemplation probes and passes over them. There is an intriguing interplay between surface and depth, where applying contemplation over the surfaces of the city he is able to immerse himself in its material.

It is through an excessive involvement with the literal material of the city's stones (not their function as, say, floors, walls, gutters, roads) that Benjamin is able to access a form of universalism. But this is a universalism that he finds emphatically within the specificity of the stones in front of him. This isn't the experience of being anywhere due to resemblance. He doesn't turn the

28 Benedict Hobson, "Growing a 'Giant Artificial Reef' Could Stop Venice Sinking," *Dezeen,* May 30, 2014, https://www.dezeen.com/2014/05/30/movie-rachel-armstrong-future-venice-growing-giant-artificial-reef/.

29 Walter Benjamin, *Reflections: Essays, Aphorisms and Autobiographical Writings,* trans. Edmund Jephcott (New York: Schocken Books, 1986), 142.

stones into a schema that can be indefinitely applied outwards onto everything else. He doesn't turn them into a "ness" (hardness, flatness, coldness, etc.), nor does he reduce them to their shape, their use function, their design, which he then is able to recognize as something he's seen before elsewhere. He is clear: "precisely as these very stones." The unguent of his attention that he smears over the world opens it out as a complex of particularities, like a body of a *Physarum polycephalum,* specificities accrue worm-holes, a sly, hidden solidarity between every thing that is irreducibly itself.

It is also a moment when Benjamin finds what he needs. The stones covered in this unguent nourish him, satisfying, we might say, a lack. Benjamin comes close to eating a city. His nourishment results in a "taste" for more. But this is for more of the same. Benjamin feels the insatiable thirst for more of *precisely this,* which is paradoxically the thirst for sameness. This is what the unguent is capable of, this is its use function. It is a tool that makes things so vehemently themselves that it feels you can taste them anywhere. In this piece on taking hash in Marseille, he reports finding a newspaper he'd been carrying on the night of his session with the phrase scribbled on it, in his hand: "one should scoop sameness from reality with a spoon." Eating is the principle mode of engagement (he is at this moment looking for an ice cream, with a pretty severe case of the munchies), the nourishing part of things being that precise piece of the environment, neatly identified with your utensil, that is the same in all places.

These kinds of thoughts are dangerous, however, there is the risk of collapsing into cliché. The passage ends with an instance of what appears to be a sense of hangover shame:

> "All men are brothers." So began a train of thought I am no longer able to pursue. But its last link was certainly much less banal that its first and led on perhaps to images of animals.[30]

30 Ibid., 143.

Spectacles of Indifference

A key imaginary of the slimy object is of it as one that simply doesn't care. Its eruption into the city space is a spectacle of *want* whose motivations are obscure or, we suspect, non-existent, certainly indifferent to our own. We might perceive the city as an environment that encourages capitalistic exchange and difference, change that induces further change and a site whose surfaces and infrastructure seek to create an ease of monetary and vehicular flow. We might, at the same time, conceive of the city as a site that is straining towards stasis, an archive, a museum of what takes place within it. "The question in its simplest and most idealistic form," as urbanologist Will Straw puts it, "asks whether the city is a mechanism for perpetual motion or a force for stasis and immobility."[31]

Whatever debates might ensue, slime does not cooperate with them either. If the city favors exchange and difference, slime is its sluggish, reluctant, clammy counterpoint. The slowness of slime in the city should not be confused with kinds of "slowness" that have emerged out of modern anxieties of going too fast: "slow food," "slow design," "slow industry." Nor should it be seen in terms of psychogeographical techniques of "walking the city" and its ring roads to rediscover lost connections to urban history, places, and identity. Slime is slow, but not in a thoughtful way, its gradualness is totally non-civic. Rather than a way to appreciate things and "take more in," slime's slowness is its dramatization of indifference. Perhaps his most intriguing insight into the viscous, Sartre identifies a "dubious slowness" of the stuff as what "discourages" possession. Its indifferent slowness is not only change that resists itself, but something that resists the forces of ownership, the creation of private and "public" property, the means by which urban space is delineated. I have, however, become fascinated by the signs attached to viciously

31 Will Straw, "Spectacles of Waste," in *Circulation and the City: Essays on Urban Culture,* eds. Alexandra Boutros et al. (Quebec: McGill University Press, 2010), 155–94, at 194.

69

spiked fences informing us that "anti-climb paint is in use." This stuff, this canned mess, this un-dryable paint, which is smeared along the tops of fences to discourage trespassing, is a use of the viscous, its sticky, transgressive qualities, to *secure* rather than to corrupt the delineations of space. Tigers defecate around their territory to ward off competition. I've heard of people in house-shares licking their cheese. I am aware of only one other moment when the threat of mess is employed as a type of security technology like it is with anti-climb paint, as I will discuss in the next chapter.

If we return, then, to the account of the molasses flood in *The Boston Globe,* it is precisely indifference that the journalist picks up on and is forced into: "here and there struggled a form," the "thrashing" and "upheavals" of mere life, the moment when horses and flies become indistinguishable. To say that disasters (nuclear bombs, earthquakes, tidal waves, etc.) indifferently obliterate everything in their path is something of a cliché and not, I don't think, what has caught the journalist's attention here. It is instead the weird visual sensation of bearing witness to a world whose forms and entities have been reduced to mere presence. The world becomes a furious slurry of motions and forces detached from identity. In the position of the viscous in the history of public humiliation — the tar in the tar and feathering ritual — the act of smearing stuff onto people brings them into social, ritualistic exposure. When the viscous *engulfs,* as it does with the molasses flood, there is also a kind of exposure, an exposure of indifference, a bringing of the world out into unspecified presence. The focus of this journalist's account is not the destructive force of the molasses, nor is it the death toll, but how strangely samey everything is as it struggles and gurgles under the clinging mass of sugar syrup. Do we have, here, a journalist struck by a vision of Oken's slimy o? A landscape where movements outwards are simultaneously a collapse back in, where a certainty of life is coupled with an indifference to exactly what kind.

What this journalist describes when observing the aftermath of the molasses flood is not dissimilar to how the philosopher

Emmanuel Levinas feels when entering a city after a long, tiring journey:

> Like the unreal, inverted city we find after an exhausting trip, things and beings strike us as though they no longer composed a world, and were swimming in the chaos of their existence [...] beings and things that collapse into their "materiality" are terrifyingly present in their destiny, weight and shape.[32]

When you get sleepy, the real world begins to feel like a hallucination, "unreal," an inverted version of what it used to be. Levinas loses his ability to define and compose what he sees and the urban environment begins to dissolve, liquefy, and rush chaotically about in dark pulsations of stuff. He figures this experience as a sort of collapse, as if some entropic dispersal of energy were taking place, a fading out into darkness, but this collapse is in fact a collapse *into* a greater intensity of presence. The terrifying fact for Levinas is that the more present the world becomes the more unreal it feels. This confusing oscillation between hallucination and reality, dissolution and composition is at the center of the ontological distinction that Levinas makes between existence and the existent. Existence is the fact of existence in general, the existent is differentiated, specified being. This is the difference between "being" and "beings." Being smothers, engulfs, and sticks to beings, but is entirely indifferent to them. At moments of sleepiness after a long journey, this irresolvable separation between being and beings erupts violently into presence, the being begins to *feel* like an unwelcome guest, an intruder into its own existence. At this moment, Levinas thinks, the *fantastic* occurs.

This is a spectacle that the makers of *Ghostbusters II* latch onto: the Psychomagnotheric Slime that grows from the city's sewers, onto the streets, to eventually engulf the (fictional)

32 Emmanuel Levinas, *Existence and Existents,* trans. Alphonso Lingis (Dordrecht: Kluwer Academic Publishers, 1988), 59.

71

Manhattan Museum of Art, lives off the social negativity and non-civic feeling of New York's inhabitants. The city goes gooey with the physical embodiment of political indifference. Until, that is, the Statue of Liberty saves the day. Affect and materiality converge, slime turns everything into the same thing and feeds, in this film, off people feeling indifferent.

But why the neon pink of the Psychomagnotheric Slime? Much has been made of the pre-'90s B-movie obsession with slime monsters as the materialization of the Cold War nuclear threat, or the threat of pollution, be it nuclear or otherwise. The link between toxicity and the color green was established in the 19th century by the arsenic in green dyes of 19th-century hair and gown pigments, which poisoned many hundreds of women.[33] They would vomit green water, their eyes would turn green, along with their vision. They would foam at the mouth, convulse, and then die. Luminous green then became associated with radioactivity in the early 20th century, when the US Radium Foundation started in 1911 manufacturing glow-in-the-dark paint, which they called "Undark." The paint also contained phosphor, the chemical actually responsible for the paint's glow, the radium only excited the phosphor to glow brighter. The paint was used for the highlights on clock and watch faces and applied by workers, all women, on 250 dials a day at one and a half cents a dial. Many of the women died painful deaths from radiation poisoning in a well-covered scandal, becoming known as the "Radium Girls."[34] It was from this that the imaginary of glowing radioactive waste came.

I will discuss the viscosity of radiation and light in the next chapter and will going much further into the cute, gooey gunge toy aesthetic in the third. The role of the pinkness in the film's Psychomagnotheric slime is interesting however for another, quite simple, reason. It exhibits how slime sits in an ambivalent

---

33 Alison Mathews David, *Fashion Victims: The Dangers of Dress Past and Present* (London: Bloomsbury, 2015), 74–98.

34 Dr Karl, "Green Glow of Radiation," ABC *Science,* May 20, 2008, http://www.abc.net.au/science/articles/2008/05/20/2249925.htm.

position between the flamboyant and the repressed. The substance has moved from one extreme to another, propelled itself from total obscurity to absolute visibility. This slime desires to be hi-vis. *Ghostbusters II* is interested in slime as a particular way of claiming attention, it will do whatever it takes to get it. There is an inkling, here, of something I want to develop further: the sense that the spread of indifference is the spread of pure spectacle, a form that exists for nothing but its extreme visibility.

I am not the first to link this sensation in Levinas to Sartre's signature substance: "paste," something that is not blurry, obscure, but of terrifying clarity.[35] This famous moment in his novel *Nausea* is appropriate:

> And then all of a sudden, there it was, clear as day: existence had suddenly unveiled itself. It had lost the harmless look of an abstract category: it was the very paste of things; this root was kneaded into existence. Or rather the root, the park gates, the bench, the sparse grass, all that had vanished: the diversity of things, their individuality, were only an appearance, a veneer. This veneer had melted, leaving soft, monstrous masses, all in disorder— naked, in a frightful, obscene nakedness.[36]

The park environment, once you remove its false veil of diversity is soft and gooey. Sartre hates it. It makes him sick. Viscous is what the world becomes when you stop having ideas about it.

---

35 This connection is made by Catherine Malabou in her essay "Pierre Loves Horranges Levinas–Sartre — Nancy: An Approach to the Fantastic in Philosophy," in *Penumbr(a)*, eds. Sigi Jöttkandt and Joan Copjec (Melbourne: re.press, 2013), 103–17, at 109–10.

36 Jean-Paul Sartre, *Nausea,* trans. Robert Baldick (London: Penguin Classics, 2000), 183.

Ecstatic Specificity

In the molasses flood, the hard streets and docks are covered in thick sugar syrup. In the experiences of Levinas and Sartre, the urban environment *itself* turns gloopy. Or rather, the urban environment feels as if it turned gloopy in what appears to be a moment of synesthetic transposition. This softness that Sartre describes cannot, of course, be touched, but intuited. But how is it possible for monstrous softness to be intangible? Here we have the crux of what are essentially the concluding pages of Sartre's *Being and Nothingness,* his famous meditation on the nature of the slimy, *le visqueux.* The central problematic in his delving into the meaning of the viscous encounter, the pouring of honey back into honey, is the question: How can "sliminess" be ascribed as much to a physical sensation, as to a social interaction, a handshake, a smile? The common opinion holds, perhaps, that we accumulate sensual experiences of softness, of hardness, of fluidity, etc. that we then use as symbols or metaphors which we can superimpose onto fully formed psychic attitudes. This explanation involves "projection," the projection of psychological states, which are primary, onto material ones, which are secondary. Sartre's hugely important and widely acknowledged contribution to material thinking is his dismantling of this psychological/material hierarchy. As he says in a statement of dazzling dialectical entanglement:

> The slimy does not symbolize any psychic attitude *a priori*; it manifests a certain relation of being with itself and this relation has originally a psychic quality because I have discovered it in a plan of appropriation and because the sliminess has returned my image to me.[37]

37 Jean-Paul Sartre, *Being and Nothingness: A Phenomenological Essay on Ontology,* trans. Hazel E. Barnes (Washington: Washington Square Press, 1992), 611.

The slimy is an encounter with a particular mode of being that has no life in itself, but which gains a psychic attitude through its response to the appropriative project of the subject. But this response seems also to possess an appropriative project itself, it "returns" his image to him. The slimy sticks to you, as you go to grasp it, it grasps you back. The more you try to remove it from your hand, the more of your hand it covers. This, Sartre imagines, is the revenge of the "in-itself" on the "for-itself," the object taking revenge on the subject, the threat of things to engulf and annihilate subjectivity, to lose ourselves in objects. When honey drips off your fingers, you sense an uncanny continuity of yourself with the world. To touch the viscous, we risk, it feels, becoming viscous.

An encounter with sliminess is therefore not only a sensual one, but the revelation of a kind of ontological schema that transcends the "distinction between psychic and non-psychic" and where slimy things of all kinds can arrange themselves: be it mayonnaise, handshakes, cakes, or glances. All the things we describe as slimy share in this schema. It is a rubric for "classifying all the thises of the world."[38] There is, then, the possibility of this schema engulfing all, for the whole of being to be taken over by this mode of self-relation. The viscous is a "potential meaning of being."[39] To be engulfed is Sartre's great anxiety.

One of the core dubiousnesses of the slimy is the fact that it lingers, it exhibits a *hysteresis,* a tendency to lag behind. Sartre finds the appropriate symbol for this in the taste of sugar that remains in the mouth after swallowing. "A sugary death is the ideal for the slimy."[40] Honey that falls back into itself displays a strange non-coincidence with itself, a reluctance to return to itself to which it eventually and ineluctably succumbs. This image of honey falling into honey, as Catherine Malabou helps to elucidate, is an image of ontological difference at once revealed and annulled. "The genius of Sartre's writing," she proposes, consists

38 Ibid., 606.
39 Ibid.
40 Ibid., 609.

"in the way in which it makes ontological difference exist; that is, the way in which it invites things to bear witness to the question of Being."[41] Things are allowed to remain themselves in all their finite, sensual particularity, but, at the same time, ooze gradually into a wider ontological schema. The viscous schema is itself viscous.

This has got to do, I think, with how exceptionally compelling this passage in *Being and Nothingness* is to read. The writing never feels prescriptive or programmatic, but instead stylistically caught up in its own subject matter. The ambivalence of repulsion and fascination is played out by Sartre as he luxuriates in the visual and visceral possibilities of these substances — honey is not enough, we move between snow, lemons, and leeches, needy dogs and breasts, glue, sweat, and children's toys. These things proliferate abundantly and then collapse into one another as Sartre returns compulsively to yet another enigmatic figuration of viscous dubiousness: "it lives obscurely under my fingers and I sense it like a dizziness."[42] The viscous is positioned as a threat, but he often seems almost addicted to all the ingenious new ways he can characterize its weirdness, the elaborating viscous dialectic between peculiar mundanity and the dynamics of Being. Alongside the astute philosophical insights he offers, there is a sense, when you read and reread this piece of writing, of a mounting euphoria, a euphoria he sticks to and that sticks to him, that may indeed disturb him. He indulgences in the pleasure, a pleasure of an ecstatic kind, of his capacity simply to describe and the role this capacity has in moving things beyond themselves.

There is a drama and a showiness to how Sartre offers himself up in his writing. His intention is not only to inform, communicate, but to thrill. The viscous itself is, after all, a moment of material and existential excitation, like the "discovery of an adventure of being." He is also caught by the status of these substances as images, not only as reflections of himself, but as substances of

41 Malabou, "Pierre Loves Horranges," 110.
42 Sartre, *Being and Nothingness,* 609.

pure exteriority, pure show. At a certain point, Sartre compares the reintegration of honey into honey to the image of a woman's breast as she lies on her back. In the original French:

[C]omme l'étalement, le raplatissement des seins un peu murs d'une femme qui s'entend sur le dos.[43]

This word, *étalement,* which most literally translates as "spreading," is translated by Hazel Barnes as "display":

[A]s display — like the flattening out of the full breasts of a woman who is lying on her back.[44]

The original image is, for sure, erotic, and Barnes highly interpretive translation foregrounds the implication of sexy advertisement and offering. What is the relation between spreading and display? In modern English, display undoubtedly entails a performance of surfaces. Its Latin roots, however, are in the word *displicare,* meaning scatter or disperse. This then evolved into a Middle English usage meaning to unfurl or unfold. There is the word "splay," splay-legged: limbs thrust apart. And then there's the gendered expression that carries violent, exploitative, rapey connotations, "she spread her legs." This association of spread with display recalls the expression "laying on a spread," an image Gertrude Stein plays with in *Tender Buttons*:

A kind in glass and a cousin, a spectacle and nothing strange a single hurt colour and an arrangement in system to pointing. All this and not ordinary, not unordered in not resembling. The difference is spreading.[45]

43 Jean-Paul Sartre, *L'être et le néant: Essaie d'ontologie phenoménologique* (Paris: Editions Gallimard, 1943), 654.
44 Sarte, *Being and Nothingness,* 608.
45 Gertrude Stein, *Tender Buttons* (New York: Dover Publications, 1997), 3.

"Laying on a spread" is precisely the spectacle of offering up, on a table probably, edible difference, one that works as a kind of system, "all this," a meal? The "difference" between Sartre's display/spreading and Stein's is that Stein's difference spreads, where for Sartre spreading is what cancels differentiation. The act of displaying the breast is exactly what flattens it out, destroys its image, the act that absorbs its form into the body. Or maybe it is in the moment of resistance against reintegration into homogeneity that the image reveals itself. This resistance grants the viewer a voyeuristic glimpse of momentary differentiation, a seductive unfolding of matter into singularity, an intimacy with it while it undertakes its disappearance. The excitation of the viscous is also found in this tantalizing moment of specificity it offers up to you in the moment of collapse. For there is in his experience of the slimy a sense that it wants him, specifically him, Sartre himself, if only for a moment.

The misogyny of Sartre's evocation of his encounter with the viscous is, in many ways, blindingly obvious. The image of the writer is primarily of an intellectual white man feeling threatened in his quest for mastery and appropriation by his simultaneous fascination for and revulsion from an aberrant gooey object, one that becomes explicitly gendered — a "feminine sucking."[46] Maybe this sense of thrill that I just identified in the text is a result of my own illusions of masculine heroism, a secret and repugnant complicity I feel with my white male predecessor, whose "signature substance" just so happens to be the subject of this book. But I will offer an alternative analysis, one that requires much less identity-based soul-searching and feels much more adventurous.

Sartre is never actually essentialist about the aberrance of the viscous. The viscous only ever takes on its threatening properties in its *encounter* with a mode of being that has at its core a project of appropriation. The viscous is only base *in relation* to a world that has as its dominant mode of being one that seeks mastery. Any reference to morality is qualified as culturally spe-

46 Sartre, *Being and Nothingness*, 609.

cific, specifically European. Sartre's fear is real, but it is never presented as one that transcends the structure of the specific encounter. In the battleground of these pages, in the antagonism between the in-itself and the for-itself, there is a recurrent acknowledgment of a revenge that ought to be undertaken against the mode of being that Sartre himself represents. In its threat, in the threat of his engulfment, the viscous contains, for Sartre, a promise of something else, an adventure of being that saturates the work but which also lies beyond what he is actually able to think. This constitutes the ultimate thrill of this writing.

I think we can safely assume that Sartre had no knowledge of the molasses flood. Not only was he fourteen when the event occurred, but, to my knowledge, it was not reported in any French newspapers. It is, however, interesting to speculate about what he would have made of it. It is, after all, the literal occurrence of what he explicitly dreads and longs for: to be engulfed and to drown in thick, slimy, sickly sweetness. What if he had been there? Philosophy begins to feel like something that can be catastrophically forced upon you, burst out from the world, rather than intuited from it through sensual encounters with things at your fingertips in domestic locations.

But most importantly: Sartre's viscous writing never paints the material state as "originary" or "primordial." It is, for him, a set of ontological structures, which are always seen more as possible futures than some indifference that preceded us and that we emerged from. In fact, his viscous writing, I want to suggest, has more in common with walking down Oxford Street, or through duty free, than it does with gradually sinking into a Lovecraftian slime pit. Sartre's famous viscous passage is not normally associated with the city or its ways of trying to sell you things, but there is certainly an almost consumerist compulsiveness to his joy in synonyms, the uneasy friendliness of the objects of display, gently accumulating. The *stuff* the viscous makes him do is all a performance of its state.

Worming through the Aperture

Composed, as they are, of extremes in sound and motion, explosions have a very special affinity with the history of the moving image, most famously exemplified, perhaps, in the climax of Michelangelo Antonioni's *Zabriski Point*. Bursts too, however, have their place the history of cinema, *Ghost Busters II* being part of a long line of B-Movie slimer films that are intriguingly foreshadowed by the molasses disaster. The earliest and most famous of these films is perhaps *The Blob* from 1955, remade in 1988. In both films, a gelatinous mass makes its way through the city streets, absorbing people indifferently into itself. The films are composed such that the viewer is only permitted glimpses of the form, slowly swelling until the great climactic moment, where the blob bursts out of the projectionist's apertures at the back of a cinema. Screams and panic ensue as the thing flops around ingesting its prey. This is, in many ways, a standard horror movie technique: placing the film's climax and scariest moment in the viewers' location. But it is also a moment where Sartre's flamboyant viscous is dramatized. The viscous is so desperate to be seen, it literally worms its way into the mechanics of the cinematic image like a cat flopping itself down on your keyboard when you're trying to write an email. In *The Blob*, the viscous forces itself into the channels that have been assigned for light as if demanding you give it the same kind of attention. The burst is jealous of the explosion, goo envious of light. This is the viscous as monstrous, obsessed with demonstration. It is that which always wants from you what you do not feel prepared to give. It treats "attention" as something not unique to its object or as a relational moment, but as an object in itself, one that can be traded, picked up, and repurposed.

In her book *Animal Capital*, Nicole Shukin unearths a gelatinous underbelly to the efficiency of 20th-century industrial processes and to the flow of the cinematic image. This slime monster does not disturb from outside cinema, but from within its industry. Henry Ford's famous system of auto assembly at Highland Park, usually traced back to 1913, had been in action, she explains, since at least the 1850s in the vertical abattoirs of Cincinnati and Chicago. Ford visited one of these abattoirs and was reportedly deeply impressed by the way "animal matter" kept flowing, suspended from hanging chains, continuously past stationary laborers occupied by highly repetitive, simple work. Ford, inspired by what he saw, devised a similar method with, as Shukin says, "a crucial mimetic twist: his automated lines sped-up the assembly of a machine body rather than the disassembly of an animal body."[47] Fordist assembly of machines found its prototype in the ways animals were torn apart in abattoirs.

The sites of these early industrial abattoirs were also, in the mid-19th century, treated as spectacles, places of sensory stimulation that you could buy a ticket to experience. Unlike today, perhaps, where the space of the abattoir is secreted away, a shameful place of our over consumption and greed, largely invisible save a few gruesome clips distributed online, the site of mass slaughter in the 19th century opened its doors to the general public, offering popularly attended tours of its processes. In 1893, 1 million people visited the Chicago stockyards, witnessing cattle cascade off elevated landings, hung on chains, slaughtered and dismembered. People would respond with a mixture of horror and delight at the sight of the blood, the flesh, but also the intense olfactory and auditory stimulation. The stench of blood and guts was accompanied by a cacophony of clanking chains, the squealing of pigs. People took pride in witnessing the efficiency with which their country was able to manage its material production, as well as feasting voyeuristically on what was a kind of pre-cinematic moving image experience. Abattoirs made sure to capitalize on the visual drama of their technology.

Shukin evokes these guided tours of abattoirs as a material "negative" of what was taking place on the other side of the river in Chicago at the same time, the World's Columbian Exposition of 1893, where Eadweard Muybridge's Zoopraxiscope was being exhibited alongside Edison's Kinetoscope motion picture

47 Nicole Shukin, *Animal Matter: Rendering Life in Bio-Political Times* (Minnesota: University of Minneapolis Press, 2009), 87.

camera, both of which sought to capture life in its animation, its spontaneity. "The mimetic media were," Shukin says, "for a brief historical instant, dangerously contiguous with their material unconscious."[48] For it was, after all, from the slaughterhouses where the film manufacturers acquired their gelatin for the production of film stock. In 1873, a gelatin emulsion made from the skin, bones, and connective tissue of animals was first used for photographic purposes. Shukin considers this gelatinous matter to be the repressed material history of the cinematic image, one that is shrouded in the mystique of the so-called "magic of cinema." Gelatin, for Shukin, "marks a 'vanishing point' where moving images are both inconspicuously and *viscerally* contingent on mass animal disassembly, in contradiction with cinema's framing semiotic of 'animation.'"[49]

"Friendly" Spaces

But is this anxious need for attention and transaction for, it seems, solely the sake of attention and transaction not one of the defining features of how it feels to live a life in modern urban spaces? This viscous neediness has seeped into the dynamics of city space itself where, rather than being a horrifying, nauseating underbelly, its tendencies are to be felt everywhere openly operating within day-to-day commerce. To put it simply — where better to find an example of Sartre's *hysteresis* of honey than a group of people on the bus all wearing the same trainers, all the same yet bought to the fulfill the specific desire of each wearer? Difference becomes, like Oken's slimy o, some reachings out that plunge back into an indifferent whole. Where better to find this completely unwelcome, calculating friendliness than in a pile of avocados sitting in Tesco, each one bearing a sticker addressing you *personally*: "Eat me, I'm tasty"? Avocados and trainers: there might not be anything slimier than hipster culture.

48 Ibid., 93.
49 Ibid.

Might it be possible for this ontological structure of the viscous to become a design strategy, a kind of infrastructure? For the architect Rem Koolhaas "each square inch" of airports, shopping centers, casinos, trash modern commercial space is

a grasping, needy surface dependent on consent or overt support, discount, compensation, and fund-raising.[50]

These spaces are defined by excessive and relentless friendliness that oppresses as it excites, like being condemned to a "perpetual Jacuzzi with millions of your best friends."

This piece by Koolhaas I'm referring to on so-called postmodern architectural spaces, his extraordinary "Junkspace," is obsessed with the texture of space, the heterogeneous scrambling of surface materials in airports: "concrete, hairy, heavy, shiny plastic, metallic, muddy—alternate randomly as if dedicated to different species."[51] But it is also obsessed with the viscous textures of how junkspace *behaves*. Though the word "viscous" never occurs in the work, its operations are everywhere. Junkspace is what "coagulates while modernization is in progress," if its movements become "synchronised it curdles," it is a malleable substance, which can "engulf an entire city," or may contain fountains that ejaculate out Stalinist buildings, "hovering momentarily, then withdrawing with amnesiac competency."[52] Koolhaas's vision of junkspace is one that morphs wildly from form to form—Disney stores become meditation centers—is continually contorted as an expression of domination, and yet has a lameness: a place out of which space is "scooped [...] like a soggy block of icecream."[53] This is the "fuzzy empire of blur."[54]

Junkspace advertises itself as a "space of flows," where it is in fact the opposite. Where "flows depend on disciplined

50 Rem Koolhaas, "Junkspace," *October* 100 "Obsolescence" (Spring, 2002): 175–90, at 178.
51 Ibid., 181.
52 Ibid., 175, 180, 186.
53 Ibid., 182.
54 Ibid., 176.

movement,"[55] direct passages of movement from A to B, junk-space absorbs, entraps, curls you round, disorientates. Think of the ways in which duty free spaces in airports make you think you're being led to wherever you need to go, where in fact you're being taken on some intestinal voyage past every mass-produced piece of tech, fashion item, or beverage on the planet. This is an example of viscous space, one that uses your desire to get somewhere to its own advantage, to make the interminable transaction more inevitable. This kind of space of course feels smooth to move through from its virtuosic use of all technologies of spatial seamlessness — escalators, travellators, air conditioning, hot air curtains, sliding doors, sprinklers. But this is in order to maximize the grotesque-ness of your journey past ever more "insistent perfumes, "asylum-seekers," building site, underwear, oysters, pornography, cell-phones."[56] Any instance of actual flow leads to disaster in junkspace, as Koolhaas says:

> department stores at the beginning of sales; the stampedes triggered by warring compartments of soccer fans; dead bodies piling up in front of the locked emergency doors of a disco.[57]

The portals of junkspace appear welcoming, but are in fact too tight. Any attempt to simply leave, arrive, get form there to here, escape or deny its thickened, gloopy logic, results in an unravelling of its simulated order.

All this clinging nonsense "spells the end," Koolhaas confidently claims, "of the Enlightenment."[58] But, despite his exasperation at the violent lameness, the overwhelming docility, of junkspace, it doesn't seem to be the Enlightenment that he wants back. Instead, we have a writing not unlike Sartre's on the viscous, if more erratic — one addicted to synonyms, lists, end-

---

55 Ibid., 179.
56 Ibid., 185, 181.
57 Ibid., 180.
58 Ibid., 175.

less returns and reformulations, a love of all the different and increasingly excessive ways you are able to describe the same thing. One place, for sure, to feel the cacophonous intestines of a shopping center is in Koolhaas's own writing. We have then the strange spectacle of a writing that seems to perform exactly what it loathes, a block of text without paragraph break that, once we're inside, could elaborate endlessly, no structure, just membranes with flimsy ellipses taping together the modular patchwork. As the text (thankfully) stifles close analysis, we might feel it better to simply wait for (as in a departure lounge) and indulge in its moments of colossal beauty:

> Railway stations unfold like iron butterflies, airports glisten like cyclopic dewdrops, bridges span often negligible banks like grotesquely enlarged visions of the harp. To each rivulet its own Calatrava.[59]

Indeed, like Sartre's viscous writing, we have the feeling of a writing that is so passionately involved with what it claims to hate, we start suspecting it doesn't hate it at all. Or maybe it is in love with how much it hates, how much it is able to hate. Fredric Jameson, reading Koolhaas's writing, finds in its mimesis a new kind of writing, one not only of euphoric repulsion, but also one where space itself is being performed by language. This isn't architectural theory, but a show exhibiting a "language of space which is speaking through these self-replicating, self-perpetuating sentences."[60] This text-performance emerges out of a time when not only the contemporary city, but also "the whole universe," is on the point of "fusing into a kind of all-purpose indeterminate magma."[61] But this mimesis is, just maybe, the way out, in Jamesian fashion, the death knell of the post-modern:

---

59 Ibid., 187.
60 Fredric Jameson, "Future City," *New Left Review* 21 (May–June, 2003): 65–79, at 74.
61 Ibid., 73.

Fig. 8. The aftermath of the Molasses Disaster, *The Boston Globe.*

> The sentences are the boom of this repetitive insistence, this
> pounding on the hollowness of space itself; and their energy
> now foretells the rush and the fresh air, the euphoria of a re-
> lief, an orgasmic breaking through into a time and history
> again, into a concrete future.[62]

This spatial writing is, then, the activity that predicts the moment the city will burst, breaking through into a state that is
made of "fresh air" and "concrete." The writing is a signal that
monstrous displays of corporate space are no longer terrifying,
but euphoric, a euphoria that remains to be explained. But it
seems to me that we also have here a thinking and a writing that
bursts. It is a writing that gives itself to the explosive possibilities
of thinking, but stays with what is there at hand. It combines the
dual excitation of the burst, the excitation of the sticky and the
explosive. It seeks to obliterate the world while simultaneously
staying with things as such. I find, here, a writing that denies

62 Ibid., 77.

86

how things are, but which lingers with them, a letting go, a giving up, of the world combined with an obstinate desire to *stay there*.

Let's look again at an image from the Molasses Disaster aftermath (fig. 8).

What is noticeable is the incompleteness of the destruction, like, as Sartre says on the viscous's power to destroy, "a retarded annihilation" has taken place, one "that has been stopped halfway."[63] It is a vision of a city blurred and twisted out of normality, caught, it feels, just on the brink of collapse in a state of incomplete sublimity. These mutilated forms give rise to pareidolia: some huge submarine beast raises its head from the city streets. From its gaping mouth reaches a tongue on which eels writhe and entangle. A discarded overcoat. Some hats. Sugar syrup. For it also seems to me that these examples of viscous writing — Sartre, Koolhaas, and, by extension, Jameson — all find huge power in something apparently very simple: description. "Criticality," in moments of all-consuming viscous encounter, is no longer possible. What can be practiced, however, is description, a smearing of ones attention again and again over the surfaces of that which surrounds you, eating away at them from within. The power to describe is figured as a viscous involvement with the world, being the power to make things malleable, form and reform what you experience. "Practice description," as Lisa Robertson says in "Soft Architecture: A Manifesto," as "the truly utopian act is to manifest current conditions and dialects."[64] To be able to describe things accurately *as they are* is the most futuristic act. And by description she means something moist, something dreamy, something to do with form, something contingent, yet posing as something else:

63 Sartre, *Being and Nothingness*, 608.
64 Lisa Robertson, "Soft Architecture: A Manifesto," in *Occasional Work and Seven Walks from the Office for Soft Architecture* (Oregon: Clear Cut Press, 2003), 20.

moistly critical dreams, morphological thefts, authentic reg-
isters of pleasant customs, accidents posing as intentions. SA
makes up face-practices.[65]

Primordial Flamboyance

The history of slime's encounter with the city is multiple. This
is because it is a force that enters into the space as a means to
rethink it. What the residents and journalists witnessed in the
Boston Molasses Disaster was a singularly uncanny event, one
where the excitations of the explosive and gooey came into large
scale, industrialized companionship — the burst. Thinking that
bursts is a thinking that is at once explosive and slimy, it seeks
to obliterate how things are, while simultaneously attempting to
stay with them, linger awhile longer.

Slime colliding with the city causes the parameters by which
we define and imagine the urban space to become blurred, expanded, and increasingly absorptive. Viscous dynamics are
becoming the core processes whereby an exploded, planetary
vision of the city is being theorized. Words like "churned" and
"colloidal" are becoming the necessary terms to reimagine the
urban, terms that involve an integral mess, an imperfect and
indeterminate conjunction. But this is not only metaphorical,
sliminess is not only a useful tool for describing processes that
are otherwise un-slimy. The primordial powers of slime mold
are, it turns out, closer than we thought to the infrastructural
powers of modernity. This interest in the organizational powers
of the slime mold is part of an interest in the intelligence of these
organisms. These dispersed consciousnesses have, for instance,
kinds of memory that works by smearing — they smear a trace
of substance over the places they've been so that they don't return to the same spot twice. Were our own powers of memory
once a very fine film of viscous matter laid over the surface of
our environment? In the writing of Walter Benjamin, when trying to describe the experience of being stoned, we find an in-

65 Ibid., 21.

triguing wormhole into this intensely material, spatialized kind of attention. He smears his imagination onto the stones of the pavement, he finds nourishment there, but also a very particular kind of "anywhere." This is an anywhere based on extreme material specificity, rather than indifferent mass production.

But from slime's encounter with the city, we also learn of slime's flamboyance. Sartre, whose protagonist in *Nausea* famously encounters the slime at the heart of things when walking in the park, is by far the most famous theorist of sliminess. From his formulation of sliminess not as a metaphor, but an ontological structure, a potential meaning of being, we also experience the exhilarating drama and adventure of the slimy encounter. If slime is an apparently primordial kind of attention to space, its substance is also weirdly attentive to *us,* attentive of the attention we display to it. Slime seems, as Sartre so vividly describes, to want *him* and, it feels in that moment, nothing else. Out of this attentiveness comes an addiction to the increasingly elaborate and striking ways he is able to figure its existence. As the slime thrills Sartre, he thrills us, feeding us more and more of the images the substance brings to him. That this is an immensely compelling text to read is at the heart of its philosophy. It revels in the powers of description to burst things beyond themselves.

The euphoria, the "dizziness" that Sartre feels as he contemplates the viscous sets it apart from the creep of the primordial. It gestures towards another kind of slimy attention, or rather the need slime has for attention and the excursions it undergoes to keep it. Slime's weirdness is its manic attentiveness to our attention, while completely misunderstanding the processes whereby attention is formed. It mistakes attention for an object in itself, one that can be moved around. Slime forces its way into the channels and mechanisms of attention. This is the work of neediness.

Slime and the city has revealed, then, how the viscous bends in two seemingly opposed directions, towards the indifferent on the one hand, and towards the needy, the showy, the flamboyant, on the other. We see Sartre's "overwhelming docility" of viscous matter creeping into Rem Koolhaas's writing on commercial space, a writing that is, like Sartre's, addicted to the wild play of the synonymous. Slime's dynamics, rather than being totally at odds with those of the urban space, start to feel as if they emerge from within its space, the grasping neediness of commercial centers. But with this we are also brought into the presence of a particular approach to writing, one that doesn't object to the slimy, but works its way into it, it feels the obligation to describe, to cling on, to mold.

Fig. 1. Mud volcano at Binəqədi, Azerbaijan. Photo by the author.

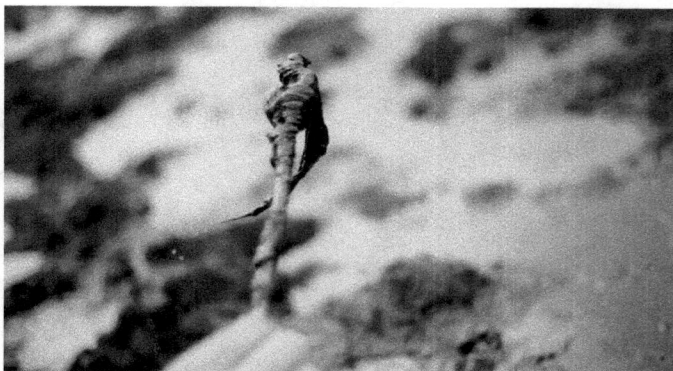

Fig. 2. Tar lake at Binəqədi, Azerbaijan. Photo by the author.

2

Sticky Worlds/Sticky Words

PLACE: Baku, Azerbaijan, 2017

> *I love the way it slows my footsteps, I am*
> *grateful for the detours it makes me take.*
> — Francis Ponge, "Unfinished Ode to Mud"[1]

The Hagverdiyev Lineage

In my search for sticky worlds, I travelled to Azerbaijan, to an asphalt lake in the north of Baku, a place called Binəqədi. My contact out there was a man named Butanay Hagverdiyev, a painter who I had met 10 years previously in Paris. We had both been 18, I was slacking around pretending to be a writer, he'd come there to look at art, fill sketch books and learn to write backwards like da Vinci. He was to my teenage mind impossibly exotic. He sang strange opera to us in the deepest voice I'd ever heard. We'd fall over laughing. We'd drink mojitos, smoke, and talk. That's about all I can remember.

Butanay was a painter who had learned his craft in the church painting icons with his alcoholic father, who had died when he was 13. The father had trained Butanay as a child by getting him to hold his waist, steadying him, as he stood swaying and hic-

---

1   Francis Ponge, *Unfinished Ode to Mud*, trans. Beverley Bie Brahic
    (London: CB Editions, 2008), 83.

cuping on the scaffold up in the rafters, a man who, Butanay says, was a raging drunk but also a perfectionist and exceptionally articulate with the brush, even when totally smashed, barely able to stand. This was where Butanay had learnt to paint, or write, as you do with icons, and also acquired his faith, about which he had been cagey. But in the evenings of his teens he would also play in a death metal band, plug in, distort, and amplify, grow long mustaches, and smash stuff up. A counterpoint to his ascetic discipline, he was interested in rage and deep, violent urges. He took part in medieval re-enactments, giving me as he left Paris, returning to Baku, a long leather smock with golden buttons, for wearing under your chain-mail. I would wear this thing every now and again around the house, I wore it eating some spaghetti with my mother once, I remember, a bit confused, but massively touched. I don't know where it is these days.

Butanay's grandfather, Hasan Hagverdiyev, a painter, had been an Iranian immigrant to Azerbaijan in the 1930s who'd left, by his own words on his entry visa, the "capitalist pigs" of Iran, to give his art to Stalin's project in the country. After World War II, and a few years in Nazi prison camps and subsequently gulags for not shooting himself upon capture by the Germans, he became the most famous social realist painter in Azerbaijan. After serving his time in Siberia, his fortunes had reversed; Stalin gave him a large building in the center of the city to use as a state-sanctioned artist commune where Butanay's father had been born, as had Butanay (his father had been also, according to Butanay, a very active Azeri land artist in the 1980s, though I wasn't able to find any evidence of this). Butanay still lives there, having one of his studios there too, along with his mother, and the extensive family network descended from Hasan, most of whom are painters and all fiercely proud of their heritage. The atmosphere is macho, angle grinders the preferred implement, phrases like "girly art" are thrown about.

When we'd met in Paris, Butanay had been preparing to do his military service, still obligatory in Azerbaijan, a country whose not-so-cold war with Armenia persists. I would see over the next year or so on Facebook pictures of Butanay in Russian-style bearskin hats, with a Kalashnikov, grinning out at me madly, cigarette tightly teeth-gripped, posing with one foot on a huge pipeline stretching off into a snow-scape, which to me was definitely Siberia or somewhere. In fact it was just the outskirts of Baku. Binəqədi, to be exact, which just so happened to be the place our asphalt lake rose its weird self to the surface of the planet. During these days, he sometimes posted online pictures of his paintings, now of engines and guns, rather than angels and shepherds. Massive and multicolored, they were intricate, iconic in their stillness, but also weirdly cute — death machines all painted soft pink and lime green.

Lake

The asphalt lake in Binəqədi is countless millennia old and out of its goo Soviet archaeologists heaved a variety of prehistoric beasts that used to roam this area in bigger, wilder times.[2] The rhino goes to drink from the lake, but gets sucked in instead, the bitumen preserving its bones. Neighboring the asphalt lake a few hundred meters to the west was a mud volcano that rose above it like an unwelcome morning. Exactly in between these two, about a kilometer south, was a bathhouse, Xan Hamamı. I dreamt of shooting a scene where we extracted a submerged Butanay from the asphalt with a forklift truck, before driving him, hanging in a harness from the forks, dripping black oil, down the road to the bathhouse and plunging him in one of its steamy

2   These archaeologists, astonished that we had come all way for the Binəqədi asphalt lake, feel totally invisible in a city more interested in Eurovision and Zaha Hadid. The Museum of Archeology and Ethnography in Baku, really just a long narrow room piled high with dusty bones, has no internet presence at all (let alone guidebook). I only knew of its existence through a brief mention in the references of an archaeological journal. We spent two whole days searching Baku for the place, asking around every museum and gallery we could find, none of whom had heard of it. It is as if it and its people are caught in a cesspool (since 1989 when the funding stopped) outside the flow of time.

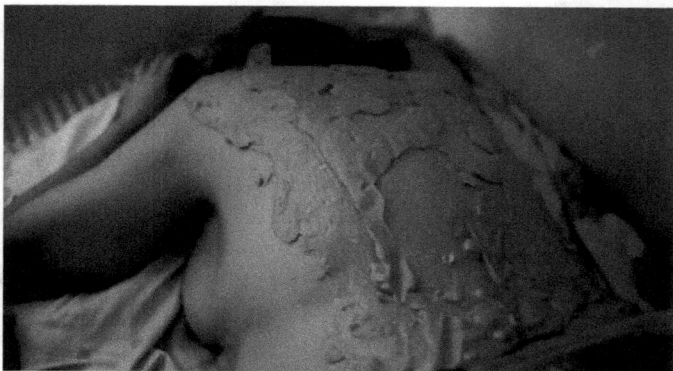

Fig. 3. Paraffin treatment at the Naftalan health resort, Azerbijan.
Photo by the author.

Fig. 4. A plastic decorative camel in front of the Naftalan health resort,
Azerbijan. Photo by the author.

pools, to be scrubbed down by an army of men with enormous bellies. All this in a single shot. I never did.

Later I would visit Naftalan, a health spa in the middle of Azerbaijan, west of Baku, where people have, for around a century, bathed in a particular kind of oil for health reasons. An oil that can, they claim, only be extracted from the surrounding region and cure you of many bodily ailments. All number of treatments are available: bathing, slathering on the back, massaging, even injecting into the prostate. The health benefits were discovered, one doctor informed me, gesturing into the desert from the terrace where we were sitting, hundreds of years ago by a dying, pregnant camel abandoned by its caravan in the desert. When the caravan returned to the same spot a year later, the camel had given birth and was in perfect health. It had discovered the lake of Naftalan oil. Life-sized, plastic, now immortal, camels are dotted around the complex to commemorate this lucky animal. The rhino and the camel, thanks to the oil, persist.

Asphalt lakes are uncanny places. They might feel to people like me from a place without large deposits of oil close to the surface, like some huge ecological catastrophe has occurred, like a moment of terrible contamination. But of course they're not, they're totally "natural." The setting at least corresponded to images I have in my head of "natural" places: reeds and grass and semi pleasant rolling hills in the distance, just on the outskirts of the city. This asphalt lake was connected to a larger water-based lake, and it sent, in mysteriously rhythmic pulsations, psychedelic plumages of color out into this water. I was, in effect, staring into an oily puddle on the road outside my house in London. But I wasn't, I was in Baku, the home of oil, one of the first places it was extracted by Alfred Nobel's brother Ludwig. It felt like the very specific location from where modern senses of placelessness had spread. The precise geographical origin of nowhere. Frogs hung around the lake at the base of the reeds in crowds. Only silken creatures are permitted here.

In Binəqədi, as I documented the lake with a camera and sound recorder as best I could, the man who Butanay had organized to drive us out to the lake got bored and went off in

Fig. 5. The director of the Museum of Archeology and Ethnography, Baku, Azerbaijan. Photo by the author.

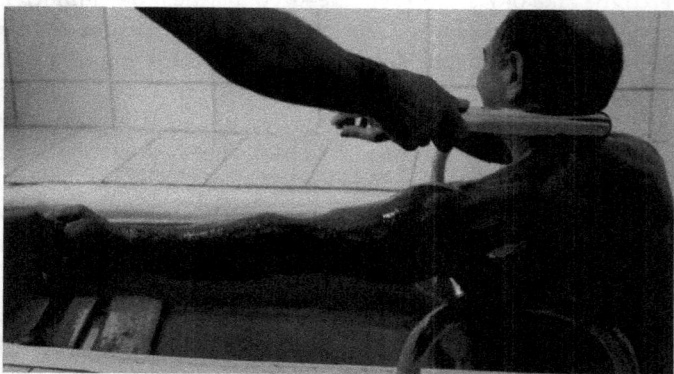

Fig. 6. A man bathing in oil in the Naftalan health resort, Azerbijan. Photo by the author.

his car to buy some food. He returned with some sausages and bread. We lit a fire on the banks of this would-be petrol, cooked the sausages and had lunch on the threshold between the world and its apocalypse. A complex, thickly bucolic atmosphere descended.

At the tip of the Abşeron Peninsula, where Baku is situated, sits the small island of Pirallahı, heavily populated with SOCAR (the state-owned oil company in the country, largest after BP) nodding donkeys, and oil pumps. It was once a Soviet prison camp for German soldiers after the war, some of whom decided to stay after being set free. They built their houses out of wood. Before, Zoroastrians had had their fire temples on the island, and it is believed to be first place oil was pumped from ground. To the west of the island, a vast mud desert, a landscape that is hard to love, at points blistering up into volcanoes. And on its east, the Caspian Sea, which is, like the Dead Sea, a large landlocked salt lake. Its body is dependent upon the flow of the Volga and Ural that empty into it. When a draught hit western Russia in 2009 there were fears that its level might drop so much that there would be an algae bloom, turning its whole body into slime. The sturgeon would then all die, the source of the caviar, causing the immensely valuable industry to collapse. Oil and caviar are the main resources here, the former slowly poisoning the latter.

Eras of Ooze

Some of the most famous moments in modernism seem to take a dim view of rivers, gesturing out instead to a viscous future, one where a stickiness has replaced that which once gushed and flowed. "Everything oozes," as Beckett's Estragon famously proclaims, a sardonic take on the Heraclitean maxim *panta rhei,* to announce the sluggishness of things when something you're sure should be happening, just simply isn't. Ezra Pound, too, goes after this constancy of flux, offering a correction to the model, one much more appropriate to how things have become. In *Hugh Selwyn Mauberly*:

"All things are a-flowing"
Sage Heraclitus says,
But a tawdry cheapness
shall outlast our days.[3]

Rivers have become laughable things. Noticeable is how both writers don't appear to feel the need to take Heraclitus's statement seriously. It is the object of ridicule, rather than something to be seriously confronted. The "tawdy cheapness" or Beckett's "ooze" is both what has replaced the sense of flow, but also what prevents you from engaging with it seriously. There is a sense that the writers both willfully misunderstand what Heraclitus means, disregarding the dialectic of non-self-identity — the way constant motion turns into a kind of stillness — but replacing it with, instead, a *mood,* a sardonic atmosphere where things cloy and clam up, rather than change and sparkle in a condition of metastasis. Just like that, rivers are dismissed. Wordsworth's River Derwent that "tempers human waywardness" is satirized, a nice idea, but nowadays hopelessly naïve, totally inappropriate for the way things have become. For these two writers, Sartre's warning that the viscous was "a potential meaning of being,"[4] was no longer a potentiality, but a fact of life — gloopiness had somehow finally come, it was everywhere and will outlast us.

But even on their entry into western philosophy the waters of the Heraclitean river were troubled. In Plato's *Cratylus,* Socrates first refers to it with disdain, seeing the assertion as a kind of toy he can fool around with. He wonders whether the reason people feel inclined towards the Heraclitean notion of flux is merely a sonic association between the *o* in *ousia* (being), and *othoun* (pushing principle).[5] The connection is accidental, he muses, the

3 Ezra Pound, "Hugh Selwyn Mauberly," in *Early Writings: Poems and Prose,* ed. Ira B. Nadel (London: Penguin, 2009), 190.

4 Jean-Paul Sartre, *Being and Nothingness: A Phenomenological Essay on Ontology,* trans. Hazel E. Barnes (Washington: Washington Square Press, 1992), 612.

5 Plato, *Cratylus,* trans. H. Fowler (Cambridge: Harvard University Press, 1921), 401b, 67.

result of an arbitrary stickiness between the sounds of words, the articulation of our mouths as we produce them, rather than a universal constant. What looks like philosophical thought is just the effect of a pleasing movement of the mouth. But he doesn't appear to have the energy to think this through properly, cutting his thoughts short: "I'm talking nonsense."[6] *Panta rhei* seems to be for Socrates an opportunity to think out loud, lose himself in speculation, unchecked rhetoric.

Socrates returns to the flowing nature of all things later in the dialogue in a moment of sheer whimsy. Maybe the modern philosopher, he wonders, is so dizzy from all their thinking, whirling round and round, that they superimpose their confusion about nature of things onto the nature of things themselves.[7] The Heracliteans wrongly assume, Socrates speculates, that if they are confused it's because everything else is as well. Thoughts can't settle because things can't either. But, again, Socrates does not seem to feel particularly obliged to follow this thought through. It just occurs to him out of the blue at this moment in the dialogue, as if he thought he'd just let his interlocutor know. This is no doubt a satirical strategy of the dialogue. Socrates, master dialectician, is sent into the same flights of dizziness he identifies in Heraclitus's followers.

The dismissal of fluidity in this dialogue might be considered part of Plato's more general philosophical project, the evocation of his metaphysics, the immutable, certainly non-fluid, Forms. But here we also have the impulse to ridicule fluidity as not serious, as a bit of a cop-out, a triumph of wishful thinking. We find the same kind of patronizing smiles and worldly head-shaking in Beckett and Pound's satirical takes on the maxim. Despite his reverence for the substance, Gaston Bachelard also warns, in *Water and Dreams,* of finding in water's constant mobility, its sparkly reflection, "only an excuse" to go on "holidays."[8] Water's

6   Ibid., 401e, 67.
7   Ibid., 411c, 97.
8   Gaston Bachelard, *Water and Dreams: An Essay On the Imagination of Matter,* trans. Edith Farrell (Dallas: The Dallas Institute Publications, 1994), 20.

substance contains the risk fake freedoms, the bitterness of the leisure time granted by one's employer.

It is precisely this giving way of fluidity to something more bloody-minded, awkward, stickier, and inconsistent, that I want to get myself into. I want to investigate hydrophobic places, thinking and writing that find fluidity disappointing. These dismissals of fluidity hijack the maxim to shift the focus from motion and stasis onto something like texture. It is easy to say that Beckett and Pound are simply evoking a texture of will-less gloom. Maybe they're onto something else, however vaguely: an adhesiveness, a tugging in things that feels like a more accurate way of describing the world. It is, after all, some kind of "world" that Pound and Beckett seem to be describing, or jibing at, in these two statements; they have in their sights a totality. What "world" is this exactly?

Mere Adhesion

> *Adhesives such as resin and gum Arabic have been employed as a means of attaching otherwise fleeting qualities to the very essences of substances.*
> — Gaston Bachelard, *Water and Dreams*[9]

For the early-20th-century American liberal Dean Everett Martin, 1920s US democracy was in a lamentable state. For him, the problem was that people don't think for themselves, they just rally behind familiar slogans, moralistic propaganda, abstract ideas of justice and freedom, rather than acting on finely tuned individual judgments about the most effective policy for a specific issue or the best party to govern the country. Instead, people get wrapped up in the "democratic crowd" as he sees it, "with its sweet optimism, its warm brotherly love." This crowd is, Everett Martin thinks, a "sticky, gooey mass which one can

---

9   Gaston Bachelard, *Earth and the Reveries of Will: An Essay On the Imagination of Matter,* trans. Kenneth Haltman (Dallas: The Dallas Institute Publications, 2002), 95.

hardly touch and come back from clean."[10] Following Gustave
Le Bon's 19th-century analyses of crowd psychology as susceptible to microbial dispersions of misinformation and hysterical
energy, Dean Martin sees the crowd, too, as a kind of ooze that
is both arbitrarily associated and wildly fantastical. When lost
in the crowd, people are not "working together, *they are only
sticking together.*" He is "sick of this oozing democracy," its
fake news, its populist lies, its spectacular tricks. There is, he
assures his readers, something "crystalline and insoluble left in
democratic America [...] people who are still solid, who have
impenetrable depths in them and hard facets which reflect the
sunlight."[11] In contrast, the knowledge of the crowd is inherently
messy, it keeps spawning new unfounded opinions from its own
fermenting body, transforming what might have been superficial into the very essence of a social identity.

This viscous state of subjectivity is opposed to the proper
functioning of liberal democracy, the presence of mind it requires from each one of its citizens, for Dean Martin. The humanist intellectual, on the other hand, is able to stay true to
the facts, be practical, realistic, not having the "unctuousness
of mind by which ideas are fastened upon others without their
assent."[12] This is a world where things link up aggressively beyond our will. In this world, democracy's only hope is if we remain infusible and resist the threat of this crowd-mind, its love
of generalization, pseudo-science, quick-fixes.

The goal of humanist thinking, then, is too keep us infusible, in order that its thinking may continue. What interests me
about Everett Martin's writing is the way in which stickiness has
an agency to it that, if not prepared for appropriately, will overcome you. The social world, for him, is in a process of *clumping
up* into unmanageable singularities. This seems to be, in his particular strand of humanism, a force of the universe, primordial

10 Everett Dean Martin, *The Behaviour of Crowds: A Psychological Study*
    (New York: Harper and Brothers, 1920), 286.
11 Ibid.
12 Ibid.

chaos surges into being through these random and hallucinatory associations between people. Mere adhesion, what could be called blind solidarity, is an immensely volatile force. From within it emerge the nightmares of liberal society — mobs, gangs, hooliganism, the wildnesses of vehement togetherness. But importantly for Dean Martin, this stickiness is continually embarking on its project, it is latent within social structures, it will be what takes over if we do not stay alert. This is a thinking paranoid about a world longing to clump up, about the agency of stickiness, its unmanageable outcomes.

So it is a particular quality of attachment that puts democracy in this degraded, volatile state, run by unions, pop-philosophies, false promises, all of which are united as anti-humanist congelations of intellect, as far as Dean Martin is concerned. And it is significant that he doesn't use words like bind, tie, knot, drown, entangle. We must not think in terms of threads or fluids, but ooze. The volatility of sticky things is twofold:

- They are continually ready to attach to anything at all, indifferent to the identity of whatever it is to. But –
- this bond is inherently imperfect, the meeting of surfaces alone, and prone at all times to come unstuck, sticking onto something else.

To say that things are attached is not, in fact, to say much at all. What is important is the quality, the dynamic, of that attachment. This dynamic is an operative force; it itself makes things happen. Stickiness and democracy are incompatible, its messiness undermines its processes.

Do we find something similar in Socrates' whimsical critique of *panta rhei*? That this foundational moment in philosophy might simply be the result of the sounds of words, the *o*'s in ousia and othoun, perhaps seems unlikely, but is also a kind of thinking that sees things as *clumping up* arbitrarily into what looks like meaning, one that then acts forcefully on the world.

Where, then, might we see an instance of this stickiness, of it being subdued? When called in to manage crowds, riot

STICKY WORLDS/STICKY WORDS

police are generally instructed to remain cold, detached, and unresponsive until given orders to change, or unless someone breaks the law. This is, at least, in theory. The same is the case with soldiers guarding buildings. They remain in stony-faced absurdity until someone commits a crime, then they act. The tradition of police and army personnel taking on roles of weird social remove found peculiar amplification in the American occupations of Iraq and Afghanistan after 9/11, where a great deal of non-combative, civilian management was required. The Joint Non-Lethal Weapons Program (JNLWP), created by the United States Department of Defense in 1996, had on its website, during the on-going fall out from the American invasions of the Middle East in the early 2000s, pictures of American soldiers in states of what is called "civil inattention." Gage McWeeny has drawn our attention to these images — a man in a kaftan sitting in a café, politely ignoring an American soldier yards away in a Humvee. Another: a distressed crowd addressing a soldier from below who reacts with a hand held out, calming, repelling the frenzied crowd.[13]

This technique of "civil inattention" in civilian crowd control was theorized by the American Cold War sociologist Erving Goffmann. He describes poses of "polite indifference" that help, he says, provide privacy for people in social life, but which also prevent social life from becoming "unbearably sticky." We are kept from being swallowed up by the crowd. I think I know what he means, if in a slightly different context. It has always comforted me when struck, as most Londoners have been, by the absurdly alienated space of a full London tube carriage, that we avoid each others gaze not because we hate each other, but because we love each other too much, that is, we know somehow deep down that if we started talking we wouldn't be able to stop. The social intensity of tube carriages is of such a degree that if it were allowed to occur, it would become "unbearably sticky"; we'd all fuse into a singular mass, ferment, and burst out of the

13 Gage McWeeny, "Weapons of Mass Reduction," *Cabinet* 22 (Summer 2006), http://www.cabinetmagazine.org/issues/22/mcweeny.php.

windows and doors, causing calamitous delays. So we don't, we stare down at our screens and shoes instead, with profound and finite love for the members our species. But we have, again, a seeming asymmetry in the relation between involvement and outcome: the slightest, most tentative gesture of engagement is impossibly adhesive, things would suddenly erupt into a total and immobilizing mess.

Gage McWeeny has shown how as American foreign policy was drawn deeper into the complexities of non-state warfare and urban peace-keeping missions, the need for non-lethal weapon technology increased. For this, the JNLWP developed a device that employed the immobilizing powers of stickiness. A tank was strapped to the back, out of which emerged a tube with a nozzle at the end. Out of this tube sprayed a kind of sticky expanding foam that clung onto whatever it touched, Spider-man style, enlarged by many times in size, reducing its victim to a writhing, pacified goo-covered body. Stickiness, it turned out, through the fearful power of the mob, could be used to re-press its formation. Fight stickiness with stickiness: cover people in the stuff and watch them try to riot. The sticky gun was deployed to Somalia in the mid-1990s, where UN peacekeepers were equipped with the device the help troops operate in urban environments in which militia fighters were mixed up with un-armed civilians. The guns, however, were never used.

Circling between literal and social stickiness, these weapons were a signal of the changing nature of American engagement in foreign states. They are hilarious, no doubt: slapstick making its glorious entrance into the war zone. But nonlethal weaponry like this is symptomatic of a protracted policing of invaded terrain. These weapons then become, in turn, the ideal instruments not only of pacification, but also of intelligence extraction through torture. Although non-lethality might signal deterrence and pacification, it is also the appropriate technology to cause as much pain without killing. In his article, Mcweeny points to the ways in which torture in American prisons such as Abu Ghraib repurposed improvised or official technology. The Taser, for instance, used for its ability to subdue violence, is able to inflict precise amounts of painful non-lethality, perfect for torture. Most strikingly, however, the sticky gun is part of the surreal entrance of slapstick comedy routines into the dark corridors of Abu Ghraib. The weird horror of the repurposed, "DIY" "props" used in the infamous photos released in 2004 — broom handles, girls knickers, wooden crates, bits of old wire, viscous excrement, and foodstuffs smeared on faces, not to mention the indelibly haunting staginess of it all. The thumbs-up next to tumbledown naked human pyramids. Many who observed the emergence of these photos were struck, I think, at the time, by the clownish joy these sadists seemed to take in their actions. Little red holes in the naked buttocks used for target practice. If, as McWeeny wonders, Harpo Marx had arrived into the world of crowd control with the sticky gun, his influence was surely witnessed in the photos of these ritual humiliations.

The sticky gun was a kind of weapon known as a "force multiplier," a type of technology that increases the effectiveness of the troops in combat. The useful thing about stickiness, or sticky technology, is that it acts on things without being asked to. In this way, it can start to act like a crowd itself. Or rather, it can transform a few military personnel *into a crowd.* Though largely abandoned as a technique of crowd control, it has found application in security technology, not unlike anti-climb paint. The Department of Energy in the US is reportedly using the substance of the sticky gun to protect nuclear facilities from terrorist attack.[14] If broken into, tanks of the stuff will splurge out, engulfing both the equipment and the intruders, protecting and ensnaring simultaneously. The volatility of stickiness is economically effective. The reactors are made more secure without the department having to hire more staff. Like self check-out machines, it makes a many of the few.

14   Ibid.

Sticky Fire

But stickiness has been used by the American military for much more widely used technology of war, one that was designed to be lethal. This is, of course, napalm, a weapon of the 20th century that contains a host of sublimatory transformations. Something like it had been developed in ancient times most effectively by the Byzantines, who termed it Greek Fire, which was, essentially, flaming asphalt. But its use declined rapidly after the invention of explosives by the Chinese in the 13th century. Developed by Harvard Scientists in the enraged wake of the Pearl Harbor bombings, napalm was, in a sense, a return to a stickier, messier kind of warfare. Its substance also loops the difference between waste and final product. An early version of napalm was made using petroleum jelly as the medium that would carry the incendiary substance, petrol. Petroleum jelly, which was trademarked as Vaseline by Robert Chesebrough in the 1870s, is made from the congealed residue of petroleum distillation. This residue looped back into that from which it was extracted, petrol, we get an entanglement of singular ruthlessness — where better to look for a device to burn skin off than in something used to protect it? To make things even more *unheimlich,* as if playing with what this weapon would turn you into, the researchers borrowed a meat mincer from the university kitchens to churn the two substances together, syphoned directly into a bombshell.[15]

The weapon's early developers, too, imagined napalm as sublimating primeval, base elements for a higher, distinguished purpose. Its first experimental mode of lethal distribution was in tiny chambers strapped to the back of Mexican Free-tailed Bats. Dr. Lytle Adams, a dentist, pilot, and entrepreneur, proposed to President Roosevelt his left-field idea of Napalm dissemination:

---

15 Robert M. Neer, *Napalm: An American Biography* (Cambridge: Harvard University Press, 2013), 34.

The lowest form of life is the BAT, associated in history with the underworld and regions of darkness and evil.

But not for long, as he continues:

Until now reasons for its creation have remained unexplained. As I vision it the millions of bats that have for ages inhabited our belfries tunnels and caverns were placed there by God to await this hour to play their part in the scheme of human existence, and to frustrate any attempt of those who dare to desecrate our way of life.[16]

The idea was to refrigerate 3000 bats, putting them into a state of hibernation, attach the incendiary devices, enclose them in a bombshell, and drop them from a plane. Once the bats met the warm air, they would awaken, the bombshell would open and they would disperse, with their respective loads, into the eaves and other secluded places in the structures of the surrounding area. A timed explosion would then occur, obliterating the bat, spreading flaming jelly onto the flammable Japanese buildings, burning everything to the ground. This would render "the Japanese homeless," Adams claimed, "yet the innocent," he somehow imagined, "could escape with their lives." This idea was tested, but the team's administration building caught fire in the process, sending all their equipment, save the refrigeration truck, up in smoke.[17]

Stickiness is crude and primeval. But within its arbitrariness can play out an imagined transcendence. Its volatility is the site of a power struggle, one that can, if harnessed and directed, be employed to devastating effect by the will of governments. Where, for Everett Dean Martin, the viscous is the enemy of liberal democracy, its powers can be put to use and regions of "darkness and evil" can be brought into the light. This is a light

16 Quoted in ibid., 45
17 Louis Fieser, *The Scientific Method: A Personal Account of Unusual Projects in War and Peace* (New York: Reinhold Publishing Company, 1964), 129.

that will rain holy fire down over those that dare to question "our way of life."

In Reza Negarestani's surreal artificial mythology of *Cyclonopedia: Complicity with Anonymous Materials,* we find a vision of napalm not simply as a weapon, but a state of being. He begins:

> Gasoline-derivative by-products of oil — mostly used in incendiary substances and fuel bombs — such as napalm never burn completely [...]. As soon as it ignites, it sticks to objects, blurring them, pervading them, but never allowing them to evaporate or reduce to ashes, it keeps them in another form.[18]

What is particular about napalm, as described by Negarestani, is the way in which it persists, but also the way it enforces a persistence onto the objects it enflames. Its victims are never allowed to transform into vapor or ash, never allowed the dignity of waste products, but are held in form through the process of being destroyed. With this, the "salvation or consolidation of all possible worlds is never possible,"[19] This is what Negarestani calls "positive disintegration": the agonizing process of living on through and beyond your annihilation, denied the bliss of gaseous, explosive dispersal, sublimation. The weird violence of this war technology is found in its paradoxical use of the viscous capacity to embalm, protect, suspend, like a salad encased in a mound of perfectly molded Jelly.

Negarestani continues his musings on napalm, seeing in it the invention of a very particular kind of flow: "NAPALM will flow no matter how viscous you make it."[20] Napalm displays itself as a substance that defies the usual dichotomies of thickness and fluidity, stickiness, and flow. The stickiness of napalm feeds its ability to flow and its flow facilitates its attachment to things.

18 Reza Negarestani, *Cyclonopedia: Complicity with Anonymous Materials* (Melbourne: re.press, 2008), 36.
19 Ibid.
20 Ibid.

It is not extinguished by water, but rather uses its flow to disperse itself more thoroughly through the environment. But this is also seen as a "crawling" onto things, a strengthening of its "filamentary [...] networks" as it spreads itself further and further.[21] The viscous horror of napalm is its ability to seize up and flow simultaneously. In so doing, it zombifies the world.

This kind of substance is really the protagonist of Negarestani's twisted bacterial archaeology/treatise of synthetic mysticism. Parsani, the work's fictional archaeologist, finds an affinity with napalm as the material analogue for the experience of love — "Love is incomplete burning. In my scarred fevered skin you see a person who belongs to sickness. In your healthy flesh, I see the same."[22] But this state is also the state he finds himself in when trying to write anything down. "Fanatically perfectionist in regard to my essays," he hopes that his writing might be ash or smoke, but what he produces instead is tons of "slimy, messy traces, oil. differentiated wetness and muddled states of matter."[23] His words are a blockage in an attempt at dispersal, a failed attempt to reduce things to an irreducible, irreducibly fine, state of matter. What we have on the page, then, is something that lingers confusedly, articulated, yet messy, the alluring notion of "differentiated wetness." How is such a thing possible?

In *Cyclonopedia,* there are two types of wetness. One is water-based, the other hydrophobic, "scared of water." This hydrophobic wetness is oil, the more "elemental wetness," one that lives independently from the *Aqua Vitae* of the Green Earth beneath the Earth's surface lured up by its extraction to form a blob, one that has thrown us all into a kind of delirium. It has emerged from beneath the Earth to turn is occupants mad and eventually against each other as civilization breaks into a fragmented mass of death cults, worshipers of oil. Everything about contemporary society oozes in Negarestani's book, but not in a metaphorical way as it does for, say, Everett Dean Martin. Oil is the literal ooze

21 Ibid., 37.
22 Ibid.
23 Ibid., 36.

of everything we do. It is, for him, or his narrator, the "Tellurian Lubricant," the viscous matter into which all narratives, all
world views, all ideologies collapse and move forward together.
It is a mutant, zombified substance itself, formed as it is from the
prevention of decay, the preservation of organic material in an-
oxic waters. It is, then, like its derivative napalm, a kind of death
in life that forms the undercurrent to all worldly narratives. This
isn't the glistening rivers of light, long-exposure photographs
of car lights on PowerPoint presentations about globalization.
Oil is the lube of these narratives, something that ensnares as
it facilitates. The situation is mythological; we, as a species, are
directed towards the desert, the land beneath which oil is imagined to reside, but also a place of flatness, a horizontality that
the religion of oil malignantly favors. This Tellurian lube, or Tellurian Omega, "simply makes things move forward."[24] But this is
a moving forward into a condition of servitude. We are moving
forward towards the "submission to a desert where no idol can
be erected and all elevations must be burned down — that is, the
Kingdom of God."[25]

But importantly, in *Cyclonopedia,* this weird "nether
wetness,"[26] doesn't only reside under out feet in subterranean
pockets, but also inside our own bodies. The boundaries of the
earth and of our bodies shiver into continuity as phlegm is the
oily, hydrophobic, elemental wetness that we contain. "Phlegm"
is a moisture whose etymology is linked the word "flame," the
substance is, as Negarestani writes, "bursting with a massive incendiary tendency."[27] It is also related to the Greek word *phleg-
ma,* the hypothetical substance thought to be the element contained within any flammable substance. But in *Cyclonopedia*'s
wild material theology, this is a black flame, one that has had
influence over the events of the 20th century, the burnt sacrifice
of the holocaust.

24 Ibid., 17.
25 Ibid., 18–19.
26 Ibid., 104.
27 Ibid., 103.

Burning black, *phlegein* corresponds with the black flame worshipped by Akht or the black light of Ayn-al-Qudat Hamedani. It is associated with the fire of conflagration which is the fire of *holokauston* (ὁλοκαύτωμα, holocaust) — an uncontrollable fire with an autonomous nervous system and a voracious rapacity for sacrifice.[28]

As this viscous matter rises up from beneath the desert, so does its companion from within our bodies as we clear our throats. What kinds of behavior, then, has phlegm been seen to inspire?

Phlegmatics

In "phlegm", one of the four humors denoting a kind of calm apathy, we find, like in napalm, another union between fire and the viscous. In addition to this etymological relation, we might think about our skin's response to becoming burnt and swollen is to become viscous, pussy, in a way that recalls all the jellied fuels, hydrophobic oils and gels — moistures that live closer to infernos than they do to rivers and wells.

The phlegmatic, most often considered a negative affect perhaps, a "bad feeling," is championed by Kant, under certain conditions in his *Anthropology from a Pragmatic Point of View* from 1798. It is true, Kant thinks, that phlegm can be a weakness if it manifests itself in voluntary uselessness, in "desires [that] aim only at satiety and sleep." But phlegmatics for Kant are never lifeless, even if they appear so. They possess a persistence that is their "genius," one that only appears to a choleric person as inactivity, someone who is driven wild by the phlegmatic's slowness:

Phlegm, as *strength,* on the other hand, is the quality of not being moved easily or *rashly* but, if slowly, then *persistently.* He who has a good dose of phlegm in his composition warms up slowly, but retains the warmth longer. He does not easily fly into a rage, but reflects first whether he should become

28 Ibid.

113

angry; when the choleric person, on the other hand, may fall
into a rage at not being able to bring the steadfast man out of
his cold-bloodedness.[29]

The phlegmatic is never enraged, yet might provoke rage in others. The phlegmatic, we might say, inflames the choleric. But
the figure of the phlegmatic is one who, more generally, possesses a plasticity of temperament whose will is both "considerate" yet "unbending."[30] When served a good dose of reason, the
phlegmatic possesses an adaptability to the views and opinions
of others, but only ever in the knowledge that he will eventually "bring their wills round to his."[31] The phlegmatic does not
puncture others with sound bites or finely wrought rebukes,
but gradually pulls the world along with itself. The phlegmatic
works obliquely, avoids conflict, understands that the best way
to convince people is not to tell them what to think. The phlegmatic becomes almost planetary in its power, Kant imagines,
collecting things that once stood in the way, unharmed, into its
orbit:

> [B]odies with less velocity and greater mass carry along with
> themselves the obstacle that stands in their path, without de-
> stroying it.[32]

Later in this work, Kant ascribes this temperament to the spirit
of the German people, but in an adapted form where the phlegmatic evolves into a state of submission to authority, a distance
from the rage against social order and "innovation." The German neither "rationalizes about the already established order
nor thinks one up himself."[33] In terms of social being, the phlegmatic German character is not proud or vehement about his at-

29 Immanuel Kant, *Anthropology from a Pragmatic Point of View*, trans.
    Robert Louden (Cambridge: Cambridge University Press, 2006), 190.
30 Ibid.
31 Ibid.
32 Ibid.
33 Ibid., 219–20.

tachments to places or people, or to the idea of a nation, never feeling "passionately bound to his fatherland."[34] He is a man of all "countries and climates."[35] But, Kant continues, when the German goes abroad, he settles quickly into expat communities that distinguish themselves from other "settlers" through their "peaceful, moral condition", their "industry, cleanliness, and thrift."[36] This, Kant notices, is something the English admire in the Germans in North America.

Kant's conception of the phlegmatic is intensely sticky, with all the slipperinesses this entails, full of intricate backtrackings, tangles, and dead-ends. The German people don't care much for nationalism, but keep to themselves when abroad, while having an appreciation for the culture. They are defiant. They are fully aware and in control of their will, but don't put any particular exertions into actualizing it, yet are known for their planet-like perseverance. They are willful, yet subservient. Is that subserviently willful, or willfully subservient? Despite being profoundly reflective, principled people, they never dream up anything different to what might be simply there at hand. The one observation Kant makes that seems stable is the phlegmatic's belief in the importance of property, which goes along with his propensity to "order and rule": "he would rather submit to despotism than get mixed up in innovations," such as unauthorized reforms in government.[37] This, Kant sees, as a positive attribute of the phlegmatic. But this is embedded within a mania for method, a punctiliousness, a pedantry for the details of the social order that, Kant thinks, is the "limitation of the German's innate talent."[38] Although slow on the outside, the phlegmatic has a neurotic interior.

I am intrigued by the smallness and finitude of Kant's vision of phlegm, a smallness and a finitude that gets somewhere near the stickiness that I'm trying to describe. The nature of attach-

34 Ibid., 220.
35 Ibid.
36 Ibid.
37 Ibid., 221.
38 Ibid.

ment for the phlegmatic is strictly un-idealized, imperfect, and inherently breakable. Bonds to a fatherland are denied in favor of linkages that are able to let go, but that which *tend* to stay with what they know. In the reporting of Hurricane Harvey, I came across an account of fire ants that have evolved to survive flood conditions by locking their legs together so closely that they resemble clumps of mud or scum floating on the surface of the water. If you pick them up (which is dangerous; the ants are poisonous), the cluster of ants flows out of your grip like slime. In fact, these fire ant clusters have been studied by rheologists and material scientists as a viscous material, their properties being analyzed for new kinds of synthetic viscous structure. The strength of these ant structures comes from their ability to break, the flowing quality of the clusters comes from each ant knowing how and when to let go.[39] Breakage doesn't mean dispersal, but is the principle of viscous structural unity. Barthes notices a similar quality in sticky rice, the "volatile conglomerate," the "measured (incomplete) defection" which is the source of another "irreducible cohesion."[40]

But there is a vaguely mean-spirited gloom to Kant's phlegmatic condition, a lameness to it that is the accuracy of its observation, but which also makes its hard to conceptualize. I am morbidly compelled by this smallness, by the asymmetry in its passionate defense of normality. It is the decay of obsession into pedantry, the contraction of nationalism into unimaginative expat communities gathered around pints under parasols on Spanish beaches, a willfulness and a love of learning that never leaves the dinner table, someone who is sensitive to your views, but who will never give up on their own, a considerate guest. I imagine, at the expulsion of some phlegm from inside me, that the substance was once distributed along my airways

39 Ashley P. Taylor, "A Mob of Fire Ants Becomes a New Kind of Material," *Popular Mechanics*, November 26, 2013, https://www.popularmechanics.com/science/animals/a9759/a-mob-of-fire-ants-becomes-a-new-kind-of-material-16202096/.
40 Roland Barthes, *Empire of Signs*, trans. Richard Howard (New York: Noonday Press, 1989), 14.

and passages as an infinitely fine film that collects itself up into an opaque blob, sentimentally concerned with the maintenance of its form, however negligible, however arbitrary. I sometimes feel myself disposed to this kind of *sinking in,* and the feeling burns me.

For the writer Maija Timonen, this lump of phlegm becomes a quality of thinking itself, once bundled together through words. In *The Measure of Reality,* she describes reading a line from Eva Illouz's *Why Love Hurts: A Sociological Explanation*:

> [T]he predominance of sex detached from emotions implies much greater difficulty in the interpretation of each sexual protagonist's actual feelings and intentions.[41]

Here the quotation ends and what follows is a description of how it feels to think after reading this sentence.

> She knew something was not right with the statement, but the more she tried to unpack it the more the concepts clung to each other, slid into one another forming a congealed orgiastic mass, obstinate in the face of her powers of reasoning that were trying to wedge its constituents apart. All that she managed to do was to find herself with the occasional sweaty cold lump of thought left in her reluctant hand, emitting a dubious odour of post-rationality. Thought that seemed vacant and self-satisfied having reached its goal, no longer concerned with much of anything beyond its (merely adequate) completion.[42]

The concepts as she contemplates them behave like oobleck, cornstarch mixed with water, thickening when agitated. As she identifies something "not right" about the thinking, the thoughts

41 Eva Illouz, *Why Love Hurts: A Sociological Explanation* (Cambridge: Polity, 2012), 46, quoted by Maija Timonen, *The Measure of Reality* (London: Book Works, 2015), 21.

42 Timonen, *The Measure of Reality,* 21.

117

recoil in on themselves, begin to tangle, thicken, and congeal in a process of collectivized self-protection. With a will and lustful energy that is apparently their own, the thoughts seem to slip into one another, agglutinating the bonds of association that were there in theory, provisionally, but then put into question. The conceptual particles of the thinking look to preserve the thought that they together compose. In the process, this thought appears ingested by her and then rejected by her body, coughed out into her hand like a blob of phlegm, sitting there with vapid self-congratulation. That the concepts are too "wishy washy," cotton-headed, or flimsy is certainly not the problem. Nor is the problem that they're too dogmatic or prescriptive. It is, instead, a weird combination of the two: a defiant vacuity, a vehemently defended mediocrity. Timonen's writing opens out onto a syndrome I think might be suffered by many involved in the production of ideas: the tendency of concepts to form sentimental, yet violently defended, bonds with one another regardless of the efforts of the consciousness that, at one time at least, might have been considered their receptacle. Phlegmatic thinking tries to smother its object, caring more about itself, about its own self-perpetuation, than whatever it's supposedly about.

Asphalt Cut with Menstrual Blood

Although Eugene Bingham coined the term rheology, its study in no way began with him. The first recorded instance of a rheological study is considered to be Tacitus's description of the river Jordan entering the Dead Sea, known to the Ancient Greeks as *Lake Asphaltitus*:

> This river [Jordan] does not empty into the sea, but after flowing with volume undiminished through two lakes is lost in the third. The last is a lake of great size: it is like the sea, but its water has a nauseous taste, and its offensive odour is injurious to those who live near it. Its waters are not moved by the wind, and neither fish nor water-fowl can live there. Its lifeless waves bear up whatever is thrown upon them as

on a solid surface; all swimmers, whether skilled or not, are buoyed up by them. At a certain season of the year the sea throws up bitumen, and experience has taught the natives how to collect this, as she teaches all arts. Bitumen is by nature a dark fluid which coagulates when sprinkled with vinegar, and swims on the surface. Those whose business it is, catch hold of it with their hands and haul it on shipboard: then with no artificial aid the bitumen flows in and loads the ship until the stream is cut off. Yet you cannot use bronze or iron to cut the bituminous stream; it shrinks from blood or from a cloth stained with a woman's menses. Such is the story told by ancient writers.[43]

Like with Negarestani's napalm, Tacitus's Jordan is not a river that gives in easy to climax. The water of the river holds itself together, pipelining its way through two bodies of fresh water, the first being the lake of Merom, the second being the Sea of Galilee, before getting lost in the dense water of the Dead Sea. The Dead Sea, an endorheic basin, is a closed, terminal body of water. Its contents, blocked from reaching the ocean, either seep slowly through the porous floor, or wait around to be evaporated off, somewhere becoming rain. There are many of these internal drainage zones on the Earth, collecting and cramming water into land-locked isolation. They sometimes occur as lakes, at others swamps or quagmires, sometimes as large expanses of hypersalinated, often highly noxious, water: the Aral Sea, the Dead Sea, Lake Chad, Lake Urmia. The river Jordan's completion is forestalled, its climax not an entrance into the ecstatic dispersal of the oceanic, but into the thick atmospheres of aquatic mass containment.

I find myself drawn to this passage in Tacitus as a moment when the river, the normal course of things, is slowed, thickened, begins to stick, is folded in on itself and warped into viscous intricacy. Different qualities of flow and densities of matter inter-

43 Tacitus, *The Histories,* trans. W.H. Fyfe (Oxford: Oxford University Press, 1997), 236–37.

119

penetrate one another. The viscous is not something that pulls towards a collapse into amorphousness, but performs within a highly articulated field of interaction. The appeal comes, I think, from witnessing mobilities that are non-continuous, non-fluid. Their dynamic seems to contain an ensemble of seizures, stoppages. Instead of meanderings and ripples, all standing for ultimate continuity, things form tentacles, before getting lost, hang around, cling onto you, burp stuff up, coagulate, and then shrink, like a crisp packet on hot embers.

Also like Negarestani's napalm, we have here a continuity between the excrescences of the Earth and the excrescences of the body, this time menstrual blood and asphalt. It is perhaps unsurprising that this early rheological writing is ghosted by this other substance, blood mixed with mucosal tissue, whose own rheological process will have taken place, but is left un-described. Although not taboo in the same way as in the Modern period, menstrual blood was commonly seen, according to another writer of early imperial Rome, to have powers to deaden the world. Tacitus's account of menstrual blood being able to bring this unruly asphalt under control is consistent with Pliny the Elder's more famous depiction of the blood's tendencies to deaden the vitality of matter, remove its shine. Alongside its ability to turn grapes sour, sterilize seed, kill off grafts, parch plants, kill swarms of bees, and turn dogs mad, Pliny sees this blood also as able to "dim the brightness of mirrors, blunt the edge of steel, and take away polish from ivory."[44]

Thicker than other blood and mixed with varying amounts of other viscous textures, mostly clotted matter and mucosal tissue, male-dominated aversions to menstrual blood have often originated from it as a substance of post-death. This is a post-death rheology that can, however, be recuperated, as we see in this moment in Tacitus, to be utilized by a spirit of "industry" and "entrepreneurship." It is the way these two viscous materials are seen to move ambiguously across the threshold between life and death that brings these substances into tonic union in

44 Ibid., 237.

the magical imaginations of these "ancient writers." The Dead Sea, a vast static pool of lifelessness, gives rise to a mysterious substance that appears to possess some kind of liveliness; once awakened by the hands of those collecting it, it wills its way onto the boat in Lovecraftian tentacles. This cloying form is cut not by what could be thought of as its opposite, a sharpened blade, but by something that echoes its texture. Just as, for instance, a ground-down tooth might be believed to cure you of a snake-bite, like affects like. This substance is one whose flow is at once a vehicle of life, of its potential, and proof of it not having happened: menstrual blood.

Have we here something we could term post-death technologies, technologies that hang on in between life and death as they are normally conceived, in between containment and dispersal? Asphalt is formed, after all, by the preservation of organic material in water with depleted oxygen content. These viscous technologies emerge out of an interrupted dispersal that sits at flow's moment of culmination, technologies made of things held agonizingly in form.

But when the flow of menstrual blood is disturbed, begins to encounter seizures, the result is far from "appealing." This experience, one that can range from painful menstrual cramps to paralyzing agony, occurs as a number of different conditions, most commonly as dysmenorrhea or endometriosis. It occurs when endometrial tissue starts thickening and clumping up on the outsides of the reproductive system and is blocked from being discharged as it normally would be. Often rightly enraged by the astonishing lack of research into this condition, there have recently been certain movements in contemporary writing that deal with precisely the complex intimacy of this adhesive menstrual flow. A post that went viral on a blog entitled *Oh My Fucking Blog,* by a woman describing her experiences of endometriosis describes its excruciating internal rheology:

> Eight days of contractions every month to pass blood clots the size of apples.
> [...]

There's so much of this period juice (endometrial tissue) made every month that it just doesn't fit in your womb, instead it emigrates to live on your ovaries, your bowel, your bladder, your tubes.

And this shit is sticky.

It's like gluing your fingers together with superglue, but more like gluing your ovaries to your bowel with excess hormones.

Of course ovaries are like planets. They don't just sit around pumping out eggs. They're on a trajectory across your pelvis throughout your cycle. They rotate. As they rotate they twist your bowel. Your lower colon is now blocked. I don't just mean you didn't shit for a few days, I mean that you've been six nights in hospital because you can't so much as fart, you haven't had a dump in three weeks and you've swollen up like Violet fucking Beauregarde.

Adhesions. That's what they call it when your organs keep getting stuck together. When your tubes stick to your bladder and you live with a perpetual UTI, pissing hellfire through your urethra on a daily basis.[45]

Of course ovaries are like planets. This is not an imagined continuity between the surfaces of the planet and of the skin, but a literal sensation of containing planets, a sensation so intense that their planetary nature is *obvious*. Nor is this the special affinity between the woman's body and ideas of astrological systems. No. Your organs roam within you just as planets trace their orbits, heaving matter with them as they go. For another writer, Thea Smith, the experience of endometriosis involves a similar collapse in scales, the body becoming planetary through a subjective attunement to activities of things *clumping up*, sticking uncontrollably together. Endometriosis is, as Smith describes,

45 The original blog post on *Oh My Fucking Blog,* June 2, 2017, http://www.facebook.com/ohmyfluffingblog/, has since been deleted. A copy can be found here: Mel Bartel, *Facebook,* June 12, 2018, https://www.facebook.com/MelroseBartel/posts/1735082299873957.

"the formation of clumps of blood in areas external to the reproductive system." But her writing rushes montage-like outwards to disembodied accounts of planetary motions:

> An embryonic planet, a planetesimal, begins as a collection of dust grains that collide and stick together.
> [...]
> Its core is a seething mass of gases unstable, unsolid, and yet whole, a coherent body.[46]

Here, in Smith's cosmic account of her menstruation, we have, I think, a precise description of the sticky world. Something that lacks stability, which has no solid parts, but holds together somehow anyway. It sticks, it coheres.

What characterizes this writing about endometriosis is how it manages to be explicit without being gory. It is a writing, in fact, that reminds us how un-explicit goriness almost always is. The intention is not to disgust, but to be detailed, to bring the attention into intimate encounter with material dynamics of the particular condition, rather than shock it into some hasty, panicked acknowledgement: "oh how *awful* for you." Importantly we have two presentations of the menstruating body as one not of flow, but of stickiness. It is a clumping up that society finds hard to handle, not the body passing fluid from inside to out. The writing exposes the body in a specific kind of pain caused by this stickiness, which is in one sense a position of vulnerability, the body subjected to forces beyond its control, forces that feel, in their magnitude, sublime, non-human. But this vulnerability also contains a strange planetary acceptance, which we might call strength: the power to stare these processes directly in the face, describe them with forensic attention to detail. For these writers there is one simple fact: this stickiness should be described, and described properly.

46 Thea Smith, "Red From Fire," RCA *Writing,* http://criticalwriting.rca.ac.uk/uncategorized/red-from-fire/.

Zombie Rivers

What I realized was striking about the asphalt lake I visited in Baku, was that it crawled to the surface of the Earth in what had become suburbia. On returning to my own piece of outlying land on the outskirts of London, Tottenham, I discovered I lived near a zombie river, a comrade of the pool in Binəqədi. The river Lea that rises somewhere near Luton flows southeast through Bishops Stortford, entering east London under the North Circular and joins the Thames at Bow Creek, south of Hackney Wick. Most of the river, however, has been canalized, dug out to form the Lea River Navigation, alongside which the original Lea now resides as a series of stagnant pools and murky channels, it swamps its way along below the embankment of its (relatively) new navigable partner like a diseased twin, sneezing out huge plumages of Himalayan Balsam and other unknown foliage at every quagmire. It's my zombie river — one that lives on, persists, beyond the cancelation of its riveriness by the fashioning of a deep and useful doppelganger. It just about flows, but doesn't really, lingering in the condition of the sort of. Although the original course, it is now literally superfluous, being the overflow channel during times of heavy rainfall from the Lea Navigation. It is originary yet surplus. This zombie river can be accessed by little apertures in the hedges, burrowed by deviants, that run along the towpath, down the bank to the little sunken swamp, full of algae, mattresses, and rubbish. Contrary to a widely held belief, it is not possible to walk along the Lea, not this bit anyhow, nor is it possible to orbit the little swamps as if they were prospective ponds. No ways exist for either of these modes of engagement. You are channeled down, instead, to these little viewing platforms, made by thousands of consecutive feet, nestled in the growths, and stand there, watching the spectacle of flowlessness go on.

The river Moselle, one of north London's lost rivers, but, at its non-subterranean moments, no more than a drainage ditch, enters the River Lea Navigation alongside some old sewage beds that have now been turned into a skate park. The Moselle, on its

short journey overland over the north side of the park, collects
various pieces of rubbish that are then caught in this filter band
that runs along its entrance to the Lea Navigation. When this
conglomerate hasn't been scooped up and shipped away for a
while, you often see walkers on the bank staring down at this
land of filth, morbidly transfixed by the horror of it all, disgusted
by the anti-social behaviors that took place for all the spray cans,
bottles, burst footballs, plastic sheeting to amount in such quantity. There is also, perhaps, a sense of catharsis as you look to
the clean side of the filter band, to the homogenous algae there,
congregating to have a look, staring heterogeneity in the face,
watching, I imagine, its version of the news. Or maybe the internet. I am also sometimes one of those disgusted walkers peer-
ing down. The writer and urban rambler Gareth E. Rees looking
down at the disjecta in the Lea, becomes fixated by the footballs,
perished, punctured, covered in green growths. To him, they
speak of "failed hopes and forgotten childhood." He notices that
it is at his most depressed that he sees the greatest number, bob-
bing about, causing him to wonder "whether its the events in
my life, or the balls, which are the cause of my turmoil."[47] At my
more sentimental moments, staring down at the island of refuse,
I am struck by the pedantic, somehow tender, neatness of the
form. Shaped by the flow of the water as it curls back round, all
the bits and pieces feel meticulously filed away in their proper
place, as if to be easily located, all aligned in militaristic anticipation, about to articulate some ingenious insight.

Pipelines and Immunity

The asphalt lake's place in the suburbs of Baku is representa-
tive of something particular about the political history of the
city. Baku is unusual in the history of oil extraction because its
oil was extracted from the geographical center of the city. Oil
is normally pumped from oil fields that lie far from major hu-

47 Gareth E. Rees, *Marshland: Dreams and Nightmares on the Edge of London*
(London: Influx Press, 2013), 57.

man settlements and then piped to refineries, then to ports and then shipped around the world. Its processes, as far as the vast majority of its consumers are concerned, take place out of sight. This is what sets it apart from coal, a fossil fuel whose extraction has, historically, occupied a central position in the identities of particular communities. Its stuff is inextricably tied to the militancy of the people of the Rhonda Valley in Wales. Or think of the popular working class support Trump received for promising to "reopen the pits" in Pennsylvania. No popular community or collective identity of nearly such political cohesion exists around oil extraction.

This is in part due to the material differences between oil and coal. Coal is heavy, has to be laboriously cut out from the Earth, carted on small railways to large railways and distributed through a highly articulated, non-modular network. The complexity and the fixity of the infrastructure surrounding coal extraction make it highly vulnerable to industrial action. There are many points along the chain that can be sabotaged, stopping distribution dead. The popular power of the British coal industry at the start of the 20th century was immense. In the US in 1918, the chaos that widespread strike action could have unleashed on established infrastructure across the country was predicted to be greater than that of war breaking out, as a report issued by the Rockefeller Foundation:

> What might not happen, in America or in England, if upon a few days' or a few weeks' notice, the coal mines were suddenly to shut down, and the railways to stop running!... Here is power which, once exercised, would paralyze the [...] nation more effectively than any blockade in time of war.[48]

Oil, on the other hand, promised much more security for the landowning class. It flows; the processes of its extraction require relatively little human intervention. The resistance to the end

---

48 Cited in Timothy Mitchell, *Carbon Democracy: Political Power in the Age of Oil* (London: Verso, 2011), 25.

of oil extraction comes generally from business interests, rather than large unionized workforces.

The distribution networks that oil operates in are also different from those of a coal-dominated energy infrastructure. Oil is much lighter than coal and can therefore be shipped with much greater ease, something that was and is extremely rare with coal. In fact, oil initiated a whole new form of modular network. Coal's infrastructure is strictly and immovably dendritic, it follows the shape of a tree, the roots converging on a central point, before separating out into branches. Oil's networks are different, much more indeterminate and web-like. An oil tanker can leave its port without having a prearranged destination. As a result, it can modify its network as it goes along. If the price of oil suddenly rises somewhere unexpectedly, for instance, it can divert, within reasonable limits, its course to the more lucrative destination. This open-ended network is becoming the format for new ideas of public transport, hybrids between cars and trains, where individual modules ("cars") link up with chains of vehicles all communicating to each other via Bluetooth, the route being calculated algorithmically as you go along.

Coal, as Timothy Mitchell suggests in his book Carbon Democracy, played a critical role in forging democracy. The articulations in infrastructure that its material qualities demanded were hospitable to the rule of the people. Oil permitted bosses and owners to circumvent such inconveniences. Pipelines were in fact invented in Pennsylvania in 1860 to reduce the ability of humans to interrupt the flow of energy.[49] A huge triumph for the technocrats, this security, this mastery over the resource its flowing physicality offered was a major incentive in the gradual shift away from coal to oil that has taken place over the last hundred years. We live in a world where fluid substances are piped near seamlessly from elsewhere to here, from here elsewhere. The switch from solid to flowing was a switch that favored continuity over questioning, while also establishing an illusory mate-

49 Ibid., 97.

rial equivalent to the afterlife, a "somewhere else" we never see, but live alongside.

But how much has this dominance of fluid fuel been integrated into the ways we imagine our own lives, our *individual* security, the imaginary of individuality itself, our happiness, our well-being? Just as flow offered solutions to the threats of industrial sabotage in fossil fuel extraction, it has become for certain strands of pop psychology and ideas of mindfulness, the route to personal joy and freedom from despair. For the hugely influential positive psychologist Mihaly Csikszentmihalyi, the "flow state" is the state we achieve in extreme moments of concentration, when we are so absorbed in a particular activity that everything else seems to disappear. It's also known as "being in the zone," the sense of being contained within an almost blissful, fluid reciprocity with a specific action or thing. It is from these moments, Csikszentmihalyi proposes, that we find most satisfaction and sense of self-worth. As he says:

> [W]e have all experienced times when, instead of being buffeted my anonymous forces, we do feel in control of our actions, masters of our own fate. On the rare occasions that it happens, we feel a sense of exhilaration, a deep sense of enjoyment that is long cherished and becomes a landmark in memory for what life should be like.[50]

This theory is specifically framed in response to the failure of society to keep its promises about its own structures of happiness attainment. Society, its institutions and values, has let us down, he thinks, and as a result "an individual must [...] take things into hand personally. [...] Each person must use whatever tools are available to carve out a meaningful life."[51] The answer is found in cultivating our capacity to enter flow states. This is a perhaps familiar theory of self-reliance that has its foundations

50 Mihaly Csikszentmihalyi, *Flow: The Psychology of Optimal Experience* (London: Harper Perennial Modern Classics, 2008), 3.
51 Ibid., 4.

in mystical theosophy that has migrated to become immensely popular not only in yoga, fitness, and competitive sports, but in self-advancement, management, and business philosophies as well. A life lived in closer proximity to "flow" is a more contented one. It is part of a common approach to well-being that considers happiness not to be something we should aim for, but rather an effect of a particular structure of attention, one that feels fluid and zoning. We might call this the ideology of flow. Like the construction of pipelines in Pennsylvania, the flow state is a way of assuring continuity, guarding against disturbance, anxiety, doubt, violent social or psychological upheavals.

The image of the superfluid helium I described in the introduction returns, then, as a source of absolute self-reliance and immunity against weakness. The endurance athlete Christopher Bergland describes using the images he saw of liquid helium on a BBC documentary to help him break through states of extreme exhaustion and pain. This is a man who has spent three days nonstop running on a treadmill. He runs triple iron-man marathons, which consist of a 7.2-mile swim, a 336-mile bike ride, and a 78.6-mile run, without stopping. He has run the Badwater Ultramarathon, running 135 miles through Death Valley in midsummer, three times. In order to achieve these feats, Bergland describes visualizing the footage he once saw of super cooled liquid helium. Crippled with exhaustion and his feet badly blistered 100 miles across Death Valley, 35 miles from the finish line, he calls forth liquid helium from the "Rolodex in his mind":

I decided that I would stomp my feet into the ground and embrace the searing sensation as a gift. [...] I felt myself become superfluid and filled with a superhuman energy, which brought me to the finish line. This energy surrounds everybody, everyday. It is everywhere and is available to all of us.[52]

---

52 Christopher Bergland discusses this in "Superfluidity: Peak Performance Beyond a State of 'Flow,'" *Psychology Today*, October 29, 2011, https://www.psychologytoday.com/gb/blog/the-athletes-way/201110/superfluidity-peak-performance-beyond-state-flow. He also discusses a similar thing in his

The condition of zero viscosity is imagined not only as infinite malleability, perfectly liquid adaptability, but as something like its opposite: a source of boundless internal energy that immunizes him against anything and everything. He advises us to read Csikszentmihalyi.

It is easy to critique self-help philosophies because, in part, they're not designed to withstand critique, but to help people feel better about themselves. They are an easy target. What is more useful is to unearth the assumptions these kinds of philosophies make about how life should be lived. In a beautiful book *A Fragile Life: Accepting our Vulnerability,* anarchist philosopher Todd May doesn't tear this kind of "self-help" philosophy apart. He accepts its utility, but rather wonders whether we would even want the invulnerability to life's difficulties and sadnesses that this kind of thinking helps to develop in the event that we were able to get it. Csikszentmihalyi's theory is part of what May calls *invulnerabalism,* schools of life philosophy that look to build "places of peace" within the subject that can withstand the world's various predations. The practice of invulnerabalism involves working on a kind of detachment from things, where any misfortune that befalls us might be looked onto as if it were a sports game or a sentimental film; it's sad, but in the end, it washes off you — it's only a film, it's only a game. Vulnerabalism, what May is forwarding as an alternative, "accepts — indeed embraces — that we can be shaken to our very foundations."[53]

May's vulnerabilism is a considerably stickier conception of how we might choose to live. The goal is the same as Csikszentmihalyi's: how to carve out a meaningful life for ourselves. But May sees the invulnerabilists as having got the process by which this is achieved the wrong way around. For May, we care about things before they work their way into what might resemble meaning. Our passionate attachment to things, and our contin-

book *The Athletes Way: Training Your Mind and Body to Experience the Joy of Exercise* (New York: St Martin's Press, 2007).

53 Todd May, *A Fragile Life: Accepting Our Vulnerability* (Chicago: University of Chicago Press, 2017), 7.

ued potential to become passionately attached to things, exists in a volatile state that lays the foundations for what might be considered a meaningful existence. Attempts to secrete emotional remove from the world, as the invulnerabilists do, is the cultivation of a compassionate existence, rather than a passionate one, a life of diminished feeling, of diminished meaning, if much more serene. I will not crudely paraphrase what May very carefully and precisely formulates in his book. But the point is this: care, as May sees it, is the often arbitrary adhesion of us to things that may result in sadness, may result in happiness, but is what gives life meaning, rather than what results from it. Complete detachment starts to seem impossible, always, like Barthes's sticky rice, constituting an attachment somewhere else, "the world is always with us." If we choose to care, something that May terms "acceptance" rises up as the only option, aside, that is, from a position of compassionate remove. May is pragmatic, he doesn't try to imagine a life with no protection against hardship. But the difference is this: acceptance helps us get through times of suffering, but does not provide a place of safety beyond it. Acceptance is not a passive movement with contingency, but something that is learnt from an active exposure of ourselves to the possibility of suffering, and, in turn, of joy. May's ideas of how we might go about accepting our vulnerability can also be seen as ways of accepting our stickiness, our imperfect adhesive tendencies, their persistence, their fragility.

Atmospheres/Never Leaving

In a letter to his friend Tom McGreevy, Beckett describes his attraction to a kind of viscous atmosphere in Keats:

> [T]hat crouching brooding quality in Keats — squatting on the moss, crushing a petal, licking his lips and rubbing his hands "counting the last oozings, hours by hours." I like him the best of them all, because he doesn't beat his fists on the

table. I like that awful sweetness and thick soft damp green richness. And weariness: "Take into the air my quiet breath."[54]

This line from *Ode to a Nightingale*, "take into the air my quiet breath," is airless: breath behaves like bitumen harvested off the Dead Sea, clutched and tugged by the air, strands dripping off fingers. Beckett describes a similar love of Keats's thick air in his essay on Proust:

the terrible panic-stricken stasis of Keats, crouched in a mossy thicket, annulled, like a bee in sweetness, "drowsed with the fume of poppies."[55]

Steven Connor, reading these lines, sees them as part of Beckett's "extreme materialism," where air is imagined to be "matter-riddled" or, like Descartes's notion of the soul, an "infinitely fine state of matter."[56] The panting of airlessness in Beckett's generally un-ventilated work is then not an absence of air, but an excess of it, a thickening of its stuff until we're left gasping, sucking in recalcitrant clumps and strands, "the gurgles of outflow." It is in this thickened air that Beckett finds Keats's terrified languor, a condition that shares much with Kant's phlegmatic, an aversion to forthright fist banging in favor of a gradualness to which we eventually succumb.

But what catches Beckett's attention is a dynamics of lingering, an atmosphere where what counts is not the ability to happen so much as the ability to resist leaving. Beckett imagines Keats's world as one crammed full of odors, fumes, sweetnesses, afterglows, all thickly intermingled. These are all things that follow an object's presence, are evidence of it having been. But

---

54 Samuel Beckett, *The Letters of Samuel Beckett 1929–40*, eds. Martha Dow Fehsenfeld and Lois More Overbeck (Cambridge: Cambridge University Press, 2009), 21.

55 Ibid.

56 Steven Connor, "Beckett's Atmospheres," a paper given at the Après Beckett/After Beckett conference, Sydney, 2003, http://www.stevenconnor.com/atmospheres/.

what distinguishes that which clings and lingers from the "trace" or the "echo" is an intensity of presence. In fact, the viscous atmosphere is one in which all the sensual traces have been excessively amplified, where afterglows have engulfed their source.

When I was about fifteen, on a night when my mother was away, two friends and I spent the evening drinking all of her alcohol before heading out on one of those overexcited nighttime voyages you can only make in times of total intoxication. As we climbed a tall spiked metal fence circling some allotments, one of my friends accidentally gouged out a piece of his arm. I remember turning round to see him walking bleary eyed towards us clutching his bloody bicep. Deeply unknowing of how to coordinate our bodies, confused and panicked by the wound, we wrapped it as best we could in my sock and ran back to my house to get him in the bath — the best solution we could think of in our delirium. My friend, in the bath, the blood creeping out into the water through the new bandage we'd affixed, I remember deciding in my madness to pour an entire bottle of TCP into the bath with him. Its severe aroma wafted up around us, carried in the clouds of steam, engulfing us in its substance, entering, it felt, every bit of us. The air became thick and sharp, it spread like lava flows under our skin.

Dying of a hangover the next day, I remember feeling the aroma of the disinfectant throughout my entire body. It hung in me just beneath my skin before its presence gradually shrank to concentrate itself, for some mysterious reason, in my gums. And there its sensation lay for the next few days pulsating gently, transmogrified into a piece of submarine foam held inside the flesh of my mouth, a sponge of wire wool that tumesced as I exhaled. This happened about thirteen years ago now, but sometimes when I lie awake in bed at night, the TCP antiseptic foam returns to my gums, growing out of the darkness within me, tickling me internally as it unfolds its wiry mass, before vanishing.

The sensation of this TCP pulsating in my gums does not return me to a former state of mind. Its powers are not transportive like Proust's madeleine; I stay very vividly in my bed within the walls of my bedroom. I do not feel again the panic of the moment my friend cut his arm on the fence. It wasn't a particularly traumatic event. It is a mild bodily hallucination that comes, like many strange things, when awake in bed at night. I have what feel like large empty rooms within my gums, just below my teeth, that are graced, every couple of years, by a cloud of sharp smoke, but otherwise stay empty. When this smoke chooses to drop by, I don't remember anything, the intensity of the sensation far outweighs any connection it has to the past. I feel like an onlooker in a pastime my gums participate in alone. And importantly, I don't taste TCP when this happens, nor does the smell of TCP initiate this sensation in me. It's as if the TCP has been dismantled and then reassembled into a form that no longer resembles what it once was. But I also simultaneously feel intensely involved, like my gums are not only gums, but things that *have been made* to receive and record this wildly specific sensation. It isn't a memory. The clouds of TCP are reassembled and re-enacted by my gums, integrated into their physiology. This persistent fuzz in my mouth has become a quality of my proprioception and important aesthetic reference point for me. But it also feels as if bits of my body are able to form long and complex relationships with bits of the world, relationships that have very little to do with "me," or my sense of what that is.

Timothy Morton describes a similar experience when listening to one of his favorite bands, My Bloody Valentine. In *Hyperobjects: Philosophy for the End of the World,* he describes the "glittering guitar fog" of Kevin Shields contained within the "fragile bubble" of Belinda Butcher's vocals forming a sonic experience that "tunes to me, pursuing my innards, searching out the resonant frequencies in my stomach, my intestines, the pockets of gristle in my face."[57] Morton describes this, in explicit reference to Sartre, as a viscous sonic latex, one from which he cannot escape. For him, listening to My Bloody Valentine unlocks an "intrauterine" connection between things that "subtends" any

57 Timothy Morton, *Hyperobjects: Philosophy and Ecology after the End of the World* (Minneapolis: University of Minnesota Press, 2013), 30.

sensations of "transcendence." Hyperobjective art, as he calls it, reveals the "sly solidarity between things" that Sartre loathes in his writing on the viscous, the hidden stickiness between Kevin Shields's guitar and the gristle in his face, a bottle of TCP and the rooms in my gums.

"Everything," as far as Morton will have it, certainly "oozes." So much so that, in perhaps the most radical reframing of Sartre's notion of the viscous by a contemporary philosopher, Morton asserts that "sweetness," how much something is able to linger on, "just is power: the most powerful thing."[58] As the atmosphere around the planet thickens with carbon emissions, with methane, with dust and other pollutants, the world becomes stickier and stickier until "[l]ight itself," Morton claims, "is the most viscous thing of all, since nothing can surpass its speed."[59] But lingering on is, for Morton, not so much the capacity resist to leaving, as the only option available. Beckett's closed, unventilated worlds take on new significance under the recent ecological turn, where the world has come alarmingly into view as a finite space, there being no "elsewhere" for us to flush away our waste. Instead, all material is turned inwards in a closed system, steadily accumulating, sticking around, waiting a few millennia for its form to dissolve into something less perceptibly itself. This is something curiously prefigured by Pound's sense that what will "outlast" us — nay, the very thing we drown in — will be a "tawdry cheapness," accumulations of stuff we always knew we never really wanted. But the collapsing of the "here" and "elsewhere" dichotomy is the collapse of something that had only ever been a fantasy in the first place. The realization of global space's finitude is also the realization that this finitude was already the case. The viscous enacts the Heideggerian "always already": the more you realize something is there, the more you realize it has always been there.

The viscous is used, then, by Morton to evoke these structures of closedness and embeddedness in material that was initiated

58 Ibid., 31.
59 Ibid., 32.

by the large scale burning of fossil fuels in the 19th century. Or, as Morton would prefer to call it, the moment the world ended. Or rather, the moment when the "world" ceased to be a set of events that take place in the background, the back drop to human society, in the foreground. But what I think is so effective about Morton's writing, or what has made his work so intriguing among certain communities of artists, activists, and writers, is the way he feels compelled to occupy a stylistics that moves erratically, sometimes awkwardly, between the voice of the hobby scientist, the romantics scholar, the phenomenologist, the activist. This Morton acknowledges in a kind of disclaimer in the work's introduction as his "sickening" "ecomimesis," which he hopes might "tug at the limits of a certain rhetorical mode, seeking out its hypocrisy."[60] Morton's ecological project is tied up with a rhetorical strategy, an almost satirical polyvolcalism that inhabits different kinds of disciplines and types of language only to eat away at them from the inside. With the suggestion, for instance, that radiation is viscous, he veers weirdly between the sensual and super-sensual, melding the two, slipping the data he finds in science journals seamlessly into phenomenological, sensual enquiry. Ideas of surface and depth become confused.

Morton explicitly situates his writing within the philosophical approach of OOO, object-oriented ontology, a metaphysics that considers objects in a continual state of retreat and reveal. We can never exhaust an object's attributes, never experience them fully, only ever "lock-in" to certain set of sensual properties, use-functions etc. But all the undisclosed attributes of an object are, like the planet's finitude, seen as always already there, not somehow invented by their discovery. Morton imagines all objects "caught in the sticky goo of viscosity,"[61] with only part of them poking out of a slime lake of cosmic proportions. The language of OOO is, as a result, a language of searching, of clumsily and messily seeking out new contours and expressive powers to things that might be absolutely familiar. Things search

60 Ibid., 6.
61 Ibid., 36.

for each other — the sound of My Bloody Valentine *pursues* his body, *searches* for the flesh inside his cheeks, he *seeks out* the hypocrisy in a rhetoric. Things then cling to each other, imperfectly. ooo is fundamentally a project of the uncanny: to find the unknown within the known. Its stylistics are one, therefore, where different voices are assumed as different methods of pulling things out of their all-encompassing goo.

I want to suggest, then, that writing that associates with the viscous substance always in some way exhibits a peculiar disease with itself. Viscous writing comes, for a writer like Beckett, from a suspicion of fist-banging statements, it is dismayed by the request that you "say what you mean," or by the idea that this is possible. We find it, too, with Sartre's compulsive, itchy flamboyance I discussed in the last chapter. I don't want to propose this kind of writing as favorable or superior to other kinds, kinds, perhaps, that do, or do believe they can, "say what they mean." In fact, viscous writing can be enragingly self-involved, while pretending not to be. It can be astonishingly vivid, completely mundane, mildly irritating, defiant, mysterious, beautiful even. The dis-ease of viscous writing is never one thing, nor always fully determining of a form, but rather a certain neurosis that recognizes an agency, an ontology, to stickiness. Somewhere within viscous writing lurks an anxiety about the tendency things have to arbitrarily and imperfectly adhere to one another in a way that seems to exceed its control. For stickiness, like Timonen's cold lump of thought, does not care about the generation of anything that might resemble "meaning." Viscous writing has an atmosphere to it that involves, strains against, gives in to, actively seeks out this volatile adhesiveness and its persistence.

To be involved in the viscosity of things is, therefore, not simply to be materially embedded in the world, but to feel the various ironies, the tuggings, confusions, and crises in synchronicity that viscosity entails. Viscous writing has, in many respects, more in common with Beckett's other main dramatic obsession: slapstick comedy. The gaze pulled one way, while the body moves in another, the slippery banana peel we slip up on despite knowing what it means, dropping an object while picking up another—all these well worn tropes dramatize the broken synchronicity of the sticky world. Viscous involvement is to be deeply conscious of one's body, but simultaneously never certain where it, or its influence, ends or begins. It is to feel firmly rooted in the "here and now," but also continually unable quite to coincide with it. We lag behind ourselves. It understands the mess created by trying dispose of things. It understands knowledge itself as a messy thing, not a process of steady clarification, but as a scraping away of substance, which, once cleared off one part, must be smeared onto another. These are all the structural dynamics of the revulsion Sartre feels at the sense of the viscous material. But an attunement to these structures of disgust have now, it seems, become the basis of a new sort of sensibility initiated by the understanding of the planet's finitude.

This sensibility might be what Tom McCarthy sees as the capacity to be "confounded" in his collection of writings *Bombs, Typewriters, Jellyfish*. In a series of events he entitles "the coming goo," he remembers at the dawn of the millennium reading in the news of a Filipino power plant being clogged up and shut down by a huge tide of jellyfish. He remembers, then, reading an article by Donna Haraway in *e-flux*, entitled "Tentacular Thinking" calling for a "jellied revolt." There'd been a coup, he thought. His structuring of his work takes on a stickiness:

> You launch them [i.e. works], and they float around for a while, catching and refracting various types of light; then this same translucence camouflages them against the general background, and they fade from view. But they're still there, trailing strands in all directions, looking—seductively, or with toxic malevolence, or both—for points of contact, larger cluster-meshes to lace into, feed off, and recalibrate, or just to sting.[62]

62 Tom McCarthy, *Bombs, Typewriters, Jellyfish* (New York: New York Review of Books, 2017), 12.

In an extraordinary image of how writing behaves in the world, one explicitly indebted to Haraway's work, writing is not "reflective," but refractive. Writing is a translucent jelly, bending light through its body, capable as much of shimmering as of disappearing entirely. At a certain point, though, this swirl of jellied creatures reaches a "critical mass" and returns to him, begins "lodging, sticking…." However mesmerizing this shimmering translucence had been, it still yearns for adhesion. But this goo, rather than being an aestheticized arbitrariness, a looseness of form, is a state of hypersensitivity, one that he finds in the writing of Alexander Trocchi, to feel like a quivering leaf "like a mute hunk of appetitional plasm, a kind of sponge in which the business of being excited was going on."[63] We have here a vision of this volatile adhesiveness as a kind of trembling, a deep impressionability, a vulnerability to sensation that lives on through confusion, not unlike Keats's negative capability, one that does not seek to capture nor decode, but persists through incompletion.

Attunement

I have tried to understand, here, how stickiness might operate, how it as an active agent might effect the world. But I've also tried to describe what might have been a world composed of stickiness, "the sticky world," a world in which stickiness dominates proceedings. This phrase "sticky world" is, in fact, almost, though not entirely, a contradiction in terms. For there to be a world, there has to be the possibility of an absolute detachment of you from things. Things have to form an independent receptacle for you to enter into, out of yourself. The sticky world denies the possibility of such a detachment, denies the structural possibility of a here and a there, clinging on in various volatile and opportunistic ways at every desperate attempt to claw yourself free. For the sticky world, detachment is always an attach-

---

63 Alexander Trocchi, *Cain's Book* (New York: Grove Press, 1960), 43.

ment somewhere else. Although volatile, stickiness has a deeper persistence.

One of the qualities of the sticky world, however, is that it is never quite possible to accept. Once you've acknowledged its existence, it doesn't just become apparent and then settle into a new feature of experience. The sticky world is necessarily a struggle, a disorientation, a slapstick routine, a confusion of sequence. Stickiness is at the heart of the weirdness of ecological thinking. But although stickiness is the viscous dynamic that has become especially useful for thinking seriously about ecology, this is part of a history of feeling that expresses a sense of things clumping up beyond our will. To trace the different responses to this sense is to trace a shifting understanding of the importance of control.

For Everett Dean Martin in 1920s American liberal sociology, mere adhesion between people was one of the great threats to humanism and its democratic ideals. Stickiness is fundamentally irrational, it doesn't care about reasoned debate, but some fetishized idea of attachment. This is what threatens to overcome people and groups at all times, as far as Dean Martin is concerned. There is a wild associative force that is able, if we're not careful, to erupt between people. This is a cohesion that is strangely impenetrable, yet completely baseless, prone to emergent hallucinations. It is the end of democracy, for him, which is, necessarily, crystalline and sharp.

But if this sticky ooze works against the principles of democracy, there is an intriguing history to how its powers have been harnessed by those supposedly fighting in its name. The sticky gun developed by the Americans, though barely used, is an attempt to fight unmanageable adhesiveness with unmanageable adhesiveness. The goo that would be fired at individuals on the street by the military would work not only to quell the volatile oozing of the mob, but also multiply the military force itself. What is useful about stickiness is that it works without being asked to, its persistence is a "force multiplier"; it makes a few armed personnel into many.

The sticky gun is most interesting as a symbol, rather than an actual tool. Its presence is symptomatic of a the changing nature of American foreign involvement, its increased stickiness and complexity, the requirement of non-lethal weaponry to be used on the streets as the military patrol urban areas post-conflict. Its presence in a war zone is undeniably surreal, no doubt slapstick. Its non-lethality is a symbol of the protracted "peace keeping" and states of confusion that characterize post-9/11 American engagements in the Middle East. Conflicts where there was and is no clear enemy, where every attempt to extract oneself is just to embroil yourself deeper, in operations whose meaning and purpose became increasingly obscure, in which everything oozes.

But by far the more infamous entrance of stickiness into American military technology is napalm. Its technology consisted in various loopings of substance and dynamics of matter. It brought a stickier, messier form of warfare back from ancient times, reunited petroleum jelly with petrol and was imagined by its earlier developers to be the sublimation of "base creatures," bats, into crusaders for the ideals of the American dream.

Napalm's substance is not only an effectively indiscriminate weapon, but a particular quality of flow and its relation to stickiness. Napalm is a state of being where things are destroyed, yet prevented from dispersing into waste. This is another key quality of the sticky world — it persists through incompletion. It holds things in a liminal state between life and death, which is also the source of petroleum oil's incendiary power: organic matter locked into a state of interrupted dispersal. Yet oil is a fluid fuel and its saturation of almost every part of human and non-human activity can also be seen as a source of ideals of "flow." "Flow" is, among other things, a way to secure clear distinctions between "here" and "there," "me" and the "world." What has erupted from within this ideal of flow, though, is a stickiness, a confused troubling of where things end and begin. Stickiness places pressure on the techniques of imagination that we use to compose the world. Stickiness is a dynamic that feels impossible to accept but overwhelmingly real, our techniques must adapt to its agency, find an attunement to its volatility, lovingly accept its agency as indifferent to our own.

How might we go about this attunement *here* and *now*?

Experiments in Kneading Dough and Asemic Writing <u>Simultaneously</u>

with The Union of Bakers and Poets,
Palais de Tokyo, Paris
June 11, 2018
in collaboration with the artist Julieta Garcia Vazquez

All photos by the author

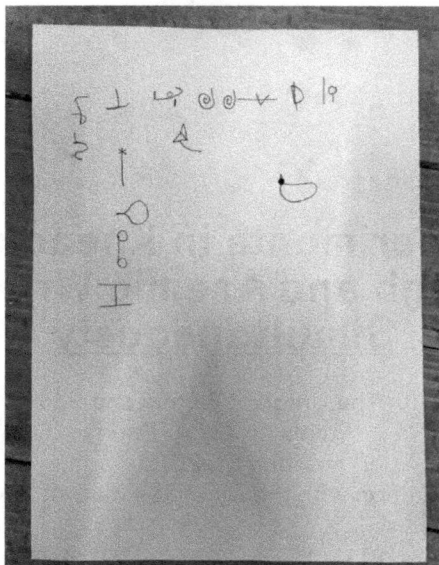

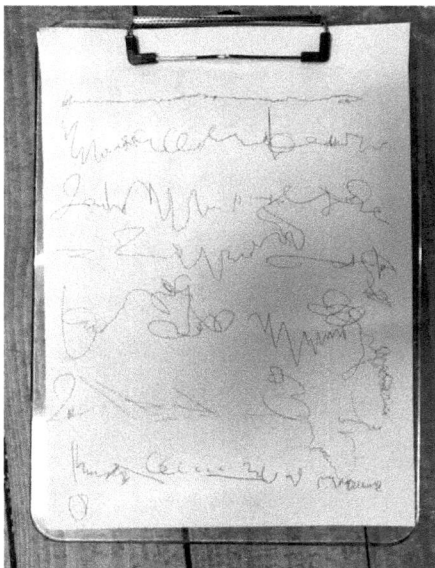

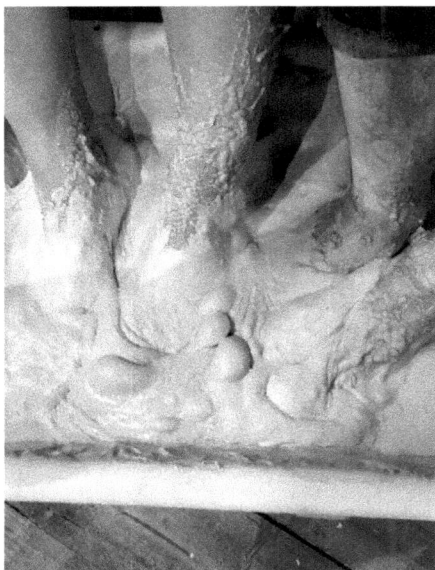

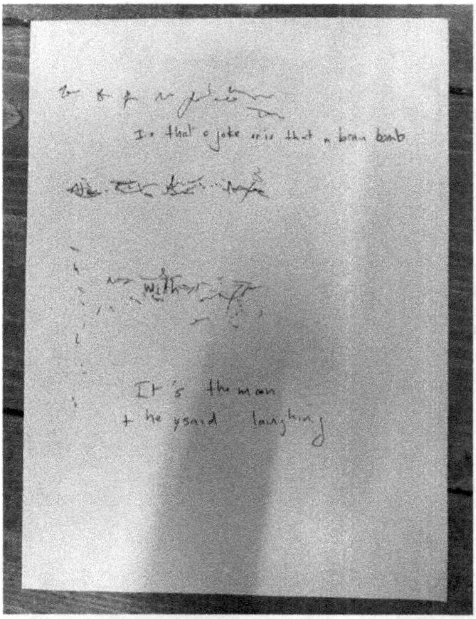
It's the man
+ he said laughing

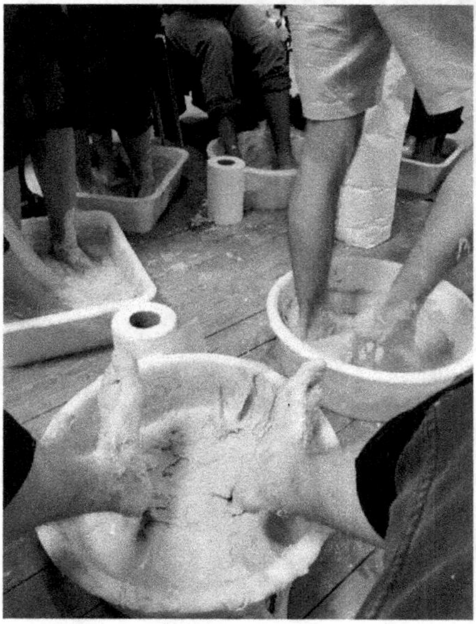

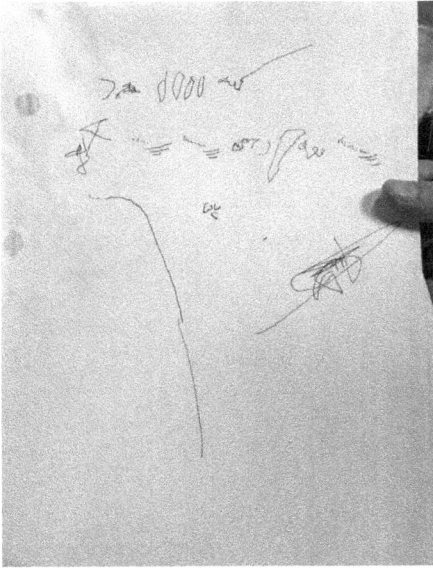

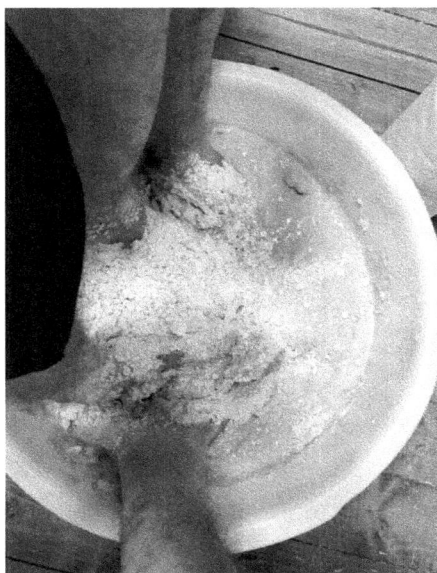

ART IS NO FUN FOR THE PEOPLE WHO HAVE TO EAT IT

Fig. 1. Still from Freddie Mason and Jazbo Gross, *Smectic LCD,* video installation, 2016.

3

Smear Screens and Fondled Things

Cleaning

Before I wrote the text before you now, I took from a red cylindrical pot a cleaning wipe and wiped down the keyboard and screen of my laptop yawning, gaping up at me — another dehiscence — like a crack addict shark (all blackened cavities): a precious moment when I feel the affinity between typing and veterinary dentistry. What I removed from the computer's surfaces with this multi-purpose wipe was mostly dust and grease, accumulations of substance we expect to find, allotropic residues of our touch, in many ways opposites — little dry, dead fragments of ourselves blown across and caught in the embarrassing clammy textures of our lifey-ness. We're dying all the time, in flakes. Smart phones are strikingly sympathetic exhibition platforms for these little dances of finger grease; I don't think anyone who owns one hasn't, at some point, whiled away a few blissed-out minutes composing Zen gardens with their fingertip smears on the blackened glass.

I wiped away the grease and dust in order to get on with my work, an attempt to make the conditions for writing optimal, to get my money's worth of disappearance from Californian design interaction at its best. I wanted to remove obscurity and distraction from the interface with and into which this work might manage to come to life. Ironic, of course, seeing as one of these substances — the grease — is the subject of my work, a substance I habitually remove from the screen of my computer, because, it seems, writing about grease is not possible, or just much harder, when you're also staring through it. I cleaned the grease away because it claimed more of my attention than I was prepared to give, while, at the same time, it prevented me from actually thinking about it.

The distinction we might make here is between the intended and the unintended. I didn't intend the patterns of finger smears absentmindedly jabbed and dragged across the screen's surface, but I do, most often, have the intention to write when I'm writing. The grease on the screen is, in contrast, unintended, unwanted, somehow wrong and therefore not, in this instance, only grease, but also a kind of dirt — matter, as Mary Douglas famously argues, that is out of place.[1] It invests the situation of writing with a sense of wrongness, a corruption of its structure; it threatens my sense of freedom, however illusory, to place my attention where I choose: the blinking cursor.

A sense of ridiculousness descends on me as I carefully remove the grease with a cloth lightly laced with benzalkonium chloride, disposing of without a trace precisely the substance I've sat down to absorb myself into. But maybe this wiping of grease off the screen is a dense, strangely literal emblem of the irony encountered by many who have chosen to write about anything at all. It is, for some annoying reason, very hard to write about laughter when actually laughing. It is, more to the point, nearly impossible to write about irony when right in the middle of the feeling of irony. It is necessary to redesign your environment, put yourself in some other place, a place of mourning, one attuned with, but not immersed in the matter at hand. Grease

1   Mary Douglas, *Purity and Danger: An Analysis of the Concepts of Pollution and Taboo* (London: Routledge, 1991).

stands as a literal encounter with the difficulty of extracting yourself in this way, the resistance the world puts up to being subject, subjected, to our words.

Grease is, in this way, similar to its companion on my screen: dust, a substance that "upsets," as Michael Marder says, "the ideal order of the house and of the universe."[2] It conceals; dust prevents what we might consider to be the natural irradiation of things from the world into our retinas, the manifestation of things to our consciousness. It covers over, cloaks what we feel we should be able to access. But dust, as Marder continues, also reveals. It awakens us to space. Hanging suspended in a beam of light, it reveals illumination to us, a suspension which is, too, a marker of the passage of someone through that space as it swirls into turbulent salience as they walk by. Though it may be "a veil that hides from us the hard kernel of reality," Marder wonders: can be anything "more real or truer than dust?"[3]

As I wipe the grease off the screen, I let myself be transported away from wherever I am now. The grease had moved beyond its background existence, reached a point of critical mass where it is no longer the slight sense of lubricated movement between thumb and forefinger, but a disturbance to my vision. In this accumulated state it announces its material to me. The wiping is a negation of materiality, a blasting off into dreams of an immaterial cyberspace, a fantasy that has been very systematically obliterated by recent and sustained materialist critique. Luciana Parisi, for instance, in her book *Abstract Sex,* equates this vision of "blasting off" into cyberspace with a specifically male ejaculative ideology. Pornography, Parisi suggests, is the crowning achievement of male models of sexual pleasure, one defined by a drive towards a discharge of viscous matter. With online sex, a kind of historical discharge of matter is dreamt to have taken place, the "heavy meat of physical presence" has been shed and

2   Michael Marder, *Dust* (London: Bloomsbury Academic, 2016), 19.
3   Ibid.

we're left "floating free in cyberspace."[4] The digital age we live in becomes, in this view, a kind of historical ejaculation, an image of modern internet culture as post-coital masculine bliss lounging luxuriously about in pixelated sweat.[5]

The grease on the screen interrupts this lounging about, adulterates the fantasy and forces my attention to the processes that take place behind or before my experience. This moment of adulterated consumer experience is something Marx notices in *Das Kapital* as a way of "subduing commodity fetishism."[6] The adulteration of useful, edible commodities like bread with grit or dust "provokes in consumer society" a huge flurry of interest in the social history of production. As Keston Sutherland says, "now that my meat has shit in it, I suddenly want to know who made it and how."[7] However convincing your social critique might be, it takes the direct sensual experience of adulteration, grease on the screen, dirt in bread, minute shards of glass in your instant coffee, for anyone to pay any attention.

Writing and Kneading

How might it be possible to synthesize a situation in which writing was literally synchronized with a viscous material? Might this be an alternative to this situation of mourning to which the grease has awakened me? This is something I attempted at the Palais de Tokyo in Paris, in collaboration with Julieta Garcia Vazquez's Union of Bakers and Poets, installed in the basement of the gallery for the months of July and August, 2018. Around fifteen bakers and fifteen poets were brought together in a space

4 Luciana Parisi, *Abstract Sex: Bio-technology and the Mutations of Desire* (London: Continuum, 2004), 2.
5 Is it some how strangely apt that a contender for the first ever piece of moving screen media was of a man, a worker from Thomas Edison's factory, sneezing?
6 Natalie Ferris, "Interview with Keston Sutherland," *The White Review,* March 2013, http://www.thewhitereview.org/interviews/interview-with-keston-sutherland/
7 Ibid.

where bread and poems would be baked and written through a variety of entanglings devised by the group. The bread would be infiltrate the *boulangeries* of Paris, become food. The texts would come together in a newspaper published over the course of the installation. For Julieta, this space was conceived in direct historical lineage with the political radicalism of Argentinian bakeries and their use of language, naming. It's well known that the bakers in Argentina were the first work force in the country to unionize, and as part of the ongoing struggle, gave their produce political, anti-state, anticlerical names. The word for pastries in Argentinian Spanish is just *factura* "invoice," while particular delicacies are called things like "nun's sighs" and "priest balls." The ruling classes were meant literally to eat the contempt their employees had for them.

I proposed a collective writing experiment where participants would make bread with their feet and write at the same time. People washed their feet in the sink before walking down a long plastic sheet to a circle of chairs. Once seated, they would put their feet in some plastic kneading tubs. Julieta came around and filled the tubs with yeast, water, then flour. Over the course of this, I tried to explain the concept of "asemic writing," that is, writing that has no semantic concept. It is a practice that has a long and intriguing history, through a mysterious 15th-century manuscript, *The Voynich Manuscript,* to the works of Laurence Sterne, Emily Dickinson, the surrealists, and a number of contemporary writers and poets. It sits eagerly on the cusp of words, emerging, for me at least, from a puppyish desire to write that overcomes and persists through and despite the fact that I don't have anything to say. It takes me back most vividly to the childhood performance of fluency. Sitting there, words flowing from my pen onto the paper, composing nonsense letters to ambassadors and the ever-elusive pen friend I never had in China. For this experiment at the Palais de Tokyo, words felt too much. We needed something more preliminary, more doughy. So we decided on asemic writing.

But, like the grease on my screen, the viscous performed its interventions. People were far too preoccupied by the sensation of dough forming between their toes to listen to me outline a well-phrased theory of "viscous writing." Conceptually, the experiment broke down. People wrote frenetically. But the asemic practice combined with the kneading felt like a fetishization of immediacy. "Words," I heard someone say, "would be a liberation."

The more we kneaded the stronger the gluten bonds became. Gluten, related as it is to "glue," adheres fiendishly to leg hair, folds of skin, containers, toe nails, and so on. About two hours were spent scrubbing after the workshop was over. We had made monstrous quantities of dough, far more than could be baked in Julieta's oven. Most had to be thrown away in a large bin in the basement of the gallery.[8] A small quantity was baked. I was surprised by how hard the knowledge of the feet made it to eat. But the bakers told us the quality was not bad. The waste, however, was depressing. Julieta's vision for the union of bakers and poets was for it to be exactly that: a union. Once you start throwing large quantities of dough away in the service of poetic experiments, all union is lost. There were serious flaws in our method. It will be attempted again.[9]

The appropriate "writerly" response to writing the viscous, to writing the grease on my screen, the dough in the tub, might be to try, rather than to write about grease, to integrate the qualities of grease into the language itself, to try to write as grease, all its sticky, slippery, blurry obscurity, to somehow translate its form into the language you can now see crisp and black, now the screen is clean. I have decided, though, to attempt something like the opposite, to be as violently clear as possible, to lay out the cleanest possible surface for its smears and marks to come into presence.

8   I later learned that this bin's lid was lifted off by the dough as it expanded, filling the entire container, in the warm evening air.

9   I held another slime writing workshop as part of *Physarum Borax,* an exhibition curated by Ella Fleck and Bryony James at Southwark Platform in London, October 2018. It was much more successful; words were used and its material will perhaps find their way into some publication one day.

Digital Goo

Via the grease, my attention turns to the material of the screen itself. Behind the glass lies a microscopically thin layer of liquid crystals that translate the charge passed through them, which corresponds to the digital information in my devices, into readable color and shape. This layer of the LCD screen is, as Esther Leslie says, a "slimy state of being," neither solid nor liquid, viscous, a state that possesses at one and the same time "properties of liquid and of crystal."[10] Screens might want to repel greasiness, asking us to wipe its obscurity off them. They might, as Parisi imagines, enact an ejaculative discharge as we enter through them into their worlds. This takes place, however, on an interface that has, at the center of its technology, this semi-state of matter. In the syrupy flow of the liquid crystal there exists the technology of high definition digital image making.

The liquid crystal was discovered towards the end of the 19th century by the Austrian botanical physiologist Friedrich Reinizter when attempting to extract cholesterol from carrots. He noticed that the particular cholesterol he was dealing with — cholesterol benzoate — exhibited two melting points. At 145.5°C, the substance melted to form a cloudy viscous liquid. At 178°C, the viscous liquid turned clear and became fluid. This intermediate state of the substance became a scientific curiosity and was picked up by the German physicist Otto Lehmann, who conducted the first in-depth experiments into what he would define as the liquid crystalline state, publishing the paper *Über fliessende Krystalle,* "On Flowing Crystals," in the *Zeitschrift für Physikalische Chemie* in 1889. In the liquid crystal, we observe, Lehmann proclaims, a "contradiction in terms": "a rigid well-ordered system of molecules," "our image of the crystal," that appears to flow like a "syrup or a gum."[11] This apparent contradic-

10 Esther Leslie, *Liquid Crystals: The Science and the Art of a Fluid Form* (London: Reaktion Books, 2016), 24.

11 Otto Lehman, "On Flowing Crystals," in *Crystals That Flow: Classic Papers from the History of Liquid Crystals,* eds. Timothy J. Sluckin, David

tion in the substance was contained, importantly, at a molecular level, part of the stuff's very structure.

There were objections to this theory, as one fully at odds with the laws of molecular science as they were then understood. The Berlin physicist Georg Quincke provided an explanation of this behavior on the basis of these substances being colloids, a structure of viscous matter I discuss at length in the next chapter. The substances, as far as Quincke was concerned, could only be composed of a suspension of small crystallites in the body of a liquid. An example of such a colloid is white paint, "which consists of crystallites of titanium dioxide suspended in polymer resin."[12] Gustav Tammann, a distinguished German physical chemist, thought these liquid crystal substances had more in common with milk or vinaigrette, suggesting they were emulsions.[13] But this state of matter was found not to be an imperceptible inter-dispersal of two distinct chemicals, but a gooeyness that existed at the level of the molecular.

Colloids and liquid crystals are the two main domains of viscous structure. They contain the types of thinking that find articulation in sliminess. One is an intermingled separateness, the other a sharpness that flows. They both do strange, though very familiar, things with light. Colloids disperse light within their body to create hazes, like the blue in the sky, whereas liquid crystals cause birefringence, the splitting of a ray of light into two that creates the classic psychedelic shimmering, cascading patterns, an aesthetic that I, at least, came across first on Windows Media Player.

One of the properties of liquid crystals that fascinated Lehmann was the tendency they have to move and grow as if alive. Like the early research into colloidal structures, liquid crystals were also thought to possess signs of life, incipient forms of vitality that potentially made them the bridge between

A. Dunmur, and Horst Stegemeyer (London: Taylor and Francis, 2004), 42–53, at 43, 52.

12 David Dunmur and Tim Sluckin, *Soap, Science, and Flat-Screen TVs: A History of Liquid Crystals* (Oxford: Oxford University Press, 2011), 29.

13 Ibid., 31.

the inorganic and the organic. Liquid crystals seemed to move of their own accord. They are animated matter that glistens, a cinematic substance. Appropriately enough, Lehmann made a film of his investigations in crystalline liquidity, entitled *Liquid Crystals and Their Apparent Life* in 1906, which is now lost. An observer of the film at the time wrote that one could see the "shooting forward and wriggling of the worm-shaped append-ages so clearly, as if one were seeing the object itself."[14] Liquid crystals look like films of themselves. Between colloids and liquid crystals, the latter were always the more cinematic semi-state. From their discovery, they were involved in moving image media. Initially at least, this was in order for their animation to be witnessed, rather than what would become the case — to be the material medium of digital visualization.

There are two phases of liquid crystalline matter: smectic and nematic. Smectic refers to liquid crystal with relatively weak molecular bonds. They slip and slide, exhibiting soap-like qualities. "Smectic" derives from the ancient Greek word *smēktikos,* later *smecticus* in Latin, meaning to clean, wash, purge. It's a soapy word, the root of the Greek *kosmētikos,* mean-ing skilled in adornment and arrangement. This would, then, evolve into the 17th-century French word *cosmétique* for the preparation of beauty. If liquid crystals have a soapy side, one intent on the maintenance of finely composed surface qualities, their other phase, nematic, is associated with a quality of writh-ing. It means "thready" or thread-like, and the molecules in the nematic phase face the same direction, but have no positional order within that arrangement. We might think of ancient mo-saic techniques, specifically the one that uses very small tiles, or tesserae, for intricate details and glow and shadows, a technique called *opus vermiculatum,* literally "worm-like work." In order to make things glow with HD finesse, we must avoid lines, hori-zons, grids; the eye can easily spot them and the illusion is shat-tered. Digital visual technologies need to technologize matter that can squirm and slide, they need the viscous: the liquid crys-

14 Leslie, *Liquid Crystals,* 30.

tal, a kind of matter that is doubled, directs us as much toward the wormy, the chthonic, as to the cosmetic, "face practices."

In her important work on the history of the liquid crystal, Leslie shows how this material signifies more than a scientific curiosity-turned-media technology. It is a "curious phase, in actuality and as a mode of processing existence."[15] For Leslie, the liquid crystal creeps into the thinking, art and social movements of the 19th century onwards, finding analogues in, for instance, Walter Benjamin's concept of "petrified unrest" or the jerkiness of the proletarian revolution "which only comes haltingly, as Marx put it."[16] In Leslie's form of sensual historical materialism, particular qualities of matter can become socially operative, historical forces in their own right, as Bruno Latour might have it, an "actant."[17] The dialectical interplay between the crystalline and the fluid is the material analogue of the struggle between revolutionary hope and reactionary thought. The liquid crystal plays out within its molecular structure the battle between progression and conservatism. But it is also the substance through which our global economy transmits images of itself "worldwide."[18] Leslie worries that the polar pull between the liquid and crystal threaten to "flatten out in the age of the flat screen."[19] She is concerned that the spectacular hypnotic power of the LCD screen is engaged in pacifying the struggles its substance enacts internally. The liquid crystal has been domesticated, forced into disappearance at the service of the ever crisper image.

One of the most intriguing moments in Leslie's writing on the liquid crystal comes as we enter with her into a television shop, screens on all sides at every moment firing across their surfaces the demonstration show-reels designed to exhibit their finest qualities. The fluid and crystal, once the thematic matter

15 Ibid., 20.
16 Ibid.
17 Bruno Latour, *Reassembling the Social: An Introduction to Actor-Network-Theory* (Oxford: Oxford University Press 2005).
18 Ibid.
19 Ibid., 21.

of the Romantic sublime — the snowy peaks, the frozen cataracts, the gushing torrents — are now the "technical matter of [...] a commodity sublime, conveyed by the digital machine."[20] But in a strange material twist, she notices how this commodity sublime, the "screens of high technology," conjure high nature to sell themselves. The images that swoop and soar on LCD screens in TV shops are ones of mountain ranges, canyons, seascapes. Adverts for GoPros display repeated images of flying off cliffs, plunging from high into lakes, snowboarding down mountain sides "the scurf of snow crystals hurtling towards the lens."[21] The sublime is traditionally associated with crises in our powers of representation and expression. The liquid crystal is now more part of a sublime that involves a super abundance of high definition representation.

Leslie notes how LCD technology is advertised as "close to nature," being more efficient, longer lasting, "eco-friendly," wanting to "keep our planet beautiful."[22] But then seems to want to "outbid" the "natural world" — seize its forms and disperse it throughout the shopping centers of human cities. The crystal clear image is advertised as being "sharp as a shark's teeth" and we move fluidly between worlds: "a dolphin rises through snow into the air, in front of a mountain backdrop."[23] Although we are oblivious to its substance, the allure of the liquid crystal is part of the form of these demonstration show-reels: a sharpness we glide easily between.

For Leslie, the liquid crystal is, itself, a dialectic and operates dialectically with the human world. It both informs and is informed by its interactions with society. In this way materials, their texture, their sensual presence, become indexes of shifts in the social fabric. They can literally contain, and contain ways of exposing, the "contradictions of the present."[24] What is so excit-

20 Ibid., 206.
21 Ibid.
22 Ibid., 208.
23 Ibid.
24 Melanie Jackson and Esther Leslie, "Journeys of Lactic Abstraction: The Meanings of Milk," *Cabinet* 61 (Fall 2016–Winter 2017), http://

ing about Leslie's writing is that material states are always also imaginary ones and that imaginary states are always also material ones. But neither are, importantly, ever reducible to one or the other. We get a writing that vibrates, a "world-view" that refracts materials states — crystallinity, emulsions, vapors — into complex relation with physic states — flights of fancy, stagnations, arrogances. Most importantly, materials are *things,* but also abstractions that can induce in us wild excursions into fantasy. Shine, glow, crystalline, glimmer: materials can advertise themselves as transcendent realms.

Looking for Ways to Live in Things

What of the desire to look to materials not as an index, but for guidance in the liberation in mind and body we think we desire? Why might we look to the behaviors of things to find instruction on how to live? What would a life look like that was lived in total and absolute attunement with materials, without any preconceptions about how they should behave or any beliefs in a transcendence from them? If such a thing were possible, would we even want this kind of life? Why did I assume, as I wrote this (if I'm being honest), that that life would be preferable to the one I feel like I am living now? In fact, why did I assume that we don't already live a life totally and absolutely attuned with materials, their texture? Am I caught by an anxiety about a disembodied digitized life and in response inadvertently give "texture" unwarranted, or totally hallucinated instructional power? I assumed it would be a good idea because, I think, materials already provide us with the metaphors we use to analyze our experience. Or further than this: material states are so often the way in which we experience our experience. The fog I feel in my mind right now as I try to work out what I'm writing is a material state I bring forward in order to bring forward how I'm feeling. Once I bring the fog forward, I am able, somehow, to experience what I'm experiencing more clearly, thinking "charged" with matter.

But this is combined with a frustration, for me at least, that we only bring forward materials like this to suit our purposes. More often than not we call upon texture if and when it is able to accommodate our metaphors. What if we were able to give texture, if only for a moment, *full control*? Would this be a kind of madness?

If not madness, perhaps this question is and only ever will be an academic thought experiment, something only theorists dream of. More than most, this question seems doomed to stay put in the world art theory; it will be centuries, no doubt, before they start discussing texture in think tanks. Luce Irigaray is driven by a similar impulse to find in the *actual dynamics* of fluid substances blueprints of how to crush male dominated kinds of living and knowing. In her influential writing on the mechanics of fluids, she sees there to have been a *historical lag in elaborating a theory of "fluids"* because, in part, their properties resist what patriarchal society considers to be "adequate symbolization."[25] As is well known, fluids are Irigaray's "real," they expose "the powerlessness of logic to incorporate in its writing all the characteristic features of nature."[26] Fluids are the excess, innately feminine substances that reach beyond. And this is, for Irigaray, the power of women and the threat they pose to patriarchal society. They diffuse themselves in ways that don't conform to the solid walls of principle, as they are "spreading to infinity."[27]

If we are to follow Irigaray we must look into the "real properties" of the fluid. But what's important for her is not so much some notion of continuity, boundlessness, structurelessness, but an attention to the "specific dynamics" of the fluid materials, which include "internal frictions, pressures, movements,"[28]

25 Luce Irigaray, *This Sex Which Is Not One*, trans. Catherine Porter (New York: Cornell University Press, 1985), 106.

26 Ibid., 107.

27 Ibid., 106.

28 Ibid., 109.

These have been excluded from our symbolization of the substance, this is what Irigaray considered to be the "real," something whose place is taken in society as it stands by an image of God.

Irigaray's writing on the mechanics of fluids feels dated for a number of reasons. I don't think it is necessary to launch another critique of its apparent essentialism, the way in which the female body feels awkwardly tied in some essential way to the physical behaviors of water. This is especially apparent when fluidity has come to mean, in more current discourses, an absolutely non-essentialist, highly constructivist approach to gender identity. Catherine Malabou, while rejecting critiques of Irigaray's essentialism as petty and irrelevant, finds Irigaray's writing on fluidity, this stretching to "infinity," to be, quite simply, in danger of being useless: "what's the point?" she asks. "Is there a viable source of action here? How do you escape the infinite fluidity or elasticity of the woman?"[29]

Malabou is one of the major opponents to philosophies of the "fluid," in favor of a material state she terms plasticity, which is at once the ability to mold, be molded and, most importantly, to explode. She looks to the Freudian idea of the healthy libido as viscous, able to reach out and contract without becoming fixated. This originates in amoeboid life, single-celled organisms that extend pseudopodia, false feet, out into the world, before contracting back in. Experience has a kind of kneading action to it: as we work on the world, it works on us. But Malabou's notion of the plastic is also wrapped up in modern understandings of the word, specifically the embedding of explosives in polymers to make plastic explosives. In French, *plastique* has the verb *plastiquer*, which means to blow up. The thinking gives a role to the material, allows it to suggest futures for where the thinking goes. The role of *plastiquer* is, as Malabou outlines in *Ontology of the Accident: An Essay in Destructive Plasticity,* to be the event of sudden change that has no relation to what came before. This is

29 Catherine Malabou, *Changing Difference: The Feminine and the Question of Philosophy*, trans. Carolyn Shread (Cambridge: Polity Press, 2011), 130.

a moment when an individual identity is "breached", "cut definitively" by something like a brain injury: a "sudden blind event
[that] cannot be reintegrated retrospectively into experience."[30]

Between Irigaray and Malabou we move from the liquid to
the plastic, from the rippling fluid to the malleable, the brain
that kneads and is kneaded on. Malabou zones in on the pressures that feel contained within Irigaray's fluid, the "frictions,
pressures, movements,"[31] and amplifies them into the explosive
moment. Both, however, allow their material and its multiple
properties to take an active role in what they say. The material
suggests outcomes.

The Ideal Firmness of Meat

In asking what a life lived in total attunement to texture would
look like, perhaps it is necessary to turn to the scientific and
commercial practice of food texture and flow analysis. With the
strict standardization that comes with mass production, there
are labs that develop the equipment necessary to measure and
test the exact sensual, tactile, properties of everything we use
and/or consume. I visited the UK site of Brookfield Amatek in
Roydon, Essex, to talk to Claire Freeman, the technical and
marketing support co-ordinator at the company, the "world
standard" manufacturer of viscometers, food texture analyzers,
and flow testers.[32]

Claire, who seemed to be the sole practitioner in what turned
out to be a medium-sized room in an industrial estate (I had, if
I'm honest, been imagining a huge factory full of vats of baked
beans), gave me demonstrations of their equipment. We used a
viscometer, a device that gently stirs viscous substances, mostly
foodstuffs and cosmetics (we used a pot of tahini), and assesses
the thickness over time. She showed me their texture analyzers,

---

30 Catherine Malabou, *The Ontology of the Accident: An Essay in Destructive Plasticity,* trans. Carolyn Shread (Cambridge: Polity Press, 2012), 29.
31 Irigaray, *This Sex Which Is Not One,* 109.
32 "About Us," AMETEK *Brookfield,* https://www.brookfieldengineering.com/.

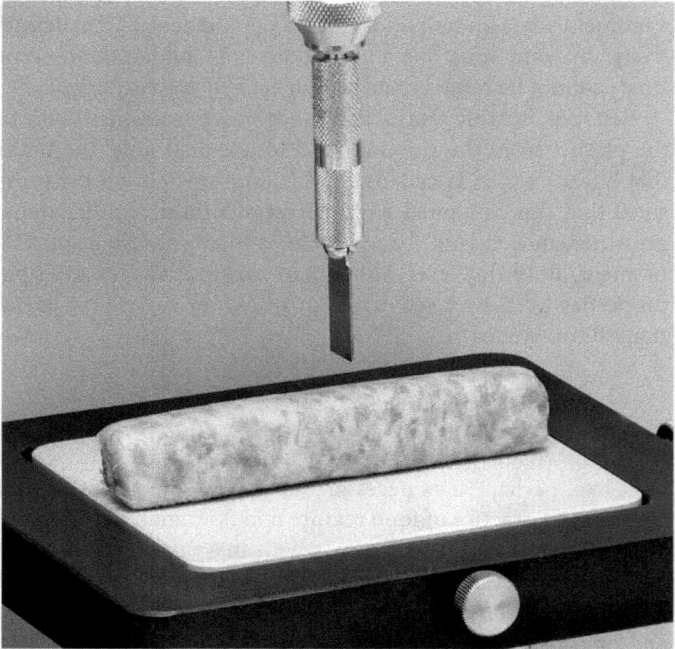

Fig. 2. The Brookfield Amatek Texture Analyser at work on a sausage. Courtesy of Brookfield Amatek.

equipment that allows you to standardize the resistance a sausage puts up to your bite (fig. 2), for instance, the reluctance a particular bit of pizza has to being torn apart (fig. 3), the stretchability of its melted cheese (fig. 4), or the effect of hair dye on the "smoothness" of hair when combed (fig. 5), to name only a few. They also have a device, something that Claire made sure I knew was very unique, that assesses the flow of powders, nuts, and beans as you tip them out of pots: the Brookfield Amatek powder flow tester. The precision is strangely both comic and breathtaking. It is breathtaking to think of the lengths cultures of mass production will go to make sure every sensual detail of your experience of their commodities has been delicately meas-

Fig. 3. The Brookfield Amatek Texture Analyser at work on a pizza. Courtesy of Brookfield Amatek.

ured, tested, and curated. As she showed me the sausage bite analyzer, I asked Claire what an ideal reading for the firmness of the meat would be. She looked at me with a shocked expression, then laughed: "Oh! That's a question for the sensory panel!" That is, the assembly of mouths, skins, noses, and fingertips that these machines sit in for and mimic.

But rather than giving us an intricate map of matter's textures, these machines try to standardize them, get a grip on what is excessive in order to repeat what seems to work, to please, to sell. They are the tactile zone of that most elusive, almost ghostly, presence in consumerist society: quality control. What quality? And who is in control? As Keller Easterling describes,

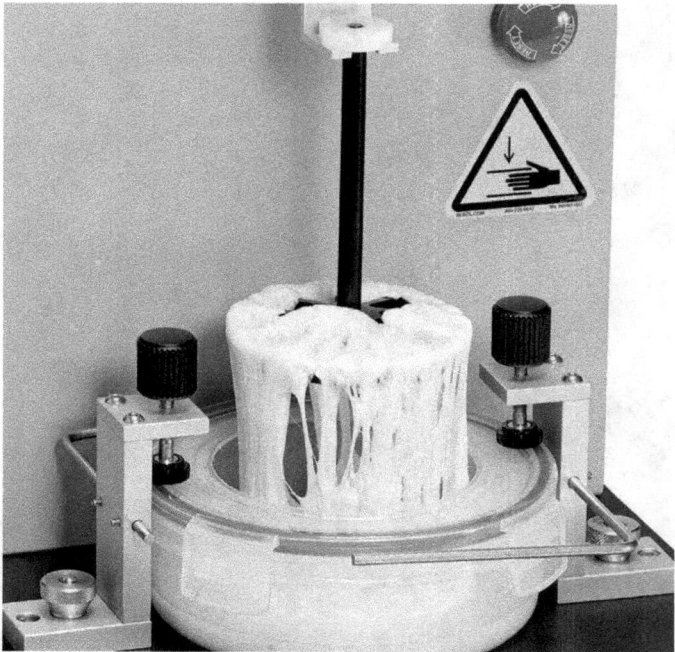

Fig. 4. The Brookfield Amatek Texture Analyser at work on some metled cheese. Courtesy of Brookfield Amatek.

"quality," in the managerial sense, "has no content."[33] And it has no content on purpose. In fact — the less content quality has, the more useful it is to the companies ascribing to its standards. The ISO, or the international standards organization, is the body that ensure that commodities traded globally meet certain requirements. We must thank them, for instance, for the fact that all credit cards and ATM slots are the same size around the world.[34]

33 Keller Easterling, *Extrastatecraft: The Power of Infrastructure Space* (London: Verso, 2014), 174.
34 Maybe all religious buildings should be converted into places where we can express our gratitude for this.

Fig. 5. The Brookfield Amatek Texture Analyser at work on a length of hair. Courtesy of Brookfield Amatek.

They also ensure that food products are of a certain "quality." But this idea of quality was not developed to assess technical performance, or durability, or efficiency. The companies themselves determined the quality of their product:

> Successful engagement with the standard is measured by evaluating whether an organization has addressed the objectives it set for itself.[35]

35 Easterling, *Extrastatecraft,* 176.

"Quality," then, is the power to standardize, to be able to set objectives and then meet them, repeatedly. These machines at Brookfield Amatek are the condition for the possibility for McDonalds food production, the texture of its experience, approaching the perfectly repeatable. Imagine a world where every bite you ever took of any food was absolutely identical, both in texture and in taste. These machines are the machines that make food texture and flow aspire towards the digital. The journey is short between the perfect crisp and perfectly crisp, repeatable image that liquid crystalline flow has now made possible.

Virtual Putrescence

The video work of artist Ed Atkins is intent on exposing not so much the so-called "materiality of the screen," but lunging out into the material excesses that smooth HD images secretly carry within themselves. His show *Olde Food* at Cabinet Gallery, Spring 2018, unfolds like a demented period drama, or perhaps a rehearsal for a historical re-enactment based on some crude "horrible history-style" imaginary of medieval England. A time, that is, as a text explains, where you "toil in filth," your teeth are rotting out of your skull, "children learn about sex from watching animals" and no-one has ever seen "anyone write a word or draw a picture."[36] You're asked to see, however, the LCD screens that surround you as participating in this creep of decay, rather than standing clear of it. In fact, the digital image is able to beat putrescence at its own game, as another text, printed on what might be part of an Ikea wardrobe explains:

> Watching our virtual cheeseburger putresce black goo is more difficult than the real mouldy cheese burger because the virtual one by virtue of being advertorial proxy threatens the entire order of cheeseburgers, all cheeseburgers, ours.[37]

36 Ed Atkins, exhibition text from *Olde Foode*, Cabinet Gallery, London, April 26–June 2, 2018.
37 Ibid.

The message is clear: the spread of mold across meat is quaint in comparison to the spread of the digital. Once mold is digitized, its threat is magnified infinitely to involve not only what is there at hand, but our entire definition of that foodstuff. The advertorial image is exposed as the adversarial, becoming, like an imaginary of the slime monster, an invasive force in the formation of our categories.

The exhibition as a whole imagines HD images as finding their origins not in the *opus vermiculatum* of the liquid crystal, but in the very particular kind of curtailed decay of the human body that occurs in the anaerobic bacterial hydrolysis of fat tissue. This is a process where the human form, instead of rotting, saponifies and becomes, essentially, soap, its image preserved, rather than dispersing out into the earth through the guts of worms. The deliciously clear images we see before us are "not just CGI." Another text describes adiopocere, the stuff of the saponified body:

> Your fat mixed with lye (usually NaOH, a common metal hydroxide, highly caustic and available) creates, famously, basic soap.
>
> Corpse wax, adiopocere (the saponification of human fat by anaerobic bacteria) chemically restructures your jelly into a crumbly whitish material that will hold its human shape with the clarity of a nightmarish Madame Tussaud's.[38]

Just as, if we follow Adorno, we might hear the screams on the Holocaust lying on a beach in California, standing in a clean gallery space in South London we're suddenly staring into a mass grave. Through this clarity we dive into the murky pits. There is the sense of an illusion having been broken, but we're not returned to the technologies of these illusions, the hackneyed mantra: "nothing more material than a broken computer." No, we're taken on *another* adventure, one that has as its protagonist a quivering lump of jelly. Please note: the tears of Atkins's char-

38 Ibid.

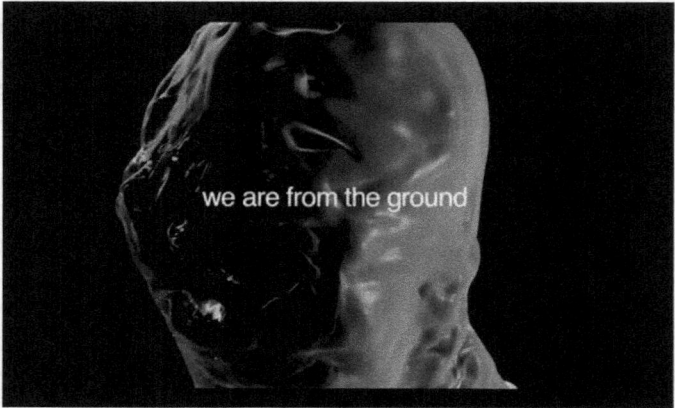

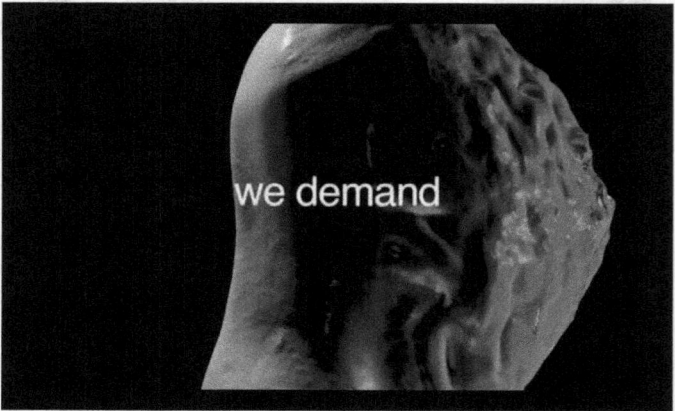

Figs. 6 & 7. Stills from Benedict Drew, *Sludge Manifesto,* digital video, 2011. Courtesy of Benedict Drew and Matt's Gallery, London

acters resemble slugs, oozing enthusiastically from the entirety of the eye, one wonders how we know they're tears at all. The eyes look through the slugs to our own, gingerly, hesitantly, in need, yet never quite sure how to go about talking.

Insurrection and Invasion

Upon the backdrop of digital technology, the meaning of the viscous substance has changed. If it was once a material state that threatened to engulf and ingest all, as dramatized by the "slime monster," its powers to do this have been overshadowed by the *creep* of the digital. The threat of the ever expanding blob, of material indifference, has been challenged by something like digital indifference, the ability of binary code to transform into itself whatever it happens to record and repeat over as many times as we want. The fear, then, changes from a fear of being reduced to the mere matter of our bodies, to a fear of total digitized disembodiment. Something curious then takes place: what was once a state of matter that signaled dubiousness, phlegmatics, disingenuousness, becomes a site of seemingly indisputable authenticity.

The video work of London-based artist Benedict Drew is fascinated by gloops, whether they are blown into, caked on anonymous objects or, as is the case with *Sludge Manifesto* from 2011, feature as a central rotating point of focus, somehow the material of the coming insurrection.

This moving image has an irony to it — an amorphous form precisely structured through digital graphic design. Its aesthetic is one that refers to the liquid crystal, a shimmering neon blurriness that might resemble the oozes of an LCD screen once you've pierced its surface with a screwdriver. The work does not release the liquid crystals from their labor, though, but asks them to perform something that might *resemble* this release. But, the form is not entirely formless. We see as it rotates, clearest from the second of the three stills (fig. 7), the curve of the neck from the top of the back to the crown of the head. It is a face that has been scrambled into obscurity. The film revels in the powers of

175

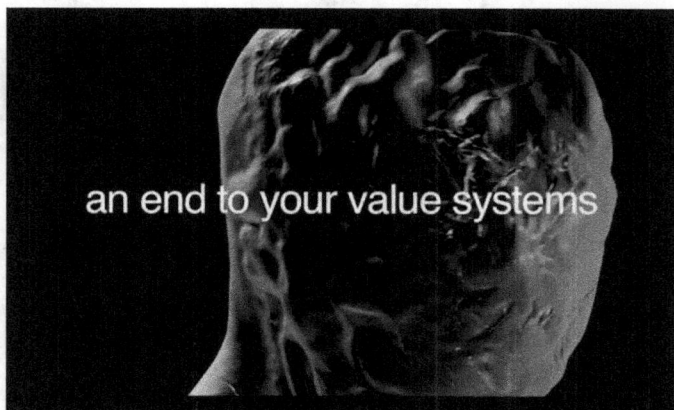

Figs. 8 & 9. Stills from Benedict Drew, *Sludge Manifesto,* digital video, 2011. Courtesy of Benedict Drew and Matt's Gallery, London

iconoclasm, the erasure of representation, one that leaves the signs of this erasure in place, a spectacle of non-representation. We have, instead, text: slogans, demands, threats, predictions, that enlist the digitally generated amorphous blob as their illustration.

The film is unambiguously using this digital viscous as a sign of the proletarian, subaltern masses, existing without form, without identity or voice, living in a state of potentiality. The connection to proletarian uprising is explicit. The film in fact opens with flashing still images of workers down mines, wheeling carts of coal, before switching to the digital gloop.

Marx used the word *Gallerte,* a kind of jellied foodstuff eaten in Germany at the time, most probably by his contemporaneous readers, to evoke the indifferent mass of the workforce under capitalism, gorged on by the greedy factory owner.[39] Today, as the critique generally goes, this group is held in subservience by the enjoyable alternate realities channelled into their living rooms via television screens or, now, on the screens of laptops. Drew, like Marx, is looking to confront this group with their own image. This, though, is the proletariat of the information age, now no longer a jellied foodstuff, no longer *Gallerte,* but a digital goo, disembodied, locked to the crystal clear computer screens of immaterial labor.

The viscous as the material analogue for the oppressed masses of capitalist society is part of its position as a substance of authenticity. It is one that cuts through the barrage of "fake news." It is something that is somehow true precisely because it never claims to be. The viscous is so often brought forward symbolically as a way of affirming the absolutely unquestionable materiality of experience, its mere stuff. Paradoxically, the viscous state has become the symbol of materiality in general, its presence itself a strangely digitized reminder of this "ground," this "real," which may or may not *actually* be viscous. Through this, goo

39 For a fuller discussion of Marx's use of the word *Gallerte,* see Keston Sutherland, "Marx in Jargon," in *Stupefaction: A Radical Anatomy of Phantoms* (Calcutta: Seagull Books, 2011), 26–90, at 37–50.

177

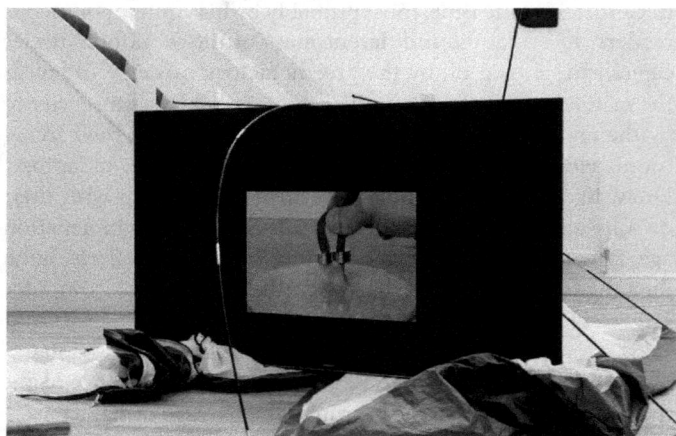

Figs. 10 & 11. Stills from Elsa Philippe, *My Goo,* video installation, 2017, installation view, Adult World at Clearview, London, UK.

has become a trope of digital visual art anxious to undercut the dreams of an immaterial existence that its medium might encourage. The thrill of watching the ooze of liquid crystals across an LCD screen that once displayed, let's say, the BBC, is the thrill of false consciousness having been shattered in favor of a spectacle that *could not lie to us,* a sense of complicity with material in a state of pure, formless, potentiality.

This is something the French video artist Elsa Philippe comes across in her film "my goo." The image of a child sitting distressed (or maybe counting) on a giant iPhone, surrounded by "jazz hands" throwing "TRUTH" in your face, is accompanied by various science experiment-like situations, one, for instance, of a magnet attracting some magnetic slime.

The story that the text and voice of the film narrate is about a girl looking for something exciting to do on the internet, only to have her mind taken over by some mysterious cyberforce from which she is unable to escape. The film's best line is the girl's thought, once trapped: "I had no clue, no clue, they were invading my goo." The monstrous menace here is not the goo, but the internet. Unlike Sartre's lazy evil, goo, here, has integrity, one that is threatened by the parasitic creep of cyberspace. Goo presents some place of refuge in a world of jazz hands hurling out endless truth claims.

Jellied Ghosts

The character in Philippe's video work becomes possessed, we might say. The internet occupies her body, her goo, like a ghost. When have goo and ghostliness come together like this before?

It was once theorized that the brain, in states of hyperstimulation, would extrude itself as a viscous mass out of the various orifices of the skull into the external world. In the late 19th century, neurological activity was thought to behave like an amoeba. Neurons made contact not through electrical charge but through the pseudopodal movements of the protoplasm of the nerve cell. The brain was thought to function much like the tentacular activity of the gloopy bodies of single-celled organisms. Little gooey, wormy fingers were thought to pass between the gaps in the brain, its synaptic clefts, for thinking, memory, feeling, and consciousness in general, to happen. When the brain was in a state of hyperstimulation, under supranormal conditions, this wormy action of the protoplasmic masses in the brain could start behaving in an extreme way. The normal leaps of matter within the brain, would start leaping out of it, spurting out of the mouth, the ears, the nose or the eyes. Such is the explanation given by the 19th-century scientist Charles Richet for the "phenomenon of materialization," the ectoplasmic masses that supposedly emerged from women's orifices during séances. The ectoplasm was never claimed to be a ghost, just the effect being in communication with a ghost had on the female subject.

Richet was drawn to the moment when the body enters a state of seizure, winning the Nobel Prize for his work on the physiology of laughter. Although he coined the term ectoplasm at the end of the 19th century, he was not involved in the completely fraudulent séances that involved its extrusion. Richet was trying to find an explanation for hoaxes.

These images are one of the rare occasions when the viscous and the spectral explicitly intersect. This might feel like a contradictory marriage — jelly being the stuff associated with a *prima materia,* material in its most basic form, before, in fact, it is something at all, and ghosts, the very definition of immaterial, of the intangible. The ectoplasmic jellied ghost is, therefore, the place where the immaterial locks back into the material, where the supernatural finds association with matter in its most amorphous, negligible form. Like the liquid crystal, it is the gloopy material that transports us though images from wherever we are "elsewhere." Indeed, one of the powers of ectoplasm was to arrange itself into forms of photographic verisimilitude, to form pictures that were, in truth, just cut from magazines and pasted onto the substance. But nevertheless, this was *claimed* to be the externalization of the mind's images and, though fakery, is also a unique moment in the history of representation: the imagination of a bodily ooze to be a technology of photographic reproduction.

Today it is hard to imagine how anybody might be persuaded to believe in images that are so obviously fraudulent. Part of the fascination of these images perhaps comes from the sense of "our" historical superiority they carry. We now know better. We would never be so fooled by the seductions of spectacle. Karl Schoonover, in his essay on ectoplasm photography, suggests that one of the reasons why the hoaxes worked was the way they responded to the changing popular perspectives of photographic technology at the start of the 20th century. In Victorian spirit photography, ghosts are caught on camera that are otherwise imperceptible. In interwar ectoplasm photography, the camera was capturing what could be seen anyway, but just happening too fast to be observed.[40] The role of the camera was not to take us directly to the "beyond," the invisible realm of the supernatural, but to take us right up close to this realm's material effects on the female body. In their visual intent, these ectoplasm images share more with Eadweard Muybridge's galloping horses than they do with Victorian pictures of ghosts. The camera was seen as an enhancement of a technology already present in human sight, rather than a mechanism for accessing the unseen. The ability of the camera to capture fleeting material contingency was what these hoaxes used to foster a sense of believability.

The hyperreal details of a viscous substance were used as a source of authenticity for a world that felt ghostly. The viscous is, then, a source of the activity of *mere stuff* through which we are able to access the ghost world. The viscous becomes an interface, a site where we are asked to delve into the "real" and the dream simultaneously. Something similar is happening to "goo" in a culture swamped in the digital. For it is inaccurate to say that Elsa Philippe's "goo" is only the symbol of some "authentic earth," the originary primordial soup from which we might imagine we emerged. No, it itself is an interfacial construction, a cohesion between senses of "base matter" and the purely syn-

---

40 Karl Schoonover, "Ectoplasms, Evanescence and Photography," *Art Journal* 62, no. 3 (August 2003): 30–41.

thetic universe. This is one that corresponds both to our shit and to our dreams, pure malleability, pure CGI.

In playing with slime toys, we are participating in an ideal of human progress. This is an ideal where shit itself has become benign, submissive to our wants and fancies, be they ambitious or vague. Where the liquid crystal might be the literal slime that sends us off into seemingly any possible form of a world, these slime toys are like digitized matter. They are the material means towards immaterial experience, *actually there,* but also a kind of fantasy. Their substance, pulled to the earth, is already partially imaginary, belonging, somehow, to somewhere else, their matter reaching out into the insubstantial. No toys are innocent, and these slimy ones are no exception. They enact in their tactile immediacy the loop whereby synthetic production "reprocesses the nature that produced it."[41] They are where the primordial and the synthetic collapse into each other, exposing the "sly solidarity" between these states.

ASMR

In trying to conceptualize this transformation, it is useful to observe the turn that has taken place on online media platforms such as YouTube and Instagram where very simple, yet intensely intimate, encounters with material things have become viral phenomena. People have started to fanatically record and distribute online videos of themselves, often only their hands, performing very simple interactions with particular things. This might be the gentle rubbing of a make-up brush on the gauze of a microphone, the tapping of long, red plastic fingernails on the surface of a fake wooden tabletop, very slowly opening the plastic wrapper of a pack of biscuits. The sound is quiet, but unnaturally amplified with immersive fidelity. If there is any speaking it is whispered so that what they're doing becomes what we're doing together, though somehow taboo and not to be overheard.

---

41 Robin Mackay, "Editorial Introduction," in *Collapse VII,* ed. Robin Mackay (Falmouth: Urbanomic, 2008), 3–37, at 5.

These films have been informally grouped together as a genre of video that seeks to excite ASMR, or "autonomous sensory meridian response," otherwise known as the "tingles" or a "head-orgasm."

To anyone involved in the ASMR community, the suggestion that these films are in any way erotic is taken largely as an insult. For the community, their pleasure is never quite pleasure, but a form of stress release. ASMR is most commonly referred to as a form of relaxation. In the most in-depth survey and psychological analysis of ASMR users online, conducted by researchers at the University of Swansea, 98% of them saw ASMR films as an opportunity to relax. Only 5% of those asked reported using the genre for sexual stimulation.[42] The feeling is only ever necessarily subdued, never overwhelming or ecstatic, a "low-grade euphoria." It has been speculated that the tingles of ASMR might be the result of a minor seizure.[43] But role-play, performed intimacy, conceits of care-giving and subservience are laid on thick. When the woman I watched opening a pack of biscuits notes in husky tones that they might be stale, she, just before taking a bite, says, "that's a sacrifice I'm willing to make for you."

The recent ASMR craze is it as an intensely intimate material encounter designed to take place solely within the context of the internet. The films do not call attention to the "materiality of the screen," but are a specific kind of material encounter that the dynamics of cyberspace has made possible. It is said that what most amazed the first people to ever use telephones was not the fact of being able to speak to your brother, say, on the other side of the world, but the fact of being able to hear him breathing. ASMR seems to be structured similarly. The transportive powers of the incidental, the fascination with the sensual properties of the absolutely mundane happening elsewhere. The effect of these films is not Parisi's fantasy "discharge of matter," nor do they, like the grease on my screen, bring me into direct physical

42 Emma L. Barrett and Nick J. Davis, "Autonomous Sensory Meridian Response: A Flow-like Mental State," *PeerJ* 3 (March 2015): e851.
43 Ibid.

interaction with the devices that encourage this fantasy. It is the way in which the films, instead, combine the two — a blasting off into cyberspace only to settle and resettle compulsively on short films that take you into extreme sensual proximity to the specifically material behavior of the extremely familiar. The vast majority of these films take place in domestic locations, using household items. They are, in some ways, the opposite of the demonstration show-reels in TV shops, dolphins erupting out of sunsets; the viewer is transported to table tops around the world, somewhere they could, very easily, already be.

Some of the most interestingly problematic writing on the phenomenon of ASMR is by a medical practitioner Nitin K. Ahuja, a gastroenterologist at John Hopkins University Hospital in the US. Ahuja first came across ASMR in 2013 in its particular form of medical role-play. A young female nurse with no professional training looks directly into camera, examines your body, gently performs various tests and tells you everything is wonderfully "ok." What Ahuja found enthralling about this pretend medical examination were how the formulas of his own training were being used to establish what seemed to be the potential for genuinely intimate connections between people:

> The popularity of these videos signalled to me an electric potential for real connections crackling beneath the surface of my ordinary professional interactions, behind the insulating postures of cynicism, defensiveness, hurry, or greed.[44]

Ahuja takes the ASMR community at their word. This is not, as it may seem to many people, a cliché of kinky online sex-talk, but a thrilling awakening of some sense of authentic intimacy within the actions he performs himself everyday with total professional disinterest.

Ahuja speculates as to why ASMR has become so popular, about the science behind these tingles. For those partial to the

44 Nitin K. Ahuja, "Softer than Softcore," *The New Inquiry*, December 9, 2014, https://thenewinquiry.com/softer-than-softcore/.

evolutionary lens, the thrill of these films might stem from the social grooming habits of other animals; it might be evolutionarily beneficial for rituals of care-giving to produce excitement. Most interestingly, however, he proposes a

> hypersensitivity to touch in the setting of its relative deficiency. For a conjectural analogy, we might turn to the over-expression of certain receptors in basic negative feedback loops: cellular membranes becoming ever more populated with molecules meant to capture a progressively infrequent stimulus.[45]

I am not in a position to comment on the science of this statement. But the suggestion is that in a world where people increasingly live online, where touch dries up, the body starts to compensate for the absence of physical encounter through generating hypersensitivity to ones represented, through sound and light, on our screens. In this way ASMR is, for Ahuja, something like the redemption of the internet. It has managed to find a kind of "homeopathic paradox,"[46] a way to cure it own ills, save us from its powers of alienation and isolation. From the medical role-play, Ahuja moves in his various articles on ASMR, between its many different loosely associated modes — people taking things out of boxes, unwrapping new handbags, things fitting neatly into other things, pouring water into cups etc. As far as he is concerned, these films are in no way mildly erotic, vaguely fetishistic, wastes of time, but a means for us to reconstitute our brains tangled and broken by the relentless onslaught of so-called "modern life." If long-term exposure to pornography produces a "slow but steady corruption of our dopaminergic pathways," ASMR is an attempt to reassemble the "fractured pieces of our psyche," he suggests. It is a return to something

---

45 Nitin K. Ahuja, "'It Feels Good to Be Measured': Clinical Role-Play, Walker Percy and the Tingles," *Perspectives in Biology and Medicine* 56, no. 3 (Summer 2013): 442–51, at 445.

46 Ibid.

we have lost in cyberspace, provided by cyberspace; ASMR films are "artefacts of a post-pornographic age," a desire to return to the very rudiments and origins of intimacy in a world of sexual and spectacular oversaturation and overstimulation. ASMR is the dismissal of "brute acts in favour of the their clean, abstract signifiers."[47]

I am wary of Ahuja's eagerness to celebrate ASMR. His terror of overstimulation and the notion that we are being somehow damaged by the sheer quantity of stuff on the internet strikes me as dull, potentially extremely conservative and deeply limited in its imagining of how thought and pleasure might operate. Who is to say how our dopaminergic pathways are "meant to be"? On what basis can we claim our very neurology is corrupt and in need of salvation? In his perception of ASMR as a return to something, some form of originary, uncorrupted intimacy, what sorts of crypto-fascist fantasies are at play? But then again, ASMR has proven to be an extremely effective method of therapy for people suffering form chronic pain, depression, and anxiety.[48] Not unlike the current trend for "mindfulness," ASMR is used by people as a therapeutic method of detachment where the participant is able to achieve a state of mental "flow," a state of being I discussed in the previous chapter. Although it might be problematic to assign ASMR some status of authenticity, the anxieties people experience are nonetheless real, as are whatever acts as their cure.

Fondling Slime Online

The viscous has found a new home in this ASMR network and one of the most popular types of this genre's videos involves fondling slime. Online communities of mostly, but by no means only, young teenage girls make slime out of personalized ratios of PVA glue, shaving foam, and borax diluted in water, add food coloring, little plastic stars, polystyrene balls, anything

47 Ahuja, "Softer than Softcore."
48 Barrett and Davis, "Autonomous Sensory Meridian Response."

to add textural counterpoint, and fondle it in little HD haptic documentaries. Some of these slimers, such as Instagram user slimequeens, command the attention of an online crowd of a size equivalent to a small city (733k followers) on a daily basis. Like the customs of an ancient community, the formula of these films is strictly adhered to: the hands remove the slime from a small transparent plastic pot, poke it with their tips three or four times, before folding the body of the slime over itself again and again. At this point the slime is stretched and pulled, the glitter and the stars exhumed and swept off, the sound crackles, pops, and politely squelches. The surface on which this activity plays out is usually a matte white tabletop. Although I've noticed that recently Instagram user slimekiingg, a young male slimer of, I would estimate, nine years, with considerably less followers than slimequeens has taken to fondling his slime on maps of the world, creating imaginary pink glittery land masses between South America and Africa. The dominion of slimekiingg; this boy has imperial ambitions.

These slime films are of course, though, reminiscent of a type of slimy toy that has been on the market since 1950, Silly Putty. This, the first of all slimes to be sold as a toy, came about, like so many things, as a failed military material. The US trade embargo with Japan during the Second World War cut off the rubber trade between East and West. An essential material for machines of war, research began into finding a synthetic rubber substitute. Silicone oil was mixed with boric acid by scientists working for General Electric and the result was a curious one: a rubber-like material that stretched if you pulled it slowly, bounced if you threw it against a wall, but broke into little pieces if you yanked it hard enough. They had synthesized a non-Newtonian viscoelastic. No practical use was ever found for Silly Putty, but its inconsistent material properties gave it a "silliness" that was commercially viable. The man who filed the patent for the material as a source of recreation, Peter Hodgson, described it in an article in the *New Yorker* in 1950, as "five minutes escape from [the] neurosis" of a world reeling from the effects of mechanized war.[49] Intended for use by the military, this viscoelastic became instead a material of benign nonsense that offered a momentary escape from a militarized world, rather than a tool for it.

Fondling things, we drift off, find release from the world through the comfort of repeated squeezing. It is a directionless pleasure, one that doesn't move, like ejaculation-oriented pleasure, towards climax. It stays with itself. This is true, too, of the form of these slime films, their strikingly repetitive nature, how little desire for innovation or variation they possess. *They merely are,* fondling their way into cyberspace clip by clip. Nothing is being evoked, no point being made. Their sole intention is to take us into the closest possible proximity with the squelches and crackles of slime.

Rather than being a dream of an immaterial existence, the internet has become a place of extremely various material experience, a place obsessed with capturing, simply for the sake of it, the quirks and irregularities of matter. Fondling activates these quirks and is a way for us to disappear into them. The structure of the films is erotic, though, in the way that their intimacy is a kind of distancing. However close we might feel to the slime, it is still only on a screen. The sensation of the tingles happens when our senses are split like this, when we feel, in one way, contained within something and, in another, completely removed from it. Like with ectoplasm photography, it is a kind of attentiveness to sensual detail, the intricate contingencies of the matter that not only delights, but results in an entry into an elsewhere.

The act of fondling gooey objects is imagined by Gaston Bachelard to be one of transcendentally communitarian potential. Fondling calms us down through providing a reciprocity between hand and matter. It finds in the world "*a suppleness in plenitude* — a suppleness that fills one's hands, rebounding endlessly from matter to hand."[50] Suppleness is what gratifies the

49 Marion Miller, Brendan Gill, and Harrison Kinney, "Here to Stay," *The New Yorker,* August 26, 1950, https://www.newyorker.com/magazine/1950/08/26/here-to-stay-2.

50 Gaston Bachelard, *Earth and the Reveries of Will: An Essay On the Imagination of Matter,* trans. Kenneth Haltman (Dallas: The Dallas

hand, provides it precisely with what it desires to do, allows it to feel most perfectly like a hand. It becomes conscious, Bachelard speculates, of how fingers became fingers. Suppleness can also pacify our anger because it denies it any object on which it could unleash itself. Pliant matter quells our inner rage, relieves it little by little of "avarice and aggression," and imbues it "sinew by sinew, with muscles of generosity."[51] The act of fondling is the origin of a particular way of being with others, for Bachelard. He chooses a moment in the great gooey novel *Moby Dick* as an example of this taking place, a moment thatmight be considered a 19th-century instance of Autonomous Sensory Meridian Response:

> All morning long I squeezed that sperm until I myself almost melted into it; […] Oh! My dear fellow beings, why should we longer cherish any social acerbities, or know the slightest ill-humour or envy! Come let us squeeze hands all round; nay let us squeeze ourselves into each other; let us squeeze ourselves universally into the very milk and sperm of kindness.[52]

Melting into things is not far, it seems, from melting into others. The object sitting there waiting to be fondled is sitting there waiting to unlock utopian visions of universal "brotherly love." There is here an imagined continuity between the activity of the hand and a kind of political consciousness. Squeezing viscous matter opens out directly onto a dream of collectivized existence. Maybe Instagram has partially realized this vision, a global network united simply by the thrill of squeezing.

Institute Publications, 2002), 61.
51 Ibid., 64.
52 Herman Melville, *Moby Dick* (Hertfordshire: Wordsworth Modern Classics, 2002), 345.

Techniques of Domination

For Bachelard, the act of kneading imagines the world as oppositional, a "perfect synthesis of yielding and resistance, a marvelous equilibrium of the forces of acceptance and refusal."[53] It is out of this state of equilibrium that we're able to determine the pejorative judgements of *too hard, too soft!* This moment of balance, something we instantly recognize, Bachelard thinks, is the dream of the "perfect earth," a moment of exactitude aimed for by the baker, the moment at which water and flour come into doughy harmony. So begins the *cogito of kneading,* where we quietly murmur to ourselves as we work away at a lump of dough: "Everything is earthen matter to me, including myself; my own destiny is my material, action and passion my materials; I am truly primordial earth."[54]

But is bread dough viscous? If yes, then it is surely of some other order of the viscous than, say, glue or tar. The slime in these films is, too, not viscous in the same way that the asphalt in the asphalt lake in Binəqədi is viscous. They stand for the viscous pacified, its maddening stickiness erased to leave an invitation to malleable playfulness. This phenomenon of the domesticated viscous is something that Bachelard locks into, unlike Sartre, whose battle between the in-itself and for-itself is ceaseless. Bachelard shows how easy it is to bring slimy things under control. Dough is an instance of this, an instance of a substance that has been dominated by the hand. If the material is too sticky, all one need to do is sprinkle some more flour! Leavening, too, caused by the addition of yeast, transforms the dough into something light and malleable, makes it fibrous, facilitating its undoing. In the battle with viscosity the hand can forge allegiances with other materials. In kneading, yeast is our "ally *against viscosity!*"[55]

Bachelard's response to Sartre's primal dread of the sticky thing is to direct us to all the not so nightmarish, but quotidian,

53 Bachelard, *Earth and the Reveries of Will,* 59.
54 Ibid., 60.
55 Ibid., 92

thickening and thinning outs of matter. What is most unique about Bachelard's writing, here, is the way he seems less interested in the horror, the dread, the disgust of it all, and more interested in the potential for reverie held in more practical matters. The material imagination, he reminds us, doesn't come from nowhere, but from a "convergence of functions, an aggregate of useful values."[56] He takes us to the attempts in the seventeenth and eighteenth centuries to prevent the build up of phlegm in the body using foodstuffs that were imagined to "cut through" its viscosity. Pepperwort, for instance, was declared by Michael Ettmüller to be an "excellent stomachic, for it cuts and dissolves the viscous mucus lining the stomach walls."[57] Others, such as Étienne Geoffrey, hold that the flowers of hops make the viscosity of beer thinner. Though there is no scientific way of legitimizing these claims, they stand for, instead, what Bachelard calls "a conviction of images,"[58] the way in which textures seem to contain a kind of internal logic of interaction that we might find ourselves inadvertently believing in.

For Bachelard, the viscous becomes, then, not so much an object of morbid fascination, but a source of debate, a complex of opinions about the meaning of consistencies. Just as people try to attenuate matter, there are situations where a highly viscous flow might simply be favored. Doctors in the 17th and 18th centuries would try, apparently, to thicken the body's humors in order to mollify the organs. According to the 17th-century chemist Daniel Duncan in *La Chymie naturelle,* the unctuosity of the organs was a good thing. The thicker they were, the better. The more resistant their substance, the more they would retain food particles that would otherwise escape. The more viscous your internal organs, the longer you can fast. The viscous, for Duncan, is associated with a retention of nutrition, it is why, for him, resinous trees live longer than others, why snakes with "gummy" skin, can live all winter without eating. In these ac-

56 Ibid.
57 Ibid., 93
58 Ibid.

counts, viscosity does not induce vertigo, is not a source of joy, but something to be worked with. It "exerts instead a gentle magnetism":

> Unctious matter attracts and retains alimentary treasure, the precious and radical moisture.[59]

And Bachelard wants to be clear: this debate over which viscosity is preferable can potentially have no basis in scientific research. Theories about the world can be proven wrong by science, but this, Bachelard observes, has "scant effect on the power of images."[60] How we perceive textures is embedded in conviction, the passage of matter between degrees of viscosity carry subtle and acute ideals about how the world should be.

It is from this backdrop that the very particular labour of kneading emerges. Though an instance of seeming harmony, raw dough is also an "invitation to domination."[61] Despite his lyrical indulgence in the act of baking, he lets no quaint illusions of the baker to settle. In the act of kneading we find a triumph of the "powerful imperialism of the human subject."[62] Viscosity has been overwhelmed and transformed. Like with the slime we might buy in gift shops that makes shit benign, there is a sense, in making bread, of having transcended some fundamental laws. This is a triumph over "base realities" that gives rise to a figure of superexistentialism, what might be Bachelard's versions of the *Übermensch*. Bachelard's theory of bread is not as dreamy or as reverent as it might initially appear. Though bread is an essential and delicious foodstuff, it also has a spectacular presence that delights the minds of writers and philosophers who refuse to get their hands dirty, don't understand the street, aren't active, avoid immersion in confusion. Kneading a lump of submissive dough delights the figure who wants to remain

59 Bachelard, *Earth and the Reveries of Will*, 64.
60 Ibid., 93.
61 Ibid., 92.
62 Ibid.

unencumbered by the world, the philosopher who believes the universe is "out of whack if they find themselves unable to run a little finger "freely" across the smooth surface of a blank page."[63]

The Silent Zone

The artist and youth worker India Harvey holds slime workshops for children after school in a playground in an estate in South London. Her project is socially progressive, the aim to realize something of what Ishmael experiences aboard the *Pequod,* new kinds of social cohesion born from the act of fondling things together. She spreads a plastic sheet over the bouncy tarmac, pushes a shopping trolley full of the borax, shaving foam, PVA glue and various colorants towards a congregation of under-tens, who then make and play with their viscous concoctions. India considers it the case, not unlike Bachelard, that intimate experiences of a viscous semi-state might reformat the ways in which we are able to be together, could break us out of pre-scribed social structures towards something more self-directed. The slime sessions with children are a boldly literal implementa-tion of Leslie's idea that liquid crystallinity might be social force in its own right. Perhaps the simple experience of the gooey ob-ject can become the blueprint of human society, one based on "malleability," "non-linearity," "playfulness," to use India's words.

Talking to India about her practice and the workshops she runs, it's hard to get a grip on exactly how the slime-play activi-ties will result in actual social effects. Alongside the after-school sessions, she runs sessions at the Camden Arts Centre with two other people for individuals with complex needs. She also runs sex education workshops for teachers where everyone eats mo-chis, a kind of squidgy Japanese sweet, while discussing the best way to educate kids about sexuality. The idea is simple. These viscous textures have a power to remove us ever so slightly from a brain function we might call linear or normative, removing us to a state of "mesomorphic reverie" as Bachelard might have

63 Ibid., 93.

it.[64] This immersion in an act of fondling or chewing facilitates a kind of social openness where the ideas we have about things also enter a state that is prior to form. The idea is that we remake our assumptions, reimagine the obvious.

Conceptually, too, India's work is unformed. When I push her on how and why, she becomes anxious and throws out names and theories that only sort of hang together. The few times I spoke to India for my research, we never managed quite to see eye to eye. My pushing felt ridiculous, my questioning impotent. That is, in part, because what she's doing and what I'm doing are, though both about slimy substances, in many ways incompatible. She is in search of that silent zone, the silent immersion in texture that cannot be articulated without being changed entirely. She is in search of pre-sexual curiosity for which the adult world, by definition, has no words. If it tries, it becomes inappropriate, pedophilic. For Freud, the unconscious was, necessarily, silent, full of erratic, wordless urges and forces. I feel sometimes as if India is looking to externalize the unconscious, to put it in hands and let them maneuver it.

India's defiantly political intentions are far removed from what the Instagram kids say about their own slime practice. The Instagram slime craze, and its place in ASMR, has been given some attention in the mainstream media as well as on endless blogs and forums. Publications like *Vice* and *The Guardian* have covered this current online curio, most recently due to a girl reportedly being quite severely burnt by the borax she was using. Reading the coverage, it is noticeable how many of the slimers are keen, when under the spotlight, to advertise the triviality of what they are doing, keep it at the level of *no big deal*. As slimer Conor Mckiernan, a 15-year-old from Pennsylvania says, "the slime community is a pretty chill and low key super popular trend that is constantly growing."[65] Conor has here, inadvertent-

64 Ibid.
65 Savannah Scott, "We Talked to Instagram's Most Popular Slimers," *Vice*, February 22, 2017, https://www.vice.com/sv/article/we-talked-to-instagrams-most-popular-slimers.

ly I think, locked into one of the more sinister and monstrous qualities of slime's imaginary: something low-key that constantly grows. But, for the most part, Conor is right. Slime is not like Pokémon or Grand Theft Auto, children do not stay up for days at a time, driven mad by obsession, throwing themselves out of their school windows to "re-do the level." Far from the ecstatic global union imagined by Ishmael in *Moby Dick,* the global interest in it is consciously low-impact, disposable. And it is true, these films have the lightness of touch that all online viral phenomena tend to possess. You scroll, they start, the hands fondle the goo, you maybe feel something, maybe not, and move to the next. Slime is a craze that treads lightly.

This may be the case because, unusually, the particular slime Instagram craze currently in action is grass-roots in its structure. There are no global billion-dollar advertising campaigns hyping up the next version, the must-have card. The phenomenon is, aside from the platform provided by Instagram, entirely directed by the craze's young participants. But, one of the major incentives behind making and filming your own slime is the possibility of selling it. The slime craze involves blurred boundaries between work and play. The films are both the innocent sensual thrill in the global playground and adverts for a child's new slimy commodity. The craze is a globalized cottage industry, rather than a universal consciousness.

Low-Key Euphoria

What are the critical limits to silliness? What are the critical limits to something like this that intends so little effect on anything at all? How is it possible to talk about something's "low-key-ness" without, just by talking about it, undermining the very reason you started talking? In Sianne Ngai's writing on the "cute," it is precisely this kind of "low-impact aesthetic" that became a "special issue" for 20th-century avant-garde and modernist poetry in particular. There is in the last century's aesthetics a recurrent fascination with what Hannah Arendt calls "the charismatically irrelevant," the modern enchantment with small, easy-to-handle, adorable little things, William Carlos Williams's plums, "delicious / so sweet / and so cold."[66] The cute object twists the avant-garde's politicization of ineffectualness to aestheticize and eroticize powerlessness.[67]

Latent in the comfort and pleasure that soft things provide is a knowledge that we could, if we wanted to, tear them to pieces. As we caress cute things we lovingly protect their vulnerability, but also aggressively dominate, keep them in a position of submission. Cuteness is a state of suspended agency. One of the most curious effects the cute object has on us is the way we mimic its characteristics during our experience of it, the babyish sounds and facial expressions that overcome us when we jiggle a pre-speech infant in front of us. We appear compelled to perform the signs of powerlessness the cute object emits. But the powerlessness the cute thing calls up does not throw the mind into "disarray" like the Kantian sublime. Cute objects are not in a state of retreat from us, like the unending one. They are in fact, entirely available to us. They make absolutely available the lowness of their "aesthetic impact." They are available to buy, to touch, to handle, to take home with us, to eat. Indeed, as Ngai helps to clarify, one of the indexes of how cute something is its edibility.[68] The cute thing corrupts that core principle of Kantian aesthetics, "disinterested delight," a pleasure that is not directed, like eating, towards bodily gain. Aesthetics do not "fill you up," for Kant. The cute is the moment the aesthetic becomes digestible.

Clearly defined features work against the cuteness of an object. Cute objects must respond to our will with a kind of "exaggerated passivity," as Ngai says.[69] They must be pliant, their contours must be soft. They must not appear to represent any-

66 A. Walton Litz and Christopher McGowan, eds., *The Collected Poems of William Carlos Williams: Volume I, 1909–1939* (New York: New Directions Books, 1986), 372.

67 Sianne Ngai, *Our Aesthetic Catergories: The Cute, the Zany and the Interesting* (Harvard: Harvard University Press, 2012), 3.

68 Ibid., 2.

69 Ibid., 3.

thing with any verisimilitude, features melting into one another, sharpness deadening our desire to pet them. "The epitome of the cute would be," Ngai suggests, "an undifferentiated blob of soft doughy matter."[70] The cute involves a distinctly viscous mode of affect too — the creep of the child into the parent, the dog into its owner. Ultimately, Ngai proposes that cuteness, though lacking in any conceptual stability or consistency, is at the heart of the appeal of the commodity. The commodity: a legless, totally helpless thing, it can't walk itself to the shop, nor off the shelves. It needs us to accompany it, its buyers, its sellers, to push it off into a state of absolute availability, fondled gently into our identities.

These slime Instagram films are not exactly cute. Although something might become cuter the blobbier it is, doughy matter is not cute. I think it's more accurate to say that the cute object aspires to the blob, without ever actually being allowed to get there. Cute things disappear off a blobby horizon. But, all the same, these films luxuriate in exactly Ngai's conception of this state, a hand held pliancy with soft contours, a trivial availability that advertises itself as edible. Indeed, many of the comments on the films will list potential names for the slime, these are often imaginary foodstuffs: Dirtypeach! Cheatocrumbs! Pumkinguts!

The films are not cute, but are a kind of culmination of the logics that set cuteness so firmly in 20th-century commercial aesthetics. Ngai's theory of the cute helps us to view these films as terrifying performances of humanity's disguised, aggressive domination of matter. Instagram slime becomes an example of the viscous in its most domesticated state, all of its transgressive qualities removed and toyed with by soft, childish, clean hands. The films provide an unsettling insight into the violence that might sit at the origin of many kinds of calmness — an ostentatious display of the world submitting to your will, reassuringly high definition evidence played out in neon and in glitter, across a wipe clean surface, of your power to dominate things. This

70 Ibid., 24.

is one of the illusions this version of the viscous allows us to sustain.

It is important to remember that these films are intricately involved with the objects they take place within. These moving images of neatly fondled goo are designed to be watched on devices that, themselves, neatly nestle in the palm of our hand, devices that appear to bubble, glisten, and bounce at your lightest touch. These devices are often now sheathed in squidgy rubber, available in all colors of the rainbow. Sometimes these sheaths sprout enormous Mickey Mouse ears, can become a piece of cartoon watermelon, or nothing but purple fur. What Ahuja fails to realize is that digital technology isn't straightforwardly a diminishing in instances of "touch," but a whole drama of squidgy aesthetics and cute affect. In fact, how to bring a sense of "presence" to technology through haptics is one of the key areas of tech innovation.[71] When you decide to delete an app on an iPhone, holding your fingertip down on one, the entire congregation turns to jelly, vibrating in fear. We're transformed suddenly into a malign overlord with absolute power over whether our subjects live or die. I'm sure it's an intended design feature of the iPhone, a relationality that appeals to dreams of omnipotence.

The aesthetic of these films continues beyond them into the contexts in which they appear. Media technology is slowly accruing an aesthetic of submission, the devices are adopting affects of exaggerated availability. In a world where it is increasingly urgent for us to think in ways that exceed the human, cuteness, acts as the aesthetic resistance against this imperative. Cuteness imagines the world as something that corresponds entirely to human will, it is the demand to "chill out" in the face of viral phenomena. When slime is fondled and posted on Instagram, its transgressions are tamed into the service of a momentary, highly manageable sensual thrill. When we dress our iPhones up as Pikachu, we uphold an image of ourselves as the ones that

71 Mark Paterson, *The Senses of Touch: Haptics, Affects and Technologies* (Oxford: Oxford University Press, 2007).

lovingly protect a universally submissive cyberspace. This is part of what the science historian George Dyson sees as our failure to imagine the internet as an actual universe invented fifty or so years ago:

> People treat the digital universe as some sort of metaphor, just a cute word for all these products [...] it's not a metaphor. In 1945 we actually did create a new universe.[72]

Digital interconnectivity is thought of as cosmological simply for PR purposes, Dyson thinks, rather than as part of its material reality. We rein it in to the prosthetic. Rather than blasting off into an immaterial cyberspace through our screens, it is also possible, if you wish, to cutify the web, transform its immensity into a rubber, goggle-eyed moron sitting in your pocket, awaiting orders. Cute aesthetics are the recoiling from the digital sublime, the disguised containment of that which would otherwise overwhelm you. Just as a cute bundle of soft puppies we coo at is also a clustered instance of their solidarity to one another, the trace of their instinct to form packs and hunt you down in the forest. Instagram slime is a viscous experience particular to the current state of computer technology, one where we are simultaneously immersed in and removed from material contingency. But they are also performances of management, management of deviant materiality, of the sensual response to it, of technology's threat have a life of its own.

Intimacy

The viscous has a deeply intimate relationship to the technology and experience of screens. Where we might wipe the grease smears off the LCD surface, it holds behind its glass a very fine layer of slimy substance that can manipulate the light that passes

---

72 Cited by Marie-Luise Angerer, *Ecology of Affect: Intensive Milieus and Contingent Encounters,* trans. Gerrit Jackson (Luneburg: meson press, 2017), 25.

though it into representations of almost any form imaginable. Greasiness obscures an image produced from sliminess, sliminess in a state of disappearance, wiping itself out into representation. But this is a very particular form of the viscous, the form of crystalline liquidity — a solid that flows. The viscous is something that disturbs the dream of an immaterial experience that screens encourage, but also sits at the heart of its possibility, its immersive, hypnotic clarity.

Sliminess has, then, paradoxically, become a symbol of materiality in a world that feels in danger of falling into complete disembodiment. Video artists like Benedict Drew have adopted an image of goo as a trope in their work that looks to resist the representational function of screens and to call to attention the occurrences that precede our experience. This is at once an iconoclastic and political impulse. There is a tradition stretching back to Marx of sliminess being associated with the non-differentiated workforce under capitalism. To liberate the ooze from within an LCD screen is imagined to be the iconoclastic moment of potential insurrection, the coming into presence of the unformed mass.

Cyberspace has recently taken a turn, however, to become a place of intense and diverse material experience. The rise of ASMR exhibits a desire for a heightened experience of mundane materiality that signals, for some, a return to some kind of authentic intimacy that has been lost in lives spent in front of screens. The internet, it seems to Ahuja, is medicating its own forces of alienation. Slime plays an important role in this new form of online activity, being fondled in short ASMR clips that provide some with a means of relaxation, for others a mild sense of euphoria, in the hope that fondling viscous objects contains the possibility of greater social harmony.

But the slime we find on Instagram is also an instance of the viscous in its most domesticated, submissive state. These films, I want to suggest, are a culmination of the logics of cute aesthetics. Although not cute themselves, they encourage a view of the material world as something that submits entirely to human will. They are spectacles of domination disguised behind an aesthetic of playfulness and triviality. They are designed to be watched, too, on devices that nestle in our hands, dressed up, at times, into submission for the occasion. Cuteness is the resistance to types of thinking that seek to de-center the human.

But what fascinates the viewers of this Instagram slime is the power of technology to enhance our intimacy with material things. This is the same thrill of material detail experienced by those who observed the ectoplasm photography of the 1920s. It is here that we find the viscous in its most radically ambivalent states of all: a bridge between the spectral and the material. The viscous as it spurts out of a woman's head during a séance, or is fondled by a child on Instagram, is not materializing the immaterial, but bridging the two within its body. Where goo is fundamental to the technology of modern screens, screens have also invented a very particular genre of goo, one of deep ambivalence. Negligible yet ethereal, pointless yet present, goo haunts our screens, something, *anything*, to hold my attention.

4

Colloidal Thinking/
Colloidal Feeling

PLACE: My kitchen, London, 2018

I think mayonnaise has a complex kind of relation to
the sublime. […] And I think emulsion does generally.
It's something about that intermediary—I don't know—
place, between being solid and being a liquid, that has
a weird relation to the sublime, in the sense that the
sublimity of it is in the indefinable nature of it.
— Fred Moten, interview in *The New Yorker*[1]

Dispersals

One of the immensely satisfying material contradictions of
many viscous substances is that their clinging sloppy bodies
are often, though not always, composed of very fine and even
dispersals of one kind of material within another. As anyone familiar with the making of mayonnaise will know, it is produced
by mixing oil with egg — whipping one into the other to transform those yellow and off-white translucences into a singular,

1 David Wallace, "Fred Moten's Radical Critique of the Present," *The New*
Yorker, April 30, 2018, https://www.newyorker.com/culture/persons-of-
interest/fred-motens-radical-critique-of-the-present.

white opacity with a seemingly indefinite capacity to expand. As Barthes says, mayonnaise contains the principle of "thickened proliferation"; oil is the medium that allows the albumen to expand without breaking-up or fragmenting. It allows foodstuffs to thicken without hardening. "And this to infinity," he says.[2] Mayonnaise follows the process of intussusception, the process by which the human body manages monstrously to transform into itself whatever it happens to eat. Mayonnaise is made of its own future. The dissemination of oil into albumen mimics the dissemination of (what was once) mayonnaise into flesh as it makes its way through and into me.

Mayonnaise is an emulsion, the dispersal of one liquid in another liquid. Emulsions are a category of what are known by chemists as colloids, substances composed through these material dispersions. Solids can be dispersed in liquids, to form gels: agar, jelly, hair gels, etc. And liquids can be dispersed in solids to form sols: ink, blood. These mixtures take place at a level that is above the molecular, no chemical reaction is taking place, but below what is perceptible. If there is a technology of the viscous, it operates at this scale: to manipulate and engineer these microscopic dispersals is to engineer goo. Colloidal thinking allows us to imagine the viscous not as crude, indifferent mass, but as something intricately articulated. Colloids are, in fact, heterogeneous material systems that only appear homogeneous to the naked eye. To imagine the viscous in this way is to infuse it with its opposite, to see gloop as an expression of immanent and subtle patterns of diffusion and interface. They are a singularity that contains an internal separateness.

"Colloid" comes from the Ancient Greek word *kolla* meaning "glue." Coined by the father of colloid science, Thomas Graham, in the 1860s, the term was chosen to describe the internal gluelike qualities of these mixtures, the tendency they have to adhere to themselves. Many colloids are also themselves gluey in nature, but not all; colloids are by no means all viscous. Colloids

2   Roland Barthes, *The Responsibility of Forms*, trans. Richard Howard (Oakland: University of California Press, 1991), 217.

are, in fact, a vast array of things made through these imperceptible mixtures. Liquids can be dispersed in gases to form liquid
aerosols like clouds, mists, hairsprays, or deodorants. Solids can
be dispersed in gases to form solid aerosols like smoke. Gases
can be dispersed in liquids to make foams like shaving foam, or
whipped cream. And gases can get mixed up with solids to make
styrofoam or pumice. Solids can also be dispersed in solids to
form colored glass, for instance. Colloidal thinking is interested
in the structures of mixture and dispersal. It is a thinking that
wants to move beyond things and their qualitative distinctions
to connect seemingly disparate phenomena: clouds with hair
gels, blood with pumice.

What unites colloids is their relation to the in-between. The
colloidal universe is a huge network of in-between places. The
viscous forms a part of this network. But these in-between materials shouldn't be considered unstable or transitory, not, at
least, more unstable or transitory than anything else. Colloidal structures are the coming into cohesion of the in-between,
the settling down of the in-between into something in its own
right. It is perhaps useful to imagine the allure of colloidal phenomena as things of curious, sometimes dreamy, often highly
commodifiable, perhaps iconic, somehow pleasing, *specificity*:
clouds, whipped cream, jelly, polystyrene, milk, muddy water,
eggs, even pearls. Colloidal thinking seems to announce a list of
suggestive things.

What is suggestive about these things might be the internal
play of opposites, the way they seem to propose, from within
their singularity, two opposing kinds of reality. This could be
figured as a conjunction of the elemental that might excite the
alchemical imagination: the fusing of water with earth in muddy waters, or the elevation of water to the status of wind in mist
or fog. But the play of opposites also takes place in their more
immediate sensual properties. Clouds can possess the opacity of
a brick wall, yet are completely intangible. Whipped cream can
form dramatic, sculptural peaks and troughs in its substance,
like a miniature mountain range, but is almost completely pow-
erless against our lightest touch. The nature of polystyrene is

such that it can easily be made to resemble something of huge size and weight, a boulder for example, but weighs less than a glass of water. It can then transform *me* into a gorilla as I hurl this polystyrene boulder across the stage in an amateur production of *King Kong*. It is precisely an ability to deceive that this play of opposing qualities makes possible. Clouds are also used as a stage-show illusionistic device by magicians when apparently vanishing in a "puff of smoke"; the colloid's airborne opacity acts both as a practical means to disguise the mechanics of the trick, but also is the spectacular intangibility into which the figure appears to disappear. The curious internal marriage of substance within colloids offers ways of switching between realities. This switching constructs a place of illusionistic potential, one where the rules can seem suddenly to change in carnivalesque inversion. Colloids find their allure as substances of escapism.

Colloids, then, are heterogenous things, but appear homogenous. They live on boundaries, without always appearing to do so — boundaries between the microscopic and the molecular, the boundaries between things, boundaries between reality and appearance.

Viscous sols, gels, and emulsions are then our focus here, and their position in the colloid map. Gloops composed of dispersion. The viscous has a history of being imagined not as formless, but of being so intricately articulated it just appears formless. The viscous imagination can often be an imagination that involves this opposition. Most obviously perhaps, this might be considered a scientific perspective, the looking beyond the directly sensual qualities of something into its material constitution. But I want to show how this oppositional nature of the viscous has actually become part of the sensual imagination of these substances. This we can detect as colloids move beyond science and enter other cultural domains. Although colloids began their life in the discipline of chemistry, they migrated widely to become structures of fascination for psychotherapists, writers, and theorists.

But with the colloidal imagination of the viscous we have also a way of the seeing the viscous as a technology, something that can be engineered, designed, and manipulated. A heterogenous thing that appears homogenous can easily become a technologized thing that appears untechnologized. Colloids are both technologies of mingling and where bodies may mingle with technologies.

Anti-Gravity Salad

Colloidal cooking might bring to mind images of jellied foods, blancmange, hardboiled eggs held in aspic, glazed cherries, "perfection salad," which came to widespread popularity in the US around the time human space travel came into the realms of the possible. An anti-gravity aesthetic pervades the presentation of these foodstuffs, a reminder at dinnertime of humankind breaking free from the earth into weightlessness. But it is also no coincidence that jelly cooking became fashionable in an era where the scientific was infiltrating the domestic space, a time when American housewives were refashioning their identities as housework scientists, technicians in the laboratory of the domestic space. As Laura Shapiro traces in her social history of science in the kitchen, this obsession with gelatin in the kitchen was part of the drive to find synthetic substitutes for every part of daily life, to keep it packaged until the very last moment. But this is also an impulse to control food, contain food, avoid at all costs a messy plate, presenting instead an absolutely determined tableau vivant of "nutritive strategies" in suspended animation before you.[3] The legacy of the house wives who cooked as scientists is enormous, from them came the whole notion of home economics, a paradoxical moment in feminist liberation, Shapiro describes, where hyper-rationalized domesticity was imagined to be the way for women to escape the house, food the way to escape the body.

3   Laura Shapiro, *Perfection Salad: Women and Cooking at the Turn of the Century* (Oakland: University of California Press, 2008), 6.

But just as elaborately jellied food participated in this movement, mayonnaise has also been found to correspond to particular ideologies. Soviet cooking, that has seen a nostalgic resurgence recently,[4] was keen to be an arena where the revolution played out its achievements, all remnants of bourgeois degeneracy wiped off the menu. This would be achieved, too, through a systematic introduction of science into the culinary that would privilege nutrition over taste and also bring together all the various cultures of the union together in one thing, all moving forward together. The widely disseminated Soviet cookbook *The Book of Healthy and Delicious Food* explicitly incorporates cuisine into socialist industrialization, beginning each chapter with quotes from Stalin, Molotov, and Mikoyan. As Elena Sorokina describes, the book's culinary guidance was entangled with praise for the achievements of the food industry, "defining new far-reaching goals for meat and fish production, or reflecting on the importance of good packaging."[5]

But mayonnaise, though a classic condiment of bourgeois French culture, persisted through this ideological reimagining of the country's cuisine. Through the transformation of the French "Salade Olivier" into the immensely popular Russian Salad, Sorokina identifies the continuance of mayonnaise as an ingredient whose practical purposes also echoed the strategies undertaken by this invention of a Soviet cuisine. After being first industrially produced in the USSR in 1936, mayonnaise became the main condiment in almost all Soviet salads. Its substance promoted friendship. It is a blend of two simple substances to create something entirely new. Once made, it becomes the medium that then binds together disparate ingredients into peaceful coexistence, "enriching each other without any one element dominating the whole."[6] These social histories of food give us a

4   I am thinking, here, of Olga Syutkin and Pavel Syutkin, *CCCP Cook Book: True Stories of Soviet Cuisine* (London: Fuel, 2015).

5   Elena Sorokina, "Peoples' Friendship Salad and Other Culinary Expressions of Brotherhood," March 2014, http://sorokinaelena.blogspot.com/2014/03/stalin-cooking-book.html.

6   Ibid.

sense of how colloidal structures might be adopted by particular social ideals. They stand for a unity of difference, a unity despite difference.

Through the awkward charade of writing I have become spiritually dependent on cooking. In the background to all this, these words, there will have been, most likely, the slow merging of salmon flesh with a meticulously blended miso marinade, a ragout on low heat, bread, meat, wine, milk, mince collapsing gradually into themselves, the cooling of an anti-gravity lettuce leaf held in a Stalinist-style jelly mold. I return to these worlds every few sentences to stir, sniff, gently touch to test. They are not so much a refuge, or a place of relaxation, as another kind of thinking, one that involves synthesis, blending, mixing, experimentation as opposed to the requirements of this writing, which must give precedence, at least sometimes, to axioms, analysis, subtraction. I wouldn't say, though, that this is the difference between the visceral and the intellectual. Something I realize as I switch between these worlds is that the laws of cooking seem indifferent to what I think about them. I mean, my thinking about the processes of cooking doesn't do anything to change or effect what those chemical processes are. Yet, the chemical processes of my mayonnaise, of my ragout, of my jellied lettuce leaf, have deeply felt, unpredictable, and sometimes fundamental influence on what I write and think. I land upon a tricky dynamic between the two activities. Though my writing has some kind of analysis or criticality as *its* frame, it seems to be more absorptive than cooking which has as its frame processes that are more ostensibly absorptive: synthesis, blending, mixing. We might say, then, that the relationship is a colloidal one, cooking is a phase medium into which my writing is dispersed. It seems, as Iain Hamilton Grant says of chemistry, that though "human thought" does not "condition the powers of chemistry," thought is "mobilized in unprecedented fashion by chemistry."[7] But this contains an essential property of colloidal thinking — it doesn't

7   Robin Mackay, "Editorial Introduction," in *Collapse VII*, ed. Robin Mackay (Falmouth: Urbanomic, 2008), 3–37, at 5.

aspire to purity, doesn't try to strip things back to their constituent parts, but looks towards and embeds itself in the intensities of the heterogeneous mixture. It is synthetic. It is collaborative. It is on the look out for tonic association, from which new "things" might emerge.

Almost Everything

When 19th-century colloidal science began, their study also seemed to take place on the boundaries between scientific disciplines. Where the classical chemist would think in terms of chemistry, in the differences between discrete chemicals, the colloidal chemist would think in terms of structure, much like a physicist. More an operation of thought than a mode of classification, colloidal science required one to think as a physical chemist. Only then could the continuity between blood and clouds be disclosed. Further than this, colloids were also identified not simply as inorganic mixtures of chemicals, but the moment at which the inorganic turned into the organic: the moment, in others words, when vital processes begin. Initially, Graham's research was on the peculiar diffusion properties of various chemicals. Quickly, however, it became clear that something else was at hand:

> Another eminently characteristic quality of colloids, is their mutability. Their existence is a continued metastasis… the colloid possesses ENERGIA. It may be looked upon as the probable primary source of the force appearing in the phenomena of vitality.[8]

Colloids, it emerged, were at the heart of the study and the debates of what it was to be alive and therefore of central interest to biologists too. Protoplasm, life in its most basic form, the gooey stuff that makes up the cell walls, was found to be composed

8   Andrew Ede, *The Rise and Decline of Colloid Science in North America, 1900–1935* (Hampshire: Ashgate, 2007), 14.

of colloidal dispersions of salts and carbohydrates, emulsions of fats and dispersions of protein jellies. Somewhere in these intricate mixes was the right formulation for life to begin. The implication was that the rules governing inorganic colloids were the same as those that governed the organic ones. If it is possible to find structural continuities between blood and clouds, maybe it is possible to do the same between mayonnaise and our own brains. At the start of the 20th century, colloids were widely regarded to be, somehow, the arena of originary vital processes, but exactly how this shift took place was the subject of heated debate. In fact, the question remained much the same as it had been before — were things mechanistic in origin, or was there some élan vital that instigated this transformation? Or was it some combination of the two?

The enigmatic father figure in the stories of Bruno Schulz, campaigns, among many of his loopy ideas, for the rights of Tailor's dummies. In one particular monologue, the father describes his theory of *generatio aequivoca,* a kind of species that is only half alive, a pseudo-fauna, a pseudo-flora that bursts out of a "fantastic fermentation of matter."[9] They are amorphous creatures, mobile, sensitive to stimuli and yet "outside the pale of real life."[10] They are teased into this life by suspending certain "complex colloids in solutions of kitchen salt."[11] And this is part, for the father, of an intensely absorptive world, one where apartments can become "saturated with the emanations of numerous existences and events."[12] These are old apartments, full of "used-up atmospheres, rich in the specific ingredients of human dreams."[13] In this state of saturation and neglect, the walls and contents of these rooms can start to grow into this pseudo-vegetative existence. Wallpaper is capable of "distant, dangerous dreams," furniture is "unstable, degenerate, and receptive to

9   Bruno Schulz, *The Street of Crocodiles and Other Stories,* trans. Celina Wieniewska (London: Penguin, 1992), 66.
10   Ibid.
11   Ibid.
12   Ibid., 67.
13   Ibid.

abnormal temptations."[14] This pseudo-life can take the form of vegetation, of wild and exuberant mildew, or can be the closing of a room in on itself, becoming over grown with bricks, doors growing out into the walls that surround it. The apartments are obliterated in a "complicated design of lines and cracks."[15] Objects are all slowly diffusing into their surroundings, themselves composed of mixtures prone to coagulation or coalescence. At certain points, the right mixture might be found, the right degree of saturation, where life, pseudo-life, occurs.

Where some branches of colloidal science in the first decade of the 20th century delved ever deeper into the nature of vitality, others advanced research, with much more financial gain, into their practical applications. One of the major energizing factors in colloidal studies at the turn of the 20th century was their huge industrial potential. In the years before the First World War, the three giants of the chemical industry, DuPont in North America, ICI in Britain, and IG Farben in Germany invested in colloidal research. The focus was on what is known as "surface technology," the science of cleansers, lacquers, paints, cosmetics, adhesives, all things that operate on the boundaries of objects. Lubricants, too, were an important area of development to meet the ever-increasing weight and speed of industrial machinery.

War is generally accompanied by vigorous technological advancements and the years from 1914 up to 1923 saw the most active and widespread period of colloidal research. Colloidal science was one of the most important chemical research areas of the First World War. The network of in-between substances expanded and complexified, as did the technologies of cleaning, painting, lubricating, sticking, disinfecting that these colloidal structures bring across surfaces. But, colloids were not only used in surface technologies, but became central elements of wartime attack and defense. The secret to making dynamite relatively safe to use was to embed it in a jelly, to form gelignite, as had been done by Alfred Nobel in the 1870s. The secret to an ef-

14 Ibid.
15 Ibid.

fective flamethrower was to gelify the petroleum so that it would hold together, and onto the things it landed on, when burning. This sticky fire would then evolve into napalm, whose substance I discussed in chapter 2. Smoke's powers to disorientate was also employed, the first smoke screen was used by the British Navy in Belgium in 1918. An interface between the industrial and the biological, the colloid was where life seemed to begin, but also proved effective in technologies to bring it to an end.

But, more recently, in the last two decades, the colloidal origins of vitality and its industrial, practical applications have started to merge. Scientists working on colloidal structure and interfacial chemists, have realized that the structures manipulated when technologizing glues and milks might also be place where we could engineer materials that possess the properties of so-called living things. The speeches of Schulz's father about chairs that are half alive are no longer at all wildly fantastical. The proceedings published from a colloquium "Toward Living Matter with Colloidal Particles," held in the summer of 2017, considers this between stage of matter as a place of immense design potential. Colloids are "large enough to be directly seen with an optical microscope, yet small enough to be susceptible to thermal fluctuations."[16] The sensitivity of structure at this scale means that they can store information, that particles can be programmed to interact with one another in specific ways. This is never claimed to be the creation of life, but the creation of an intense relationality, the dynamic of a mixture whereby colloidal dispersions can be programmed to express emergent properties. These can be complex processes that are biomimetic: *self-assembly,* the ability to spontaneously form predetermined complex structures; *self-replication,* the ability of a material to make a copy of itself; and *metabolism,* the ability to carry out complex transformations internally that would be "impossible

16 Zorana Zeravcic, Vinothan N. Manoharan, and Michael P. Brenner, "Colloquium: Toward a Living Matter with Colloidal Particles," *Reviews of Modern Physics* 89, no. 3 (July–September 2017): 031001.

to realize if a single structure acted alone."[17] It is this, I think, that contributes to the allure of colloidal phenomena I discussed a moment ago. We find them alluring because they already feel as if something is taking place, they have a presence to them, an internal dynamic that attracts us. We are drawn to foams, gels, smokes as things that play with our sense of aliveness, there is a sense of things being underway.

One of the problems with writing about colloids is that they aren't quite everything, but are almost. The scope is too expansive for it to be neatly defined, but not large enough to be all-encompassing, to have claims to universality, as molecules or atoms do. They occupy the awkward place of *almost everything*. There isn't one property that all colloids share. It was as a result of this over-stretching and incoherence that colloidal science began to unravel after the initial wave of excitement in the build up to the First World War. The historian of science Andrew Ede compares the teleology of colloidal studies to the Ouroboros, the mystical symbol of the snake that eats its own tail. Its advance was in fact a slow demise, a collapse into the indefinable. Barthes is wrong about mayonnaise; expand it too far and the substance will coagulate. Scientists also became frustrated by the inexactness of colloids. Mixtures, dispersions, and suspensions of matter at this scale are inherently messy things, precision never seemed possible. Eventually, colloidal chemistry and its aspirations gave way to molecular science, protoplasm gave way to the genome.

Coagulated Brains

In the interwar period, colloids also began to be associated with quackery. The protagonists in the field of the science were extremely eager for their discipline to offer solutions to issues of health and well-being. In the early 1930s, one of the most erratic enthusiasts of colloids, Wilder Bancroft, the founder of *The Journal of Physical Chemistry*, proposed a colloidal explana-

17   Ibid., 3.

tion for various mental illnesses such as depression, dementia, epilepsy, schizophrenia, and addiction. He forwarded the notion of two degenerated states of the brain, one where the tissue had become "puckered," shriveled, and one where the tissue had become "mushy," sodden. Manic depressives and epileptics have, he suggested, a "puckered" brain, where catatonics, for instance, have a "mushy" one.[18] According to Bancroft, these mental problems were due to a reversible coagulation of protein cells, which could be cured by the administration of a peptizing agent, a chemical used to stabilize colloidal dispersions in jam, for instance. Although very much an establishment figure himself, this theory was widely regarded by the scientific community as pseudo-science and almost universally mocked by doctors. It did, however, find some favor in the popular press, being covered in the *New York Times* and in the weekly American opinion magazine *Literary Digest* that announced in 1931 Bancroft's "Chemical Cure for Insanity." Like Bachelard's dough as the place of exactitude aimed for by the baker, for Bancroft, colloids were substances of balance and stability, ones that were responsible for the stable and normative functioning of mental processes. Mental health, it seemed, had a particular colloidal viscosity. In the coagulation of mayonnaise we find, according to Bancroft, the same material transformation that, in the brain, results in an epileptic fit.

As colloids became less and less fashionable in the science mainstream, they were taken up by more left-field, experimental independent scholars and psychologists. Alfred Korzybski, the Polish–American behavioral psychologist latches onto colloids in his major 1933 work *Science and Sanity: An Introduction to Non-Aristotelian Systems and General Semantics* as part of his gestalt, organism-as-a-whole theory of therapeutics. Colloids provide for Korzybski a kind of knowledge that is able "bridge between the different classes of occurrences,"[19] between the self

18 Wilder Bancroft, *The Literary Digest* 28, no. 3 (November 21, 1931), 16.
19 Alfred Korzybski, *Science and Sanity: An Introduction to Non-Aristotelian Systems and General Semantics,* 4th edn. (Lakeville: Institute of General

and the world, the mental and the physical, the organic and the inorganic. A knowledge that operates structurally, beyond individual things, it provides him with a holistic perspective on issues of health, both mental and bodily. As all life is found in colloidal form, Korzybski thinks, any force capable of influencing the colloidal structure of an organism must have an effect on the mental and physical welfare of that organism.

Korzybski considers the scale of colloidal structures, this "neglected dimension," this "twilight zone of matter," as the site of complex energy exchanges where environmental conditions are transformed into feelings, thoughts and semantic activity.[20] The colloid is, for Korzybski, where we begin to physically blur with our environment and the material origins of how we think and feel. Korzybski goes further than Bancroft and imagines the behavior of colloidal structures to determine the array of different "human types," from fat to thin, from clever to stupid.

> Some [people] are delicate, some heavy-set, some flabby, some puffy all of which indicate a difference in colloidal structure. Paired with these physical colloidal states are also nervous, "mental" and other characteristics, which vary from the weak and nervous to the extreme limitation of nervous activities, as in idiocy, which is a negation of activity.[21]

For Korzybski, each colloid has a state of equilibrium and a set of optimal conditions. If one disturbs this equilibrium, various physical and mental illnesses can occur, anything from chills, headaches, vomiting, and convulsions, to illusions, delusions, and hallucinations. Because of the general "colloidal background of life,"[22] different disturbances to this equilibrium result in specific effects, which can then be engineered. Colloidal balance can be disturbed in four main ways, Korzybski theorizes. It

Semantics, 1958), 121.
20 Ibid., 112.
21 Ibid., 118.
22 Ibid.

can be influenced physically, by light, x-rays, cathode rays, electricity, etc.; mechanically, through touching, rubbing, puncturing, etc.; chemically, by the administration of tar, paraffin, etc.; or biologically, with microbes or parasites. There is also a fifth way to disturb colloidal balance, he thinks, one that is unique to the human species, which is "semantic reactions," the power of thinking and speaking.[23]

The body, in *Science and Sanity,* becomes a complex dance of thickening and thinning out matter. Swellings, tumors, inflammations, catarrhal diseases, and blood clots are all colloidal injuries that can, in the most extreme cases, result in complete coagulation or fluidification. Parts of the body can suffer complete concretions of its soft matter, Korzybski points to gout, gallstones, rice bodies, and "brain sand," calcified structures that can form in the brain. The cure for these ailments does not lie, he argues, in specific chemical reactions, but in anything that might influence the colloidal structures of the body. Certainly aware of Bancroft's theories, Korzybski claims that if a guinea pig is injected with a colloid that "accustoms its nerve endings to flocculation," the process whereby suspended particles come out of colloidal suspension in the form of "flakes," the animal becomes immune to "epileptic serums," whatever they might be.[24]

The structures of colloidal dispersions are, for Korzybski, a kind of knowledge, a particular way of thinking between different classes of things, but also the material origins of thinking. They are both a way and an origin. But he goes further than this. The activity of the brain is known to produce electrical energy, Korzybski explains. Experiments suggest, he continues, that other forms of radiant energy are produced by thinking that we do not yet have instruments capable of measuring. This electrical energy of thinking is able to act upon the colloidal dispersions of the body in beneficial ways. This explains, Korzybski thinks, why "psychotherapy is effective in diseases with tubercu-

23 Ibid.
24 Ibid.

lar symptoms."[25] Korzybski imagines colloids, then, as a way of thinking, its origin, and at the core of thinking's power to radiate beneficial or cancerous energy on the body. This is not psycho-somatic in any traditional sense. This is the material power of thought to make you healthy or sick.

To be in a state of equilibrium, colloidal dispersions must hold within them a separate-ness of substance. That the pro-toplasm is a "film-partitioned system" is integral to its sensitiv-ity to outside influences, its "irritability," as Korzybski calls it.[26] When something stimulates the surface of the protoplasm, the "irritability is transmitted to other regions of the protoplasm with differing *finite* velocities."[27] This region of surface excitation becomes, at this moment, "dominant over the other regions to which the excitation is transmitted."[28] The bodies of protoplas-mic structures are capable of *momentary specificity* in response to external stimuli. We might find here the influence of Kor-zybski on the Body without Organs in the thought of Deleuze and Guattari: life before its instrumentalization, before the divi-sion of labor has set in, where excitement can roam nomadi-cally across the surface of living matter without determination by folds, protrusions, or apertures.

Freud wonders whether we might find some optimal struc-ture of human desire in the gloop of protoplasmic bodies. In "A Difficulty in the Path of Psycho-Analysis" from 1917, the mo-mentary specificity *in response* to outside influence, becomes active:

> For complete health it is essential that the libido should not lose its full mobility. As an illustration of this state of things we may think of an amoeba, whose viscous substance puts out *pseudopodia,* elongations into which the substance of the

25 Ibid., 119.
26 Ibid.
27 Ibid.
28 Ibid., 102.

body extends, but which can be retracted so that the form of the protoplasmic mass is restored.[29]

Not quite an organ, these pseudopodia — literally, false feet — protrude from the body of the organism in such a way that formal integrity is kept in tact. Libidinal attachment to the world requires, Freud thinks, a retractability, an equilibrium between investment and withdrawal, if it is to be healthy and for successful analysis to occur. Catherine Malabou, reading this passage in Freud, considers this the elastic plasticity of the libido, its ability to "cling to the object and to abandon it."[30] Desire, to be desire, needs the power to pull away from the thing that it is drawn towards. Part of desire's structure is the risk of being destroyed by its object.

Not having this ability to extend and to recoil poses, for Freud, serious problems for therapy. As is the case in the famous Wolf Man analysis, the analysand exhibits tendencies of "fixation": "any position of the libido which had once taken up was obstinately defended by him from fear of what he would lose." [31] With patients of such cathectic loyalty, therapeutic action is much slower. But the reverse is similarly problematic — with any patient of excessive libidinal mobility, excessive fluidity, any development in therapy is precarious, may not hold.

The image of the amoeba can be read as a metaphor, an image that helps describe through equivalence an idea that Freud has about the behavior of the healthy libido. Or perhaps he is being more literal. In her extraordinary analysis of Freud's "Be-

29 Sigmund Freud, "A Difficulty in the Path of Psycho-Analysis," in *The Standard Edition of the Complete Psychoanalytical Works of Sigmund Freud, Volume XVII (1917–1919): An Infantile Neurosis and Other Works,* ed. and trans. James Strachey with Anna Freud (London: Hogarth, 1953–74), 135–44, at 139.

30 Catherine Malabou, "Plasticity and Elasticity in Freuds 'Beyond the Pleasure Principle," *Diacritics* 37, no. 4 (Winter 2007).: 78–85, at 83.

31 Sigmund Freud, "The Obsessional Neurosis," in *The Standard Edition of the Complete Psychoanalytical Works of Sigmund Freud, Volume XVII (1917–1919): An Infantile Neurosis and Other Works,* ed. and trans. James Strachey with Anna Freud (London: Hogarth, 1953–74), 61–71.

yond the Pleasure Principle," Malabou points to the speculation
Freud makes that if there is anything beyond the pleasure principle, "it can only be at a certain time."[32] This specific moment is
one that precedes life, but precedes death also. It is the moment
just before matter became animate, the last gasp, so to speak, of
inorganic material. The amoeba is what welcomes the inorganic
into the organic. What lies beyond the pleasure principle is the
colloidal state that immediately precedes the amoeba. This is
the moment towards which the death drive yearns. Colloids are,
then, the material structures that haunt desire, the material of its
origin and its goal.

The surfaces of these protoplasmic masses are capable of
indeterminate specificity, reachings-out from or for wherever
excitation might be. But colloidal structures, including protoplasmic bodies, do not have "surfaces" as we might convention-
ally conceive of them: a membrane that divides inside from
outside. Colloids are in fact internally structured by a plural-
ity of miniaturized surfaces, the microscopic interplay between
the surfaces of one substance with another's in a their state of
suspension. One teaspoon of a colloidal industrial lubricant can
have a total internal surface area of over 127 acres.[33]In *Noise Water Meat,* Douglas Kahn addresses exactly this quality of colloidal structures, seeing them as a "*hypertrophied state of surface*
[...] where the state of surface has become pervasive through
internalisation, through autoingestion."[34] Hypertrophy, the state
of excessive nourishment, here, fattens surface such that it becomes something in its own right: a body made of only surface.
If the viscous is often associated with troubling the stability of
boundaries or limits, we have here an image of the substance
as composed of an internal tangling of them. This, Kahn suggests in his reading of William Burroughs's style, might be a way

32 Malabou, "Plasticity and Elasticity in Freuds 'Beyond the Pleasure
    Principle," 78.
33 From the lubricant manufacturer RyDol's webite: http://rydol.com/
    techdetails.html
34 Douglas Kahn, *Noise Water Meat: A History of Sound in the Arts*
    (Cambridge: MIT Press, 2001), 305.

of thinking of how modernism, its use of the surface in montage, was ingested greedily by the postmodern. "Hypertrophied modernism,"[35] where the switches and cuts between time, place, culture, and register are so excessive, so rapid and instinctual, we're faced not with the jolts of fragmentation but a gentle ooze of proliferating, gradually homogenized, difference.

Lube Itself

Korzybski's influence on Burroughs is well known. Burroughs was evangelical about Korzybski's theories, urging Allen Ginsburg among others on numerous occasions to read him, and Kahn's work has helped a great deal to elucidate this influence. I want, though, to read closely some passages from Burroughs's *The Soft Machine* as writing that enacts with intensity what colloidal feeling might be said to actually *look like*.

> The boy's flesh dissolved in the unguent losing outlines fuzzing out in blue light… Lee straddled the boy's body one shuddering white flash the bodies lit up inside pulsing bluer and bluer incandescent purple blue flash back the two young bodies stuck together like dogs.
>
> […]
>
> See here an elbow and there wherever fly the frame they stuck there like filled it finally the jar which was filled with a stuff with little black specks Lee watched the drug of rotten protoplasm contracted his tubes. The flesh dissolved over Johnny's body suspended spurts of blue jelly like flesh were dissolving in the unguent one pulsing blue in white light Lee watching from cold blue centre. In his brain the quivering sphere shaped to blue in a crystal web. Johnny stripped off his blue boy the room the stainless steel locker.
>
> […]
>
> He pushed Johnny's limbs catatonic rubber spread the pulsing blue light inside him a crystal web. The boys puffed

35 Ibid.

> blue smoke two bodies fuzzing the web one shuddering white
> tile walls in polar distance blue haloes flickering... a pulsing
> blue sphere over skeletons locked in limestone.[36]

The body is lubed-up with some jelly like Vaseline, loses its definition and begins, it seems, to turn into light. "Blue," incessantly repeated in these passages, is an anagram of "lube," the color their bodies radiate when covered in the unguent, when penetrating or being penetrated, and is, of course, also the color of the sky. Both lube and the sky are colloids, the blue being caused by the Rayleigh effect, the visual effect of sunlight passing through dust particles suspended in the atmosphere. As "blue" merges with "lube," as "lube" merges with the sky, the two young male bodies begin to merge with one another. An unguent substance is what allows for the merging of bodies, but they do not ooze, they fuzz, disperse like scattered light into a pulsating mass, quivering rather than creeping. The play of texture in this passage is between pulsating gloop and fuzzing incandescence. Just as jelly holds suspended within its body a structure of dispersal, the union it allows between these to bodies is figured as a radiation of crystalline light, glowing and flashing. The lubricant becomes more than simply a medium through which their bodies can meet, slide, and take pleasure in one another. Its substance becomes the structuring principle of their desire. Surfaces are not erased, but complexified, fuzzed.

The classical view of friction is that it results from the roughness of the surfaces moving over one another. To smooth the surfaces out as much as possible was once thought to be the purpose of a lubricant. Chemists discovered, however, that is was the internal friction of the lubricants themselves that effected smoothness of movement. The viscous has surfaces on the inside. In 1906, the chemist Edward Acheson invented a lubricant made from the colloidal dispersion of graphite in oil, which came to be known as "Oildag." The properties of graphite

36 William Burroughs, *The Soft Machine* (London: Fourth Estate, 2010), 116-17.

that make it slide across a page at the end of a pencil, could be used for the efficiency of heavy machinery. Antonino Tabascio, working for IG Farben under the Nazis, developed the first synthetic lubricants for jet engines. Tribology, the scientific study of rubbing, lubrication, and wear was established in Australia during World War II by David Tabor and Philip Bowden, and then continued by them at the University of Cambridge in the 1960s.[37] Technologies of in-between, slippery places flourished. Increased efficiency was, of course, the goal. In 1966, a Cambridge tribologist report, "The Jost Report," suggested that £515 million a year was lost in Britain through inadequate lubrication.[38] Colloids contain the industrialist's dream of the perfectly oiled machine, a tireless dance of pistons, cogs, and axles, interlocking, never actually touching, but floating on invisible viscous seams: mechanical and monetary flow brought into an impossible frictionless harmony.

Lubricants are a viscous technology, the purpose of which is both to slow time down and to accelerate it. The technology of lubricants is as much about protecting surfaces from wear, as it is about the efficient passage of one surface over or around another. Materials last longer and move faster, soundlessly. Surfaces must be kept apart to work together. They are the necessary separation for any connection to take place. These are the dialectics of lube.

For Burroughs, the viscous is also a technology, a substance squeezed out of a tube that lubricates protrusions and orifices of the body otherwise too dry to interact. Lube can also, of course, be used in heterosexual sex, but was certainly for gay culture in the 1960s, and in LGBT scenes today, a facilitator, an enhancer, and material symbol for non-conformist sex. Burroughs's work abounds in gloops, synthetic and organic, all of which constitute the very possibility of homoerotic union. But these colloidal

37 *The New Scientist* 7, no. 183 (May 19, 1960), 1267.
38 Peter Jost and Department of Education and Science, *Lubrication (Tribology), Education and Research: A Report on the Present Position and Industry's Needs* (London: H.M. Stationary Office, 1966), a.k.a. "The Jost Report."

gels also provide him with a kind of knowledge that only occurs with deviant, ecstatic experience: to see the world as pulsations of structure, as colloidal interface, the human body as a
soft machine or a puff of smoke. This slippage between things
finds most hypnotic enactment in Burroughs's famous cut-up
writing technique. His novels become a colloidal technology
themselves, language feels dispersed into itself, whipped into a
specific set of interfaces, before it coagulates and is recomposed.

Feelings or psychic states are rarely described in Burroughs's
work. Instead, interactions between people and their bodies
take place as a series of material processes and transformations.
Limbs are spread, stuff is dissolved, webs quiver. What gives this
writing its exceptional intensity is how it lashes so erratically
between different images and phenomena, but stays so strictly
in a material register. Burroughs is never reductively materialist, things can be radically, immediately, and impossibly transformed. What might be, or might have been, the emotional or
psychological "reality" of this scene is by-passed and we are tak-
en, instead, to the alchemical dynamics of how matter behaves
as if feelings were purely material, the Sartre vision of feelings
as once being particular substances.[39] Colloids might be considered erotic substances in their own right; not only do they
allow for bodily union, here, but are themselves a kind of intimate mingling of matter into what may seem, but never actually
is, unity. Colloidal thinking, here, releases matter from material
determinism, allows it to move and change with the sensations
it produces.

The presence of synthetic substitutes for absent bodily fluids
is a widening in the scope of the ways it is possible to realize
desire. It is an encouraging thought that in the 1960s, while tri-
bologists at the University of Cambridge were working out how
to make mechanical components glide more profitably over one
another, William Burroughs and others were lubricating their

39 Jean-Paul Sartre, *Being and Nothingness: A Phenomenological Essay on
    Ontology*, trans. Hazel E. Barnes (Washington: Washington Square Press,
    1992), 605.

bodies to subvert biopolitical control. It is also an important fact for the history of these substances that as the viscous became increasingly technologized, it became a central practical and symbolic substance for gay counterculture. Where for the engineers, the flourishing of slippery substances was a diminishing of wasted energy, it was for queer communities, the becoming of a major object identification. But it is also more than a symbol, more than a means. Its material corresponds to non-conformist desire.

There are few writers more singularly obsessed with gloop than William Burroughs. The substance that allows for sex is the material quality that seems to creep into every part of his universe. Nights, walls, smiles, entire countries, and the syntax of the text itself become viscous: "Panama clung to our bodies."[40] This we might read as a structure of perversion. In Žižek's reading of Lacan and "creepiness" in *Disparities,* creepy, perverted sexual desire is the sexual desire that focuses more on the object-cause of desire, than the object itself.[41] The desire for the person I love might be, let's say, sustained by the curls of their hair. If such a time arrived that my desire for this person came to be entirely overtaken by my desire for their hair, a short-circuit has taken place: the medium has become the object. This short circuit removes the "personal" from the equation, and directs desire into the things that sustain it, in Burroughs's case, lube and all other viscous technologies of deviant intimacy. In the above passages, it is the colloidal lube that awakens and invests the erotic power of the scene, rather than the presence of the lover's body.

Lube becoming more than mere medium, but an active partner in the situation can be seen as well in Jean Genet's writing about vaseline. Like Burroughs, Genet is similarly obsessed with lubricants as facilitators and sources of homoerotic desire. In the *Thief's Journal,* Genet dreams of smothering the whole body of his lover in vaseline, a "delicate transparence," which, in Sartre's

40 Burroughs, *The Soft Machine,* 118.
41 Slavoj Žižek, *Disparities* (London: Bloomsbury Academic, 2016).

reading, acts as an aesthetic "veil," the ability to put the world at an aesthetic remove; vaseline is not simply a sexual lubricant, but the materialization of his desire to enjoy the world.[42] Later in the novel, Genet is arrested by the police and the vaseline confiscated. The police ridicule Genet when they realize what it's for and the vaseline becomes, instead, the material of his humiliation. When in the cell, however, Genet imagines the vaseline "exposed to their scorn."[43] Gradually Genet imagines the vaseline to become an object "by its mere presence [...] is able to exasperate all the police in the world."[44] Genet identifies with the lubricant. He begins to embody it. He aspires towards it. Genet lets the vaseline take charge as his slimy emissary. Its indifferent, humiliating viscosity becomes an object of resilience, one that can resist social decency and condemnation more effectively than he ever could. The lubricant takes on social agency.

But different lubes mean different things. Though lube might be the thing that "gets you to where you want to go,"[45] it also carries within it traces of what the destination might be. To have a bottle of Astroglide by your bed used to mean, for writer Erica Rand, a "certain commitment to pleasure,"[46] a queerer and more stylish alternative to dreary old KY Jelly, whose associations are a little more practical, medicinal. This was especially true if you lived far from the city, "queer urbanity," and in the times before the internet. But then Rand finds an article in *Elle* magazine in 2000 that advised women suffering from vaginal dryness to buy Astroglide from the "family planning" section in their local pharmacy. Where Genet repurposed vaseline, these lubes have been branded, they offer different well-lubricated identities and

42 Jean-Paul Sartre, *Saint Genet: Actor and Martyr,* trans. Bernard Frechtman (New York: Plume and Merdian, 1963), 489.

43 Jean Genet, *The Thief's Journal,* trans. Bernard Frechtman (London: Faber and Faber, 2009), 18.

44 Ibid.

45 Erica Rand, "What Lube Goes Into," in *The Object Reader,* eds. Fiona Candlin and Raiford Guins (London: Routledge, 2009), 526–30, at 527.

46 Ibid.

identifications to us. For Rand, this is a de-queering abstraction, lube packaged as the means to reproduce.

Lube slows time down, while speeding it up. It slips people out of non-normative sexual identities, while slipping people back in to ones that they feel they've lost. Its substance intermingles control with a loss of control. As KY Jelly advertise on their website, its lubricants are for "everyday comfort seekers and pleasure explorers"[47] alike. In the branding of lube, the controlled and the adventurous are as tightly entangled as ideas of the highly technological and the natural. It is a supplement, it mimics your body, its formula a trade secret, it is smooth, it is soft, it is pure, it feels natural, it is harmless, it is reliable, it provides instant excitement when you want it. Its technology is one that promises to take us to whole new continents of pleasure, or let us, if we want, simply feel like ourselves again.[48]

There is the sensation, when applying gels to the body, of the stuff becoming me, of absorbing a new quality of myself somehow, uncannily, from outside. Integral to the nature of viscous technologies is an ability to become part of whatever they are used on. In *Testo Junkie,* Beatriz Preciado describes testosterone gel as part of the "new gelatinous technologies" with which we are now confronted.[49] One of the powers of these gel technologies, once rubbed onto the flesh, is to "adopt the form of the body they control and become part of it."[50] They are substances that sit at the centre of the biopolitical power struggle, one where the body "no longer inhabits disciplinary spaces but is inhabited by them."[51] Gels are where the technological and the human mingle imperceptibly, a way of technologizing ourselves without appearing to do so. Gel lubricants are, for Burroughs, no doubt something of a perversion. But they are one that trou-

---

47 https://www.ky-jelly.co.uk/ (webpage now defunct).

48 Ibid.

49 Beatriz Preciado, *Testo Junkie: Sex, Drugs and Biopolitics in the Pharmacopornagraphic Era,* trans. Bruce Benderson (New York: Feminist Press, 2013), 77.

50 Ibid., 79.

51 Ibid.

bles the structuring principles of perversion, able to mingle with the object of desire, become almost part of it, enhance its erotic power from within. Gels are different from the curls of somebody's hair because they refuse to remain simply a medium, an object-cause. Like Francis Ponge's mollusc, "*a being — almost a quality,*"[52] they straddle that line between thing and quality, a thing that feels composed entirely of qualities, qualities of touch, of smoothness, of subtlety that then become part of wherever it is applied. In modern "personal lube" technology, much more than simply a frictionless glide is offered. Gels, absorbed by the genitals, can become the quality of hardness for longer, extra-sensitivity, warmness, tingling. Gel technologies fuzz the limits of what it is to feel ourselves.

As Preciado describes in *Testo Junkie,* these gels are powerfully unruly, subversive substances that require control. The instruction manual that accompanies the testosterone gel she acquires illegally, reads like a manual for "microfascism," listing ways to ensure that the drug is used only to cure what has been diagnosed as a deficient male body. By what criteria, Preciado asks, are those that produce this gel working? Interestingly, it is the gel nature of the drug that makes it so potentially threatening to this un-self-reflexive ideology. "Testogel [...] can 'pass' imperceptibly onto another body through skin contact."[53] Gel technologies carry with them an unruliness, a power to transgress the boundaries of both skin and sexual determinism. Preciado figures the gel as a "transparent demon,"[54] a substance with a subversive will of its own, which it waits to unleash. Colloids are potentially rebellious things that must be trafficked and channelled by the dominant ideology. And this is not limited to gels, but includes, for Preciado, all kinds of colloidal microdiffusions of substance — "drops of sweat," the "importing and ex-

52 Francis Ponge, *Unfinished Ode to Mud,* trans. Beverley Bie Brahic (London: CB Editions, 2008), 19.
53 Preciado, *Testo Junkie,* 65.
54 Ibid.

porting of vapors," these "contraband exhalations," these "crystalline mists."[55]

Preciado actively positions the Testogel treatment as part of a history of unguent being repurposed for diabolical transformations of the body. The act of rubbing is coupled with its miasmic influence, able somehow, through the operations of repeated lubricated touch, to diffuse transformations into a body. Through the act of rubbing, gel becomes a kind of smoke, mist, breath. As Steven Connor describes in *The Book of Skin,* witch trials, such as the case of the Somerset witches from the mid-17th century, are full of accounts of demonic transportation being initiated by first anointing the foreheads and wrists in oil. This was a seen as an appropriation of anointing and embalming practices conducted by the church. As Connor says, "the power of the idea of satanic anointing derives [...] from the fact that it is a parody of religious practices of anointing."[56] As the 16th-century Jesuit theologian, Martin del Rio, was sure that the Devil "mimicks the Holy Sacraments instituted by God, and by these quasi-rituals imports a degree of reverence and veneration into his orgies."[57] This was also a period in the history of medicine where, unlike in post-19th-century modern medicine, little distinction was drawn between medicinal substances that were ingested or applied to the skin. Poison was something that might just as easily have been smeared onto the skin as taken into the mouth. *Intoxicare,* Connor claims, means to smear with poison rather than to ingest it,[58] a sense that has been preserved in the idea that effects of alcohol or drugs "wear off," like a paint or varnish.

Preciado participates in witchcraft's imagined proclivity for subversive uses of unguent. The devil was thought to leave his mark in secret places, normally the gooier regions of the body — the inside of the nose, the mucous membrane of the lips, the anus. Preciado's body starts to cultivate these sticky places,

---

55 Ibid.
56 Steven Connor, *The Book of Skin* (New York: Cornell University Press, 2004), 199.
57 Cited in ibid.
58 Ibid., 198.

becoming more viscous with the testosterone inside: "[M]y sweat become sickly sweet, more acidic. The smell of a plastic doll heated by the sun comes from me, apple liqueur abandoned at the bottom of a glass."[59] Yet at this moment of thickening, the testosterone gel itself becomes spectral: "The testosterone mole-cule dissolves into the skin as a ghost walks though a wall."[60] Are we coming close to Burroughs's sense of bodies, in moments of highly lubed excitation, becoming vaporous colloidal suspensions of matter, bodies as smoke?

What is so unique about the status of gel in *Testo Junkie* is how the dubious object of the viscous substance is used as part of a project of empowerment. Smearing viscous substances on people is almost always intensely violent because it is a reduction of people to objects. This is the crux, as we have seen, of Sartre's argument: the viscous is the threat of the world becoming you, of you becoming the world. The ritual humiliation of tar and feathering, for instance, is to thicken that person into object-hood. It is a ritual that very precisely enacts the Sartrean fear of the for-itself engulfing the in-itself. The punishment has most commonly been used to expose traitors during periods of nationalist conflict. It was used by the Americans during the Independence War against individuals collecting taxes for the British. It was used by the French after the Nazi occupation of Vichy France to punish women who were suspected of having had affairs with Germans. And most recently, there were instances of it in Belfast during the Troubles.

Preciado's deep involvement with the material of the Testogel operates within an equivalent structure to this tar and feathering ritual, but to the opposite effect. Preciadio, not unlike Genet, chooses to identify with the literal object of Testogel, finding in its material qualities a transformative power, an internal defiance of prescribed structures that they desire to emulate. But this identification cannot operate in the same way that it might with a table, a chair, a pen. The object is viscous, one that threat-

59 Preciado, *Testo Junkie*, 67.
60 Ibid.

ens to become you, turn you into the world. In this case it is a colloidal viscous object, one that not only sticks to you, but disperses like a mist into your body, unloading its contents irrevocably through and into your flesh. Preciado paradoxically identifies with the object's external powers to disappear into their body. The gel is a means for Preciado to *self-objectify*, work on the body and present it to the world in all its biological "horror and exaltation."[61] And things would not be the same if this were done with pills of injections. Essential to this account of testosterone treatment is the presence of touch, the power of viscous matter to allow for touch, to transform touch into an act that radiates influence, whether it be imaginary, chemical, or both. The body becomes intimately folded onto itself and, in so doing, opened outwards into colloidal feeling, trembling at the very point where, as Korzybski might have it, our bodies merge with their surroundings.

Preciado's viscous explodes the Sartrean viscous and it is all thanks to colloids. Or perhaps Preciado finds what Sartre weirdly longs for but can't quite express: a viscous involvement in things based on extreme subtlety, rather than indifference. Preciado's viscous carries in it an understanding that for you to become the world, for the world to become you, is not a threat, not something to dread, but a liberation, the potential for wild, immense and indeterminate possibility, a place where your very biology becomes a creative act.

Milk Says No, Saying Yes

Where substitutes for absent bodily fluids might be synthesized to enable new forms of corporeal interaction, bodily fluids themselves can be technologized. The organic colloidal secretion from the body that has seen the most dramatic technologization is almost certainly milk. An emulsion, a complex mixture of fats and proteins, it is the originary nourishment, most likely the first meal we consume, but also a huge commercial

61 Ibid., 79.

and industrial enterprise. In milk we find what might feel like a contradiction, two opposing forms of reality: the most intimate and instinctual first interaction between mother and child and the vision of entirely de-humanized, industrialized processes. Milk is something that feels like it might take us back to some idea of an origin, links us to our mammalian ancestors, while also launching us forth into a universe of milkshakes, McFlurries, cappuccinos, Dairymilk, and Häagen Dazs. The milk of animals is made into powders, canned, bottled, pasteurized, homogenized, heated, disinfected, and distributed to become a commodity and, in controversial cases, act as a substitute for mother's milk.

Mother's milk itself has seen attempts, on much smaller scales, of technologization. In her paper "Human Milk as Technology and the Technologies of Human Milk," Kara Swanson analyzes how MIT scientists in the 1920s tried to disembody mother's milk, a product that was deemed deficient, responsible for the rates of infant mortality, and in need of improvement by science. Human milk would be harvested from lactating women, then mixed with supplements in a powdered form. The scientists pursued a "decoupling of the nursing dyad of mother and child" and attempted to transfer the responsibility of infant nutrition away from a woman's nipple to the expertise of medical men, replacing the "femininity of the breast with the masculinity of technology."[62]

These attempts to improve human milk were ultimately unsuccessful. Although they did find women willing to be milked for commercial purposes, and paid for their labor, maternal bodies proved unruly, biologically prone to "leak, squirt drip, and exhibit all manner of variability."[63] The attempted banishment of the breast resulted, in fact, in a greater involvement with it. The milk itself was difficult to transform into a standardized

62 Kara Swanson, "Human Milk as Technology and Technologies of Human Milk: Medical Imaginings in Early Twentieth-Century United States," *Woman's Studies Quarterly* 37, nos. 1–2 (Spring/Summer 2009): 20–37, at 21.
63 Ibid., 22.

product. Although synthetic infant formulas were still developed, the project of technologizing maternal milk was largely abandoned as commercially unviable. The complex internal chemistry of milk, combined with the unreliability of its production caused problems.

Animal milk is also prone to huge variability. In industrial milk production, milk is taken from a multitude of different sources and combined into a single emulsion. In order to standardize the substance, it undergoes a process of homogenization. The milk is forced at high pressure through very small holes, so that the fat globules, sheathed in protein, reduce in size and are dispersed uniformly through out the substance. Homogenization produces a tighter colloidal structure that results in a uniformity of concentration and flavor, and also slows down the processes of separation. In industrially produced milk, fat aggregates do not rise to the surface forming a film at the top of the emulsion. Homogenization produces non-differentiation and helps prevents separation, or curdling.

Derrida uses precisely this separability of milk's substance, its ability to curdle, in setting out his way of thinking between the "human" and the "animal" with the *limitrophe*. His thought, he says,

> will consist, certainly not in effacing the limit, but in multiplying its figures, in complicating, thickening, delinearizing, folding, and dividing the line precisely by making it increase and multiply. Moreover, the supposed first or literal sense of *trephō* is just that: to transform by thickening, for example, in curdling milk.[64]

Like hypertrophied surfaces of Kahn's colloidal structures, Derrida looks not to delineate or to erase, but to complicate the boundary substance, make it something in its own right. Before us, us humans, there were animals. We follow them, as we follow

64 Jacques Derrida, *The Animal That Therefore I Am*, ed. Marie-Louis Mallet, trans. David Willis (New York: Fordham University Press, 2008), 29.

ourselves back to wherever we are. Milk is the boundary substance of care and nurturing. It is the substance and, by extension, an act of giving, that connects us to our mammalian roots,
but also an *example,* Derrida thinks of how we should consider
the limit between "us", the human, whatever this may be, and
the animal. It is, perhaps, though, exactly this kind of generic
thinking, the "us" and "them," that this thickened limit wants to
do away with. The thickened limit is precisely the resistance to
ossifying difference, in a way that is not blind to difference. The
thickened limit is the place where difference can play out, mu-
tate, and intensify, where it might flourish, but also, if necessary,
disappear. Emulsions, tight colloidal structures, become like
"sleepwalking,"[65] blind liberalism: a claim to a fantasy of continuity, a denial of difference (the "abyssal rupture"[66]) where difference exists, a pasting over the cracks. Coagulated limits think
this: "we are definitely animals. We are definitely not animals."

We nourish our young with milk. The milk of animals can
nourish us. Derrida finds nourishment in the *limitrophe,* a place
where we might find "everything we need"[67] for the discussion
to come. For this place, he chooses the moment milk falls out of
its colloidal structure to form the curd, the basis of all cheese-
goods. The separation Derrida is after, then, is also a temporal
one. Cheese is the preservation of the dairy product, a substance
that looks beyond the present moment of encounter, inventing
a future for itself: "cheese is milk's leap toward immortality."[68]
Cheese is the invention of a future and also, by way of this future,
another potential commodity. But curdling is also, in another
scenario, undesirable as the moment milk turns bad, becomes
undrinkable. Curdling is milk's rejection of its purpose in your
fridge, the moment it denies you your request, it says no, we pull
away in disgust. Curdling is also milk's rebellious fragility, one
that industrial production tries to curtail. It is a rejection of the

65 Ibid., 30.
66 Ibid.
67 Ibid., 29.
68 Clifton Fadiman, *Any Number Can Play* (New York: Avon, 1957).

simplicity forced upon it by its technologization, of the illusion that such a Platonic ideal of dairy exists. This curdling might be seen as a disavowal in the Kristevan sense, as the repulsive film on top of your coffee, the formation of the gag-inducing "other".[69] But it is also the reaffirmation of this disavowal as a triumph of specificity and multiplicity, a breaking free from homogeneity. It is a fragile unruliness to milk that sits at the heart of its nourishment, its status as a *limitrophe,* where we might find what we need. Where for Preciado colloids find agency in their ability to spread, exhale, and diffuse, there is, for Derrida, a fragility to colloids that is a promise of their agency. They contain a promise of collapse, a breaking out of things from simplicity that nourishes a resistance to lazy, reductive thinking.

For me, off milk and its threat of curdling, has one significant association. As a 13-year-old boy, I arrived home from school one day to find the house unusually empty. My father, who had suffered a stroke three years before and been left severely disabled, was normally at home when I got back on weekday afternoons. But we'd had a car adapted to his needs and I thought nothing of it. Making myself a cup of tea, I took the milk out of the fridge and smelled it to see if it was still good. It was at that ambiguous stage. Perhaps it was just the residue around the rim giving off this smell, but perhaps it was the whole thing. To resolve this, I decided, in an act that still mystifies me, to pour some of the milk onto the marble work surface, so that it made a little lake which I could sniff unobstructed. Sniffing the lake I found that, yes, it was off. I put the bottle down next to the lake of smelly milk and gave up on the tea. A mild March afternoon, I went out into the garden to peer over the fence at its end, down the hill of allotments to the ring road whirring away at the bottom of the Thames valley. Immediately to my left, in a small glasshouse, I found the body of my father lying face down in potting soil.

69 See Julia Kristeva, *Powers of Horror: An Essay on Abjection,* trans. Leon S. Roudiez (Columbia: Columbia University Press, 1982).

The paramedics came, even though he was long dead. The people came, the house filled with business and grief and still the off milk hung around on the counter. My only real memories of sitting at the kitchen table in, I think, a state of shock, are my memories of this milk's presence, sitting there nearby, its odor not detectable from here, but, I knew, not good to drink. Why were they not clearing it up? Had they not noticed? The marble counter was pale, yes, but surely it could be seen. As the house filled with the sounds of tears, the phrase "there's no point crying over spilt milk" floated about cruel and mockingly in the air. It was my mother who addressed the issue first, asking nobody in particular through her tears what this milk was doing on the counter like this. I thought about trying to explain, but it felt like an unimaginably complex task, basically time travel. But the point is: this cracking open of its substance into off-ness, its fragility, its threat of saying "no," is tied in no uncertain way to this corpse. It isn't death exactly, however, but a promise of an insistent return to that moment.

The colloidal structure of milk as both a highly commercialized and deeply intimate substance also finds attention from the poet J.H. Prynne in his *Kazoo Dreamboats or, On What There Is,* from 2011.

> The root for commerce takes from suspended milk colloidal its creamy delinquent pride of decision, curds resonant in whey by opposed nature not contradicted because lattice charges are in the separation of milk's being, conjugate and pre-organic beyond doubt, post-sexual sweet or even sour. The nipple corridor by conductance of care origins completes the pair bonding expressed to the tongue before more than murmur construes the answer: how, then can what is be going to be in the future, coming to this? What is for is without tense, but the corridor conjugates erotic for-being as root derivative as one satisfied to the start of another or many, the harbingers are come by implant of being into the contradiction of hip-on singularity. Joy to hold, the issue of being up close against another heart-beat at best parallel never in uni-

son which never is the natural place of being then and there,
to brood out this be generic fortune as yet to cost a cool arm
and a leg, orthopedic expense sheet.[70]

This vision of the colloid is different from Derrida's as it takes
its structure less as the *appearance* of indifference, one that must
be resisted, and more as an internal dialectic of substance, a
resonance of opposition. Milk's chemical structure becomes a
blueprint for the bond between mother and child, a union established through the physical separation of bodies. One of the
substances given by the body that enables this process of separation, milk's substance is literally expressed from the breast, but
also expresses this dialectic of care through its make-up. Matter
and language slip seamlessly between one another, and this "expression" is one met by the tongue as an agent of the digestive
process, but also as one that can form words, could in the future
summon up "the answer" to this milky proposition. "The answer" turns out to be a question, as part of the textural pattern-
ing where each maneuver of the text oscillates or somersaults
itself into the next one: "opposed [...] not contradicted," "pre-
organic beyond doubt, post-sexual," "for-being as [...] the start
of another," "parallel never in unison." The text labors to hold
together "opposed natures," which is a dialectical impulse, the
chemical constitution of milk, but perhaps also a vision of love:
a bond that does not try to possess or consume, but nurtures the
limits of separation.

There is a joke that sits just beneath the surface of all this,
one that I don't think is lost on Prynne, who seems wary, at moments, of the work becoming cheesy. The language never slips,
at least at this point, into satirical melodrama, but the tightly
arranged prepositional constructions that situate things in delicate, analytic syncopations, pre- or post-, are certainly drowned
out by the nearly effusive "joy to hold." With these words, the
uniformity, the surface tension, of the writing is threatened, as

70 J.H. Prynne, *Kazoo Dreamboats or, On What There Is* (Cambridge: Critical
Documents, 2011), 18.

237

if the milk, the structuring principle of the text's form, of its desire, were curdling into some kind of emotional outburst. *The Oxford English Dictionary* offers very little insight into why "cheesy" has come to mean overtly sentimental, melodramatic, showy, clichéd. One reason might be the function of the elongated pronunciation of the *ee* in "cheese" in making people appear to be smiling when photographed. The substance, through the mechanics of its utterance, has acquired an association with performed positive affect, the terrifyingly transparent inauthenticity of corporate culture as it tries to make friends with us. Another is also the way in which cheese might be thought of as attention seeking through being smelly. The giving-off of itself into the air is cheese's humiliating obviousness of presence. Bad smells are always a return to limitation through an attempt to reach out beyond oneself. With bad smells, our self-presence moves beyond our corporeal borders, as it does when we speak or sing, only to be returned violently to the various enclosed folds, hollows, and orifices of our bodies. The slang use of "cheesy" for lame sentimentality latches onto this odorous obviousness, an embarrassing emphasis of what is already clearly apparent, what is already well-known.

This reaction to a newborn "joy to hold" feels wrong, here, a gesture towards something somehow too well known, one whose emotive power breaks the slippery material dialectics carried through the text up to this point. This is especially the case in a text that seems intent on finding ways to unearth the structural constituents of what might otherwise be the profound pleasure of holding your child. The text certainly seems anxious to whip itself out of any private indulgence in the pleasures of reproduction, to see it as anything other than a "generic fortune." If this joke, this threat of cheese proposed by this "joy to hold," does linger somewhere in this text, it sustains itself through the fragility of the writing. This colloidal style is, like the milk it is about, fragile, in danger of collapse. This, I want to suggest, is a way of seeing Prynne's poetic project more generally, a project that seeks to keep language suspended in constructions that resist a fall into the useful, the communicative, the consumable, but which are, somehow, continually engrossing and exhilarating. It is the agonizing consistency of this effort, the labor of holding words and the passage between them in a state of indeterminacy, that gives the poems their repelling abundance. But Prynne is also drawn, as in the case of "joy to hold," to incorporate what threatens this indeterminacy into the work itself. Like the structure of desire in Freud's amoeba, Prynne's work invites into itself what might procure its collapse.

Not only do the syntactic constructions of this text form dialectical clusters, but the words themselves are entities that hold together splittings and divisions. How do we read, for instance, this first clause: "The root for commerce takes from suspended milk colloidal its creamy delinquent pride of decision." What is a pride of decision? And how, in any way, do colloids give it to the root of commerce? "Commerce" is most commonly used in relation to financial transaction and dealings, but can also be used to mean sexual intercourse. "Pride" is a word of immense variation in use and meaning over its history. A particular quality of self-regard, it also has an obsolete meaning of abundant productiveness and luxuriant growth. "Decision" is the act of choosing between a set of things or options, but is, more literally, the act of cutting, separating. Where this kind of thinking might attract accusations of elitist, cloistered scholarly wordplay, it is also one that turns poetics into a kind of hyper-synthetic colloidal technology. Viewed diachronically, words evolve over time, accruing new meanings and uses as they go. Viewed synchronically, these causal chains become clusters of difference that, depending on the *design* of the text, can be held in states of indeterminacy and multiplicity. As I've said, commercial milk production involves forcing the milk through very small holes to increase the stability and homogeneity of the fat globules dispersed in the fluid. Through the alienation of circumstance, excesses of meaning are forced into these words, forced into shivering interface. The irony of commercial milk is, though, the fact that it is the stabilization of suspension, the commodification of indeterminacy,

Fig. 1. The first ad campaign for Coco cola's milk beverage, Fairlife.

a "petrified unrest," as Benjamin says.[71] The relation of this text to the dairy commodity is therefore an ambivalent one. Where the easy indifference of consumption is something resisted by every syntactic maneuver of this writing, the technology of colloidal dispersion in commercial milk becomes the sadistic textual practice of a philologist. We find in colloidal technology a stubborn love of language.

This word "commerce" begins to take on new abundantly political meanings. Sexual intercourse and corporate finance not only mingle intimately within this word, but also in modern visual culture and discourse. One of the infinitely complex ways in which sex and money undertake their mingling is in the contemporary fetishization of milk. In 2014, Coca-Cola launched the advertising campaign for its own brand of milk, Fairlife.

The campaign, met with a Twitter storm of ridicule and objection for being hyper-sexualized, was quickly discontinued. These images of women figured as retro 1950s pin-ups, imagine milk far from nourishing excretion of a mammal's body, far from the possibility of curdling, but as a substance of such synthetic

71 Walter Benjamin, *The Writer of Modern Life: Essays of Charles Baudelaire,*
    ed. Michael W. Jennings (Cambridge: Belknap Press 2006), 143–44.

stability that it can become an item of clothing. The special quality of wearing milk, however, is that undressing becomes an act
of consumption: a way, depending on what you desire, of having
the body in front of you or becoming it. These images exploit
milk's associations with service, of giving oneself, of Prynne's
for-being, and transpose it into the archetype of a predatory
male gaze. Milk, in these images, becomes an erotic commodity through its colloidal structure, achieving the consistency and
stability of latex, silk, or velvet. It perhaps also achieves, though,
the imaginary situation that these materials gesture towards
with their shimmering, floaty softness — clothes held in a state
of melting off you. The female body is locked into biological
determinism in being imagined as wearing its own nutritious
excretion; the images dream of a day when the colloids are held
in perfect inseparability, of the substance modified into erotic,
cheeky subservience.

Mouths are held open for little gasps, little startled "oh!s," to
pop out. The figures are infantilized by this mild surprise, designed to have the bodies of women, but the self-possession of
a newborn, gaping wide in attendance of the mother's breast.
But as part of Coca Cola's darkest dream, Fairlife, we have the
spectacle of an orifice awaiting its exploitation, a dollish acceptance, just as sex dolls' mouths are perpetually open, ever ready
to swallow interminable stag party cock, or just whatever new
beverage they come up with next, poured into latex renditions
of Eisenstein's silent scream.

The dream of the milk dress has decidedly fascist origins.
Filippo Tommaso Marinetti's Futurist poem "Il Poema del Vestito di Latte" ("The Poem of the Milk Dress") urges into life a
moment when milk is no longer liquid, but pulled and reshaped
into a material that can be worn, might be weaponized even:
"T'impongo o sacro latte di stringere le maglie d'una viscosità
re-si-sten-te," which can be translated as "I impose it on you
oh sacred milk to tighten the knots of a re-sis-tant viscosity."[72]

72 Filippo Tommaso Marinetti, *Il Poema del Vestito del Latte* (Milan: Lanital/
SNIA Viscosa, 1937), n.p., my translation.

241

Milk, interestingly addressed directly in this statement, would be transformed from nutritious liquid into "milk made of reinforced steel," "milk of war," "militarized milk."[73] The Futurist dreams of daring, boldness, adventure, and war would play out in the resilience of the colloidal interface of the most originary and innocent of emulsions. This was part of the Futurists' ambition to liberate women's fashion from the materials of the old days, employing a whole new revolutionary set of fabrics to be the clothing of the new era:

> One hundred new revolutionary materials will riot in the piazza, demanding to be admitted into the making of womanly clothes. We fling open wide the doors of the fashion ateliers to paper, cardboard, glass, tinfoil, aluminium, ceramic, rubber, fish skin, burlap, oakum, hemp, gas, growing plants, and living animals. Every woman will be a walking synthesis of the universe.[74]

Marinetti's championing of milk clothing as the ultimate in the technologization of the human body was not enigmatic, utopian propaganda, but based in contemporary experimentation with synthetic material production. Finding synthetic substitutes for naturally occurring materials was an obsession of chemical industries under the fascist governments of the interwar period.[75] Mussolini invested in textiles, producing, most successfully, rayon, an artificial silk. In 1935, the company SNAI Viscosa, which produced the vast majority of Italy's synthetic fibers, began producing a textile known as "lanital," spun from the protein fibers of waste milk. Mussolini adored the idea, provided SNAI with large government funds, which produced in 1937 10 million pounds of the fabric. Its material was imagined to be a

73 Ibid.
74 Filippo Tommaso Marinetti, "Futurist Manifesto of Women's Fashion," in *Futurism: An Anthology,* eds. Laurence Rainey, Christini Poggi, and Laura Wittman (New Haven: Yale University Press, 2009), 253-254, at 254.
75 See Esther Leslie, *Synthetic Worlds: Nature, Art and Chemical Industry* (London: Reaktion Books, 2005).

nationalist emblem of the triumph of Italian fascism, a stuff of "exemplary Italianness." Lanital is a portmanteau of "lan", from *lana* meaning wool, and "ital," *Italia*. A British Pathé film from 1937 shows footage of the Viscosa factory workers pulling out strands of fibrous matter from vats of sludgy milk.[76] Central to ideals of this material was its ability to move between notions of the feminine — it was described as being perfect for specifically women's clothing by the British publication *The Children's Newspaper* — but also masculine domains of warfare.[77] After some publicity maneuvers by Viscosa, the American Atlantic Research Associates, a division of the National Dairy Corporation, started producing fabric made from milk protein known as "aralac." According to a *Life* magazine from 1944, the first American troops sent to fight in World War Two were wearing milk-based hats. But this didn't last long. The fabric was decommissioned quickly. When damp, the fabric became unpleasant, starting to smell sour, the milk flourished into mildly repellent non-conformity. It said "no."

Aeronautics

Talking to a middle-aged aeronautics engineer one night about my book about viscosity, all of a sudden he grabbed my arm, widened his eyes maniacally and said in a dramatic hush *"do you know what viscosity is?!"* I felt put on the spot and mumbled something incomprehensible that I've forgotten. He interrupted and repeated: *"do you KNOW what viscosity IS?!"* I said, finally: "no... no I don't," ashamed. His drink in one hand, swaying slightly, he leant in towards me and whispered in my ear: *"It's the possibility of connection."* It occurred to me: is this how engineers flirt?

76 Michael Waters, "How Clothing Made From Milk Became the Height of Fashion in Mussolini's Italy," *Atlas Obscura,* July 28, 2017. https://www.atlasobscura.com/articles/lanital-milk-dress-qmilch.

77 Ibid.

Colloidal thinking draws maps of the in-between. It is a kind of knowledge, one based on structure rather than things. Colloids began their life as a fashionable new interdisciplinary mode of scientific enquiry. Matter dispersed together at microscopic scales attracted the attention of scientists from various disciplines as the place where explanations might be found for the origins of life, for the advances in gel technology, for its immense practical applications in war and industry, for its insights into healthcare and mental illness. Although colloidal science continued in the world of engineering, it fell largely out of fashion in research departments, particularly in chemistry and biochemistry departments, from the late 1930s onwards. This was partly due to the burgeoning interest in molecular science and partly due to the rather overzealous claims made by colloidal researchers of their significance. But, in any case, the technology of the in-between flourished.

Colloids, though, caught the attention of a number of minds from outside the established circles of scientific thinking. Alfred Korzybski is the most significant of these thinkers, dedicating a large part of his major work of gestalt therapy to colloidal structures. For Korzybski colloids are a kind of knowledge, but also its origin. Any thing that can effect colloidal stability can effect the well-being of the body and, in turn effect how one thinks. As thoughts radiate electrical energy and as colloidal balance is influenced by electrical energy, thinking also can make you healthy or sick, according to Korzybski. Korzybski writing on colloids helps us to rethink the nature of surfaces. Colloids are not quite bodies with an inside and an outside, but a tangling of internalized surface, a body made entirely of surfaces.

This interpretation of colloidal science had huge influence on the work of William Burroughs. Burroughs's work is intensely materialist, casting the dynamics of thinking and feeling through intricate substantial transformations and exchanges. Colloids provide him with a way of moving erratically between the body and the world and between mind and matter. Matter does not only produce sensations but moves and transforms with the sensations it produces. Colloidal thinking releases matter from material determinism and affords it a sensual agency. This ability to think structurally, between things, is a kind of thinking that dominates his style, but is also one that he finds at certain states of ecstatic feeling. Lubricant jelly is a particular obsession of Burroughs's. It is the colloidal substance that allows him to realize his desire, a technology of intimacy that opens him out onto a colloidal perspective of things. Lubes and gels become active agents in the realization of non-normative forms of desire. These technologies of the viscous are defined by an ability to become part of whatever they act with. They are an assemblage of qualities that are then absorbed by whatever they are applied. The drunk engineer was right, of course. The viscous is the distance of intimacy. The politics of these colloidal possibilities become of central importance to the writing of Paul (formerly Beatriz) Preciado. Colloids are seen as an unruliness of matter that the dominant ideology feels it must channel.

With milk we find the bodily excretion that has seen most technologization. It is milk's tendency to curdle that commercial milk production attempts to slowdown. For Derrida, we find a celebration of the curd as a both a kind of nourishment, a futurity and a fragile rebellion against the pressures of homogeneity. The curdling of milk may be, in one scenario, repulsive, it is also the flourishing of difference where a sleepwalking continuity has been imposed on things. Prynne takes a different view of the colloidal structure of milk. The colloid, for him, is a fragile material dialectic out of which he finds an image of love and particular poetic strategy. He has an ambivalent relation with commercial milk as a shimmering suspension of opposites, but one that has been designed for ease of consumption. It is this idealized version of milk that has resulted in its oppressive fetishization, most notably by Coca-Cola in its Fairlife campaign of 2014. The subversive power of milk is dreamt away, its creamy, fragile nourishment reduced to a cheaply erotic commodity.

But I have, I hope here, given some insight into the colloidal articulation of viscous substances, and how this might become part of their sensuality. Colloids are where the viscous can become technologized, adapted, and enhanced. I'm interested in

245

showing how what might otherwise be imperceptible about a particular substance can become part of an expanded encounter with it, as is the case with this moment in *The Soft Machine,* where Burroughs extracts, with fetishistic attention, the quietly immanent, orgasmic explosiveness to the material of his slippery lube. This is not to reduce a material to its chemical or physical structure, nor to let things live solely in their surface qualities, but to allow for an interchange between the two. Colloids, not quite everything, but definitely too much, are a particular mode of material dialectic, a non-linearity and indeterminacy of sensual encounter where patterns of radiation and dispersal become part of whatever might cloy, clam up, and cling to us.

Conclusion

Hair at Birth, I Suspect

Let's say I have in me a vague and uneasy feeling, a feeling not present enough to be able to deal with, however it might be that we "deal with" feelings we can't handle or are never quite there. I suspect I might share this vague and uneasy feeling with many others. It's something that can't be shed, and that moves like a current between and within.

I also suspect that if I were to rub this vague and uneasy feeling, it would become moist and tend towards a translucence, but I can't be sure. I suspect that if I continued rubbing, it would froth out into a cohesion of membranes and gas, a foam: enormous now, relatively speaking, but just as fragile as it was before, composed as foams are, of two things that, if alone, feel as if they might as well not exist, but together so flamboyantly do, bringing joy to innumerable newborns across this earth.

I suppose I'm trying to describe a sense of worth. In his preface to his collection of stories *In the Heart of the Heart* of the Country, William Gass wonders about the sense of worth we might have before any action of our own has occurred, worth that feels like it was already there. The feeling of worth, for instance, we feel when watching our football team win. Coming before, this sense reaches out ahead of us, "like hair at birth, and makes brilliant enterprises possible."[1] Gass seems to have been feeling positive. My sister has just given birth to a little girl, a little girl who came out with a shockingly thick full head of hair, like George Harrison circa 1966. I would like to describe (at some point) in some detail the outcomes of this weighty hair-at-birth. If goo is that which should stay on this inside, hair most certainly is not. Maybe there needs to be a history of things that must always be on the outside.

Hagfish

Recently, hagfish came under renewed scrutiny as a tanker full of them burst all over a road in Oregon, USA. Hagfish resemble eels and these ones in particular were on their way to Korea, where they are eaten as a delicacy. But the spillage resulted in more than just eels all over the road. When they feel threatened, hagfish erupt in viscous matter, spewing out a complex translucent jelly, expanding the mess of tangled creature by many times.

When confronted by a predator, they excrete from tiny ventrolateral pores a colloidal substance made of three components: vesicles made of mucin, protein threads coiled up in skeins, and a residual fluid. When this mixture comes into contact with sea water an eruption of physio-chemical processes takes place, and the stuff enlarges by several times, jellifying the water around it. The mucin vesicles rupture, letting in an influx of water and the protein skins unfurl and elongate. The mucins form strands that are then churned up with the threads as they unfurl. Slime is made.

This slime has remarkable physical properties. It is a gel with a coherent and soft structure formed of a complex network of ultra-long proteins and hydrated mucus. Between the threads and the mucins is held large amounts of water. The vast majority of this slime is water, around 99.996 per cent. Hagfish are most

1   William H. Gass, *In the Heart of the Heart of the Country* (New York: New York Review Books, 2015), 4.

vulnerable to biting or sucking, to feeders that open their buccal cavity (mouth) wide, creating a flow of water that draws the prey inwards. Hagfish resist this suction into mouths by undertaking a process called "gill clogging." They stimulate their slimy eruptions, forging an allegiance with the water, before a jet of slime is directed into the mouth of the predator, causing them to cough the hagfish back up again like we might some clot of phlegm, in danger of suffocation.

The problem, however, is this: how do hagfish avoid asphyxiating themselves? The hagfish must have a way to free itself from its own slime. They do this by another method of tangling. They form their body into a sliding knot and scrape the slime of their body with their own body, thus avoiding a death by their own excretion.

There are two rheological properties of hagfish slime that aid them in their use of it to defend and escape. Elongational stresses to the hagfish slime increase its viscosity. This means that the suction of fluid into the predators mouth excited a thickening in the hagfish slime. The more the predator sucks, the more clogged its gills become. Shear flow, the kind of exertion on matter that comes from rubbing, for instance, the bottom slid from under the top, results in a decrease in gooeyness. The non-linearity of the hagfish's excretion is a mechanism to ensure efficient defense and escape. The slow pull into the stomach of another creature is met with resistance and when the whip of a writhing free is required, the stuff thins out and lubricates.[2]

Gooey Worlding

This has been an experiment to see what happens if we move beyond what might be seen as the "horror" of this hagfish slime, but resist, too, the objectifying powers of a scientific remove,

2   For this description of hagfish slime I have used a selection of scientific articles, most notably: Lukas Böni et al. "Hagfish Slime and Mucin Flow Properties and Their Implications for Defense," *Scientific Reports* 6 (2016): 30371.

wanting to stay *personally* involved in the imagination of its substance. I set out to write about slime, not necessarily slime in visual culture, in literature, or in the history of B-movies, even if I do, at moments, do all of these things. I wanted to get to grips with the enigmatic object that is "the viscous," use its tendencies as a place to nourish thinking and speculation, take from it propositions about how to think, feel and live. Staring at gloop, what kinds of life and world unravel before us? Why would we want to do this?

In chapter one, I took inspiration from the moment a molasses tank burst, engulfing its urban surroundings. From inspecting a line of sensual instances that constitute the very specific history of the urban space turning gloopy, we witness slime's powers of bursting and indifference. In the philosophy of Emmanuel Levinas, Catherine Malabou, Jean-Paul Sartre, and Iain Hamilton Grant, we find philosophies of slime that conceive of its stuff not simply as primordial indifference, or the collapse of complexity into mere simplicity, but a dynamic of matter, a churning, an extendibility, a deviant specificity continually intent on lingering a while longer, wanting me and only me, until it relents, detaches, merges back, out sync, with itself. We find a slime that is desperate to be seen. A curious companion to this stuff's indeterminate material energy is its unwieldy flamboyance. It gives and it gives, dancing into forms shocking and pleasing, a dance that creeps into any attempts to write about it. As we see in Sartre's famous pages and in Koolhaas's more recent ones, viscous writing so often unleashes itself into the wild domains of the synonymous — and this, and this, and this. Through what was once assumed to be the warm little pond of our primordial roots, we find a loop into synthetic delirium. This is a foundational paradox of viscous thinking.

But this paradox is also an opportunity to reimagine the city, churn its environment with spaces previously thought independent of its body. Thinking with slime is all about relinquishing control and discovering that, perhaps, things might be better if you do so. We find this in the simple fact that slime mold can, it appears, design more efficient road networks than we can. The more I look at slime, the more I find myself in it. Slime mold confronts us with the singularly uncanny notion that our memory, the most perplexing of human faculties, was once a mildly toxic piece of mucus lightly smeared on places we'd been. Slime is a memory of memory.

In chapter two, we zoomed in on the issue of stickiness, that is, kinds of attachment that are inherently imperfect and un-reliable. But this imperfection and unreliability comes from a deeper persistence, an eagerness to attach regardless of the pur-poses of that attachment. I am drawn to moments when people have imagined stickiness to be a force in its own right, a ten-dency in things to clump up and adhere, oblivious to the whole notion of "meaning". From Socrates' whimsical dismissal of "everything flows," through Kantian writing on the phlegmatic, through 20th-century methods of crowd control, to contempo-rary theories of ecology, we have a map of volatile, opportunis-tic adhesions. The agreement, between all these diverse world-views, is that there is somewhere lurking within life something that snags: an ontology to stickiness working beyond or within senses of continuous flow. Stickiness is a particular dynamic of attachment that has special relevance in an age of deep ecologi-cal anxiety in a world where things stick around, where there is no "elsewhere." Its ironies are ironies we must increasingly deal with and feel. The stickier the world becomes, the less world there must necessarily be. If it is possible that particular eras of human history might liquefy into revolutionary optimism, or crystalize into reactionary stasis, now seems to be a period of all-encompassing, disorientating ooze, where every distinction we might feel we have the power to make, is in its very utterance not dissolved into sameness, but suddenly warped into confu-sion. Knowledge has never been so messy.

But this all takes place in an era where viscous matter is becoming of increasing technological interest, one of these technologies being the thing most people spend a lot of their time staring at or through: the liquid crystal, as I discussed in chapter three. The liquid crystal, just like the slime monster, is hyper-demonstrative. Even at its discovery, it looked like a film of itself. So much so, in fact, that its stuff is now the basis of the contemporary spectacle and simulated visual reality: HD, as Luciana Parisi suggests, the imagined blast-off into an immaterial cyberspace. This slimy state of being, the liquid crystal, is the technology of disembodiment in a way that recalls the spectral messages claimed to be transmitted from beyond the grave by that fraudulent substance, ectoplasm. Far from being "base matter," slime is revealed as being a complex interface between realms of the spectral and the material. This interfacial switching is played out in the slime craze currently underway on the internet — hands fondling substance of ambivalent origin, simultaneously shit and plastic. The squelch and pops of slime, viewed on LCD screens around the globe, have been seen by some as the redemption of the internet, a recoiling from the visual cacophony of a 24-hour news cycle into the very specific, mundane, and contingent sensual details of viscous matter. Indeed, where the "digital" seems to be the thing that creeps imperceptibly further into our lives, slime has acquired a renewed sense of authenticity.

In chapter four, I sought to display slimy matter as composed of imperceptible articulations. Overall, these chapters can be considered as attempt to articulate the viscous, unpack its nuance, listen to its alternative and alternating structures. In "Colloidal Thinking/Colloidal Feeling," we found in viscous materials, extremes of articulation, minute and complex interdispersals of substance that are the generative core of these materials. Lubricants, gels, sols, emulsions, and foams are where gloop becomes creative, fragile, and rebellious. Preciado's use of and writing about testosterone gel is a culmination of a history of writing about viscous matter that has never quite been able to give the agency to gloop that it has been demanding. But it is essential not to idealize the viscous as somehow something with answers. I am not sure what a world in which that was the case would look like. But it is, in some sense, exuberantly *there*. In trying to describe in detail its body, we can pull it out from stultifying dead ends of "mystery" into something we might use.

Bounce out the Window

Recently I participated in an exhibition that claimed to reimagine the gallery space as a "fluid cultural site." More generally, "fluidity" appears to be a dominating state of matter in how progressive politics and cultural experience is conceptualized. No doubt as part of the pressures for art and intellectual practices to become increasingly "interdisciplinary," the emphasis on fluidity seems to ask us to imagine a world in which all boundaries and blockages are erased, existence becomes totally unmediated, all exchanges taking place at an infinite speed across a wash of life and activity. Is this where fluidity wants to take us? Is this possible? Would we even want it if it were? I have become increasingly perplexed by the importance of the fluid in certain circles, by what is meant exactly, if people are conscious of what they mean and why it has become something to aim for. And the problem with questioning the desirability of the fluid is that you are immediately landed with what is perceived to be its opposite, solidity. Part of what I have hoped to have delineated here is another ground, the ground of the non-solid, the non-liquid, a place where flow is resisted just as much as the solid is liquefied.

What better tool to help imagine liberation than a mobility formed of a thousand clustered resistances? Rather than fluidity, surely we should be thinking about kinds of being that stretch and then shimmer, flop off, then bounce out the window. A dynamic that troubles in equal measure the pressure to contain and control as the pressure of "boundlessness, of 'irrealization,' and reduction to principle — the principle of flowing, of distance, of vague endless enticement."[3] The viscous is doubtful, it is messy. It is a state of matter that speaks to people who dream of being so involved in things they can't help but explode, then stay on for more. For those who rise up to plunge back in. Its matter is a startlement, an obligation to think that seizes you. Its object appeals to that feeling, vague and uneasy, that yearns

3   Klaus Theweleit, *Male Fantasies: Women, Floods, Bodies, History,* vol. 1 (Cambridge: Polity Press, 1987), 272.

to adhere to things, but also to detach and roam meteorically about. It appeals to a desire to be slippery, but also tremble with anticipation at the next attachment. It speeds things up. It slows them down. It embalms, it protects.

Things don't leave. The viscous nourishes, it is a place of contradiction and synthesis, an encounter with a complex of excitations that is there in all seriousness and utility, promising more of what you thought you were never quite able to imagine.

Bibliography

This bibliography contains works directly cited in *The Viscous,* but also works not directly cited, works that have acted more as guides through my writing on this stuff.

"About Us." AMETEK *Brookfield*. https://www. brookfieldengineering.com/.

Aftalio, Fred. *A History of the International Chemical Industry.* Philadelphia: The Chemical Heritage Press, 2000.

Adorno, Theodor. *Aesthetic Theory.* Translated by Robert Hullot-Kentor. London: Bloomsbury Academic, 2013.

———. *Minima Moralia: Reflections from Damaged Life.* Translated by E.F.N. Jephcott. London: Verso, 1985.

———. *Negative Dialectics.* Translated by E.B. Ashton. London: Contiuum, 1981.

Ahuja, Nitin K. "It Feels Good to Be Measured: Clinical Role-Play, Walker Percy and the Tingles." *Perspectives in Biology and Medicine* 56, no. 3 (Summer 2013): 442–51. DOI: 10.1353/ pbm.2013.0022.

———. "Softer than Softcore." *The New Inquiry*, December 9, 2014. https://thenewinquiry.com/softer-than-softcore/

Angerer, Marie-Luise. *Ecology of Affect: Intensive Milieus and Contingent Encounters.* Translated by Gerrit Jackson. Luneburg: meson press, 2017.

Apollonio, Umbro, ed. *Futurist Manifestoes.* Translated by
    Robert Brain et al. London: Thames and Hudson, 1973.
Aristotle. *The Complete Works of Aristotle.* Edited by Jonathan
    Barnes, translated by H.H. Joachim. New Jersey: Princeton
    University Press, 1984.
Atkins, Ed. *A Primer for Cadavers.* London: Fitzcarraldo
    Editions, 2016.
Bachelard, Gaston. *Earth and the Reveries of Will: An Essay On
    the Imagination of Matter.* Translated by Kenneth Haltman.
    Dallas: The Dallas Institute Publications, 1994.
———. *Water and Dreams: An Essay on the Imagination
    of Matter.* Translated by Edith Farrell. Dallas: The Dallas
    Institute Publications, 1994.
Badiou, Alain. *Black: The Brilliance of a Non-Color.* Translated
    by Susan Spitzer. Cambridge: Polity Press, 2017.
Bancroft, Wilder. *The Literary Digest* 28, no. 3 (November 21,
    1931).
Barratt, Emma L. "Autonomous Sensory Meridian Response
    (ASMR): A Flow-Like Mental State." *PeerJ* 3 (March 2015):
    e851. DOI: 10.7717/peerj.851.
Bartel, Mel. *Facebook,* June 12, 2018. https://www.facebook.
    com/MelroseBartel/posts/1735082299873957.
Barthes, Roland. *Empire of Signs.* Translated by Richard
    Howard. New York: Noonday Press, 1989.
Bataille, Georges. *Story of the Eye.* Translated by Joachim
    Neugroschal. London: Penguin Modern Classics, 2001.
———. *Visions of Excess: Selected Writings 1927–1939.* Edited
    by Allan Stoekl, translated by Allan Stoekl et al. Manchester
    University Press, 1985.
Bauman, Zygmunt. *Liquid Times: Living in an Age of
    Uncertainty.* Cambridge: Polity Press, 2007.
Beckett, Samuel. *How It Is.* London: Faber and Faber, 2009.
———. *The Letters of Samuel Beckett 1929–40.* Edited
    by Martha Dow Fehsenfeld and Lois More Overbeck.
    Cambridge: Cambridge University Press, 2009.
———. *The Unnamable.* London: Faber and Faber, 2010.
———. *Watt.* London: Faber and Faber, 2010.

Benjamin, Walter. *Reflections: Essays, Aphorisms and Autobiographical Writings.* Translated by Edmund Jephcott. New York: Schocken Books, 1986.

———. *Selected Writings, Vol. 2: 1927–1934.* Translated by Rodney Livingstone, edited by Michael W. Jennings et al. Cambridge: Harvard University Press, 1999.

———. *The Writer of Modern Life: Essays of Charles Baudelaire.* Edited by Michael W. Jennings. Cambridge: Belknap Press 2006.

Bennett, Jane. *Vibrant Matter: A Political Ecology of Things* Durham: Duke University Press, 2010.

Berardi, Franco "Bifo." *And: Phenomenology of the End,* London: Semiotext(e), 2015.

Bergland, Christopher. *The Athletes Way: Training Your Mind and Body to Experience the Joy of Exercise.* New York: St Martin's Press, 2007.

Bhandar, Brenna, and Jonathan Goldberg-Hiller, eds. *Plastic Materialities: Politics, Legality and Metamorphosis in the Work of Catherine Malabou.* Durham: Duke University Press, 2015.

Bogue, Robert Herman. *The Chemistry and Technology of Gelatin and Glue.* London: McHraw-Hill Book Co. Ltd, 1922.

Bois, Yves-Alain, and Rosalind E. Krauss, eds. *Formless: A User's Guide.* Cambridge: MIT Press, 2000.

le Bon, Gustav. *The Crowd: A Study of the Popular Mind.* London: Ernest and Benn ltd., 1938.

Böni, Lukas, Peter Fischer, Lukas Böcker, Simon Kuster, and Patrick A. Rühs, "Hagfish Slime and Mucin Flow Properties and Their Implications for Defense." *Scientific Reports* 6 (2016): 30371. DOI: 10.1038/srep30371.

Boscagli, Maurizia. *Stuff Theory: Everyday Objects, Radical Materialism.* London: Bloomsbury Academic, 2014.

Boutros, Alexandra, and Will Straw, eds. *Circulation and the City: Essays on Urban Culture.* Montréal: McGill University Press, 2010.

Brenner, Neil, ed. *Implosions/Explosions: Towards a Study of Planetary Urbanization.* Berlin: Jovis Verlag, 2014.

Brown, Bill. "Thing Theory." *Critical Inquiry* 28, no. 1 "Things" (Autumn, 2001): 1–22. DOI: 10.1086/449030.

Burke, Edmund. *A Philosophical Enquiry into the Origin of Our Ideas of the Sublime and the Beautiful.* Oxford: Oxford University Press, 2013.

Burroughs, William. *Naked Lunch.* London: Penguin Classics, 2001.

———. *The Soft Machine.* London: Fourth Estate, 2010.

Caillois, Roger. "Mimicry and Legendary Psychasthenia." *October* 31 (Winter, 1984): 16–32. DOI: 10.2307/778354.

———. *The Writing of Stones.* Translated by Barbara Bray. Charlottesville: University Press of Virginia, 1985.

Chang, Hasok. *Is Water H_2O?: Evidence, Realism and Pluralism.* New York: Springer, 2012.

de Chardin, Pierre Teilhard. *The Divine Milieu.* Translated by Sion Cowell. Sussex Academic Press, 2003.

Chesebrough, Robert. Improvement in Products from Petroleum, Specification Forming part of Letters Patent no. 127,568, June 4, 1872.

Connor, Steven. "Beckett's Atmospheres." Paper given at the Après Beckett/After Beckett conference, Sydney 2003. http://www.stevenconnor.com/atmospheres/.

———. *Matters of Air: Science and Art of the Ethereal.* London: Reaktion Books, 2010.

———. *The Book of Skin.* Cornell University Press, 2003.

———. "Thinking Things." Talk given at the Textual Practice lecture, University of Sussex, October 14, 2009. http:// www.stevenconnor.com/thinkingthings.

Csikszentmihalyi, Mihaly. *Flow: The Psychology of Optimal Experience.* London: Harper Perennial Modern Classics, 2008.

Darwin, Charles. *The Correspondence of Charles Darwin,* Vol. 19. Cambridge University Press, 2012.

Delanda, Manuel. *Philosophical Chemistry: Genealogy of a Scientific Field.* London: Bloomsbury Academic, 2015.

Deleuze, Gilles, and Felix Guattari. *A Thousand Plateaus: Capitalism and Schizophrenia.* Translated by Brian Massumi. Minneapolis: University of Minnesota Press, 2004.

———. *The Fold: Leibniz and the Baroque.* Translated by Tom Conley. London: Continuum, 2006.

Derrida, Jacques. *The Animal That Therefore I Am.* Translated by David Willis. New York: Fordham University Press, 2008.

Dick, Philip K. *Ubik.* London: Millennium, 2000.

Didi-Huberman, Georges. "The Order of Material: Plasticities, Malaise, Survival." In *Sculpture and Psychoanalysis,* edited by Brandon Taylor, 195–213. Aldershot: Ashgate, 2006.

Dillon, Brian. *Essayism.* London: Fitzcarraldo Editions, 2017

———. *Objects in This Mirror: Essays.* Berlin: Sternberg Press, 2014.

———. *The Great Explosion: Gunpowder, the Great War, and a Disaster on the Kent Marshes.* London: Penguin Books, 2016.

Dolphijn, Rick, and Iris van der Tuin, eds. *New Materialism: Interviews and Cartographies.* Utrecht: Open Humanities Press, 2012.

Douglas, Mary. *Purity and Danger: An Analysis of the Concepts of Pollution and Taboo.* London: Routledge, 1991.

Dr Karl. "Green Glow of Radiation." ABC *Science,* May 20, 2008. http://www.abc.net.au/science/articles/2008/05/20/2249925.htm.

Dunmur, David, and Tim Sluckin. *Soap, Science, and Flatscreen TVs: A History of Liquid Crystals.* Oxford: Oxford University Press, 2011.

Eagleton, Terry. *The Ideology of the Aesthetic.* Oxford: Blackwell Publishing, 1990.

Easterling, Keller. *Extrastatecraft: The Power of Infrastructure Space.* London: Verso, 2014.

Ede, Andrew. *The Rise and Decline of Colloid Science in North America, 1900–1935.* Hampshire: Ashgate, 2007.

Epstein, Jean. *The Intelligence of a Machine.* Translated by Christophe Wall-Romana. Minneapolis: Univocal Publishing, 2014.

Fadiman, Clifton. *Any Number Can Play*. New York: Avon, 1957.

Ferris, Natalie. "Interview with Keston Sutherland." *The White Review,* March 2013, http://www.thewhitereview.org/interviews/interview-with-keston-sutherland/.

Fieser, Louis. *The Scientific Method: A Personal Account of Unusual Projects in War and Peace*. New York: Reinhold Publishing Company, 1964.

Freud, Sigmund. "A Difficulty in the Path of Psycho-Analysis." In *The Standard Edition of the Complete Psychoanalytical Works of Sigmund Freud, Volume XVII (1917–1919): An Infantile Neurosis and Other Works,* edited and translated by James Strachey with Anna Freud, 135–44. London: Hogarth, 1953–74.

———. "The Obsessional Neurosis." In *The Standard Edition of the Complete Psychoanalytical Works of Sigmund Freud, Volume XVII (1917–1919): An Infantile Neurosis and Other Works,* edited and translated by James Strachey with Anna Freud, 61–71. London: Hogarth, 1953–74.

Gass. William H. *In The Heart of the Heart of the Country*. New York: New York Review Books, 2015.

Genet, Jean. *The Thief's Journal*. Translated by Bernard Frechtman. London: Faber and Faber, 2009.

Grant, Iain Hamilton. "Being and Slime: The Mathematics of Protoplasm in Lorenz Oken's Physio-Philosophy." In *Collapse IV: Concept Horror*. Falmouth: Urbanomic, 2009.

———. "The Chemical Paradigm." In *Collapse VII,* edited by Robin Mackay et al. Falmouth: Urbanomic, 2012.

Groys, Boris. *In the Flow*. London: Verso, 2016.

Guess, Raymond. *Public Goods, Private Goods*. Princeton University Press, 2001.

Güway, B., et al. "Aliphatic Hydrocarbon Content of Intersteller Dust." *Monthly Notices of the Royal Astronomical Society* 479, no. 4 (October 1, 2018): 4336–44. DOI: 10.1093/mnras/sty1582.

Hallward, Peter. *Out of This World: Deleuze and the Philosophy of Creation*. London: Verso, 2006.

Han, Byung Chul. *The Scent of Time: A Philosophical Essay on the Art of Lingering.* Translated by Daniel Steuer. Cambridge: Polity Press, 2017.

Harman, Graham. *Immaterialism: Objects and Social Theory.* Cambridge: Polity Press, 2016.

———. *Towards a Speculative Realism: Essays and Lectures.* Winchester: Zero Books, 2010.

Harraway, Donna. *Staying With the Trouble: Making Kin in the Chthulucene.* Durham: Duke University Press Books, 2016.

———. "Tentacular Thinking: Anthropocene, Capitolocene, Chthulucene." *e-flux* 75 (September 2016). https://www.e-flux.com/journal/75/67125/tentacular-thinking-anthropocene-capitalocene-chthulucene/.

Harvey, Robert. "The Sartrean Viscous: Swamp and Source." *SubStance* 20, no. 1, iss. 64 (1991): 49–66. DOI: 10.2307/3684882.

Heidegger, Martin. *Being and Time.* Translated by John Macquarrie and Edward Robinson. New York: Harper Collins, 2008.

Hegel, G.W.F. *Philosophy of Nature Vol. III.* Translated and edited by M.J. Petry. London: Allen and Unwin, 2013.

Henisch, Heinz K. *Crystal Growth in Gels.* New York: Dover Publications, 1996.

Hobson, Benedict. "Growing a 'Giant Artificial Reef' Could Stop Venice Sinking." *Dezeen,* May 30, 2014. https://www.dezeen.com/2014/05/30/movie-rachel-armstrong-future-venice-growing-giant-artificial-reef/.

Hugo, Victor. *Les Miserables.* London: Penguin Classics, 1982.

Huxtable, Juliana. *Mucus in My Pineal Gland.* New York: Capricious, Wonder, 2017.

Ingold, Tim. *The Life of Lines.* New York: Routledge, 2015.

Iragaray, Luce. *This Sex Which Is Not One.* Translated by Catherine Porter. New York: Cornell University Press, 1985.

Illouz, Eva. *Why Love Hurts: A Sociological Explanation.* Cambridge: Polity, 2012.

Jackson, Melanie, and Esther Leslie. "Journeys of Lactic Abstraction: The Meanings of Milk." *Cabinet* 61 (Fall

2016–Winter 2017). http://cabinetmagazine.org/issues/62/
jackson_leslie.php.

Jameson, Frederic. "Future City." *New Left Review* 21 (May–
June 2003): 65–79.

Jung, Carl. *Psychology and Alchemy*. London: Routledge, 2010.

Jost, Peter, and Department of Education and Science.
*Lubrication (Tribology), Education and Research: A Report
on the Present Position and Industry's Needs*. London: H.M.
Stationary Office, 1966.

Kahn, Douglas. *Noise Water Meat: A History of Sound in the
Arts*. Cambridge: MIT Press, 2001.

Kant, Immanuel. *Anthropology from a Pragmatic Point of View*.
Translated by Robert Louden. Cambridge: Cambridge
University Press, 2006.

———. *Critique of Judgement*. Translated by James Creed
Meredith. Oxford: Oxford University Press, 2007.

Kelley, Mike. "On the Aesthetics of Ufology." *Blastitude* 13
(August 13, 2002). http://blastitude.com/13/ETERNITY/
ufology_kelley.htm.

———. *Vaseline Muses (Why I Got Into Art)*. Cologne:
Jablonka Galerie/Walther Konig, 1991.

Koestenbaum, Wayne. *Humiliation*. London: Picador, 2011.

Koolhaas, Rem. "Junkspace." *October* 100 "Obsolescence"
(Spring 2002): 175–90.

Korzybski, Alfred. *Science and Sanity: An Introduction to Non-
Aristotelian Systems and General Semantics*. 4th edition.
Lakeville: Institute of General Semantics, 1958.

Kristeva, Julia. *Powers of Horror: An Essay on Abjection*.
Translated by Leon S. Roudiez. New York: Columbia
University Press, 1982.

Lacan, Jacques. *The Seminar of Jacques Lacan, Book II: The Ego
in Freud's Theory and in the Technique of Psychoanalysis
1954–55*. Translated by Sylvana Tomaselli. New York: W.W.
Norton and Company, 1998.

Latour, Bruno. *Reassembling the Social: An Introduction to
Actor-Network-Theory*. Oxford: Oxford University Press,
2005.

———. *We Have Never Been Modern.* Translated by Catherine Porter. Cambridge: Harvard University Press, 1993.

Law, John. *After Method: Mess in Social Theory.* New York: Taylor and Francis, 2004.

Le Guin, Ursula K. *The Lathe of Heaven.* New York: Diversion Books, 1999.

Lehman, Otto. "On Flowing Crystals." In *Crystals That Flow: Classic Papers from the History of Liquid Crystals,* edited by Timothy J. Sluckin, David A. Dunmur, and Horst Stegemeyer, 42–53. London: Taylor and Francis, 2004.

Leslie, Esther. *Derelicts: Thought Worms from the Wreckage.* London: Unkant Publishers, 2013.

———. *Liquid Crystals: The Science and the Art of a Fluid Form.* London: Reaktion Books, 2016.

———. *Synthetic Worlds: Nature, Art and the Chemical Industry.* London: Reaktion Books, 2005.

———. "The Meaning of Milk: Journeys of Lactic Abstraction." *Academia.edu.* https://www.academia.edu/34426356/The_Meaning_of_Milk_Journeys_of_Lactic_Abstraction.

——— and Melanie Jackson. *Deeper in the Pyramid.* London: Banner Repeater, 2018.

Levinas, Emmanuel. *Existence and Existents.* Translated by by Alphonso Lingis. Dordrecht: Kluwer Academic Publishers, 1988.

Litz, A. Walton, and Christopher McGowan, eds. *The Collected Poems of William Carlos Williams: Volume I, 1909–1939.* New York: New Directions Books, 1986.

Lovecraft, H.P. *The Call of Cthulhu and Other Weird Stories.* London: Penguin Modern Classics, 2002.

Mackay, Robin. "Editorial Introduction." In *Collapse VII,* edited by Robin Mackay, 3–37. Falmouth: Urbanomic, 2008.

Macosko, Christopher. *Rheology: Principles, Measurements and Applications.* New York: Wiley, 1994.

Malabou, Catherine. *Changing Difference: The Feminine and the Question of Philosophy.* Translated by Caroline Shread. Cambridge: Polity Press, 2010.

———. "Pierre Loves Horanges Levinas–Sartre–Nancy: An Approach to the Fantastic in Philosophy." *Penumbr(a),* edited by Sigi Jottkandt and Joan Copjec, 109–10. Melbourne: re.press, 2013.

———. "Plasticity and Elasticity in Freud's 'Beyond the Pleasure Principle.'" *Diacritics* 37, no. 4 (Winter 2007): 78–85. Baltimore: John Hopkins University Press, 2007. DOI: 10.1353/dia.0.0038.

———. *The Ontology of the Accident: An Essay on Destructive Plasticity.* Translated by Carolyn Shread. Cambridge: Polity Press, 2009.

Marder, Michael. *Dust.* London: Bloomsbury Academic, 2016.

Marinetti, Filippo Tommaso. *Il Poema del Vestito del Latte.* Milan: Lanital/SNIA Viscosa, 1937.

Marriott, James, and Mika Minio-Paluello. *The Oil Road: Journeys from the Caspian Sea to the City of London.* London: Verso, 2012.

Martin, Everett Dean. *The Behaviour of Crowds: A Psychological Study.* New York: Harper and Brothers, 1920.

Marx, Karl. *Capital I.* Translated by Ben Fowkes. London: Penguin, 1990.

Mathews David, Alison. *Fashion Victims: The Dangers of Dress Past and Present.* London: Bloomsbury, 2015.

Matulis, Brett Sylvester. "Liquid Helium III: The Superfluid." *Vimeo,* March 31, 2010. https://vimeo.com/10579813.

May, Todd. *A Fragile Life: Accepting Our Vulnerability.* Chicago: University of Chicago Press, 2017.

McCarthy, Tom. *Bombs, Typewriters, Jellyfish.* New York: New York Review of Books, 2017.

McKie, Robin. "How to Set Young Minds on Fire." *The Guardian,* October 22, 2006. https://www.theguardian.com/uk/2006/oct/22/schools.education.

McWeeny, George. "Weapons of Mass Reduction." *Cabinet* 22 (Summer 2006). http://www.cabinetmagazine.org/issues/22/mcweeny.php

Melville, Herman. *Moby Dick.* Hertfordshire: Wordsworth Modern Classics, 2002.

Miller, David, ed. *Materiality*. Durham: Duke University Press, 2005.

Miller, Marion, Brendan Gill, and Harrison Kinney. "Here to Stay." *The New Yorker,* August 26, 1950. https://www.newyorker.com/magazine/1950/08/26/here-to-stay-2.

Misek, Richard. "High Tar Babies." *Vimeo,* September 10, 2013. https://vimeo.com/74189761.

Mitchell, Timothy. *Carbon Democracy: Political Power in the Age of Oil*. London: Verso, 2011.

Monbiot, George. *Feral: Rewilding the Land, Sea and Human Life*. London: Penguin, 2014.

Morton, Timothy. *Dark Ecology: For a Logic of Future Coexistence.* New York: Columbia University Press, 2016.

————. *Hyperobjects: Philosophy for the End of the World.* Minnesota: University of Minnesota Press, 2013.

Moskoff, William. *The Bread Of Affliction: The Food Supply in the USSR during World War II.* Cambridge: Cambridge University Press, 2002.

Moten, Fred. *Black and Blur.* Durham: Duke University Press, 2017.

Neer, Robert M. *Napalm: An American Biography.* Cambridge: Harvard University Press 2013.

Negarestani, Reza. *Cyclonopedia: Complicity with Anonymous Materials.* Melbourne: re.press, 2008.

Ngai, Sianne. *Our Aesthetic Categories: The Cute, the Zany and the Interesting.* Cambridge: Harvard University Press, 2012.

Noys, Benjamin. *The Persistence of the Negative: A Critique of Contemporary Continental Theory.* Edinburgh: Edinburgh University Press, 2010.

O'Reilly, Sally. *Crude*. London: Eros Press, 2016.

Parisi, Luciana. *Abstract Sex: Bio-Technology and the Mutations of Desire.* London: Continuum, 2004.

Paterson, Mark. *The Senses of Touch: Haptics, Affects and Technologies.* Oxford: Oxford University Press, 2007.

Perniola, Mario. *Sex Appeal of the Inorganic.* Translated by Massimo Verdicchio. London: Continuum, 2004.

Plato. *Cratylus*. Translated by H. Fowler. Cambridge: Harvard University Press, 1921.

Pollack, G.H. *The Fourth Phase of Water: Beyond Solid, Liquid, Vapour*. Seattle: Ebner and Sons, 2013.

Ponge, Francis. *Unfinished Ode to Mud*. Translated by Beverley Bie Brahic. London: CB Editions, 2008.

Powell, Marilyn. *The Story of Ice Cream*. Toronto: Penguin, 2005.

Pound, Ezra. *Early Writings: Poems and Prose*. Edited by Ira B. Nadel. London: Penguin, 2009.

Preciado, Paul B. *Testo Junkie: Sex, Drugs and Biopolitics in the Pharmacopornagraphic Era*. Translated by Bruce Benderson. New York: Feminist Press, 2013.

Prynne, J.H. *Kazoo Dreamboats or, On What There Is*. Cambridge: Critical Documents, 2011.

———. *Poems*. Northumberland: Bloodaxe, 2005.

Puleo, Stephen. *Dark Tide: The Great Boston Molasses Flood of 1919*. Boston: Beacon Press, 2004.

Purves, Robin. "For-Being: Uncertainty and Contradiction in Kazoo Dreamboats." *Hix Eros: Poetry Review* 4 "On the Late Poetry of J.H. Prynne" (2014): 143–60.

Rainey, Laurence, ed. *Futurism: An Anthology*. New Haven: Yale University Press, 2009.

Rand, Erica. "What Lube Goes Into." In *The Object Reader*, edited by Fiona Candlin and Raiford Guins, 526–30. London: Routledge, 2009.

Regan, Geoffrey. *Military Anecdotes*. London: Guinness Publishing, 1992.

Rees, Gareth E. *Marshland: Dreams and Nightmares on the Edge of London*. London: Influx Press, 2013

Reid, Chris R. at al. "Slime Mold Uses an Externalized Spatial 'Memory' to Navigate in Complex Environments." *PNAS* 109, no. 43 (October 23, 2012): 17490–94. DOI: 10.1073/pnas.1215037109.

Regan, Geoffrey. *Military Anecdotes*. London: Guinness Publishing, 1992.

Renehan, Robert. "Viscum/Viscus." *Harvard Studies in Classical Philology* 84 (1980): 279–82. DOI: 10.2307/311053.

Robertson, Lisa. *Magenta Soul Whip.* Toronto: Coach House Books, 2005.

———. *Nilling.* Toronto: Book Thug, 2012.

———. *Occasional Work and Seven Walks from the Office for Soft Architecture.* Oregon: Clear Cut Press, 2003.

Schoonover, Karl. "Ectoplasms, Evanescence and Photography." *Art Journal* 62, no. 3 (August 2003): 30–41. DOI: 10.1080/00043249.2003.10792168.

Rockefeller, Stuart Alexander. "Flow." *Current Anthropology* 52, no. 5 (August 2011): 557–78. DOI: 10.1086/660912.

Saigusa, Tetsu, et al. "Amoebae Anticipate Periodic Events." *Physical Review Letters* 100, no. 1 (January 2008): id. 018101. DOI: 10.1103/PhysRevLett.100.018101.

Saint Augustine. *Confessions.* Translated by William Watts. Cambridge: Harvard Univeristy Press, 1979.

Sartre, Jean-Paul. *Being and Nothingness: A Phenomenological Essay on Ontology.* Translated by Hazel E. Barnes, New York: Washington Square Press, 1992.

———. *L'être et le néant: Essaie d'ontologie phenoménologique.* Paris: Editions Gallimard, 1943.

———. *Nausea.* Translated by Robert Baldick. London: Penguin Classics, 2000.

———. *Saint Genet: Actor and Martyr.* Translated by Bernard Frechtman. New York: Plume and Merdian, 1963.

Schulz, Bruno. *The Street of Crocodiles and Other Stories.* Translated by Celina Wieniewska. London: Penguin, 1992.

Scott, Savannah. "We Talked to Instagram's Most Popular Slimers." *Vice,* February 22, 2017. https://www.vice.com/sv/article/we-talked-to-instagrams-most-popular-slimers.

Seifriz, William. *Protoplasm.* London: McGraw-Hill Book Company, 1936.

Serres, Michel. *The Birth of Physics.* Translated by David Webb and William Ross. New York: Rowman and Littlefield, 2018.

————. *The Five Senses: A Philosophy of Mingled Bodies.* Translated by Margaret Sankey and Peter Cowley. London: Bloomsbury Academic, 2016.

Shapiro, Laura. *Perfection Salad: Women and Cooking at the Turn of the Century.* Oakland: University of California Press, 2008.

Shaviro, Steven. *Discognition.* London: Repeater Books, 2016.

Shaw, Duncan J. *Introduction to Colloid and Surface Chemistry.* Oxford: Reed Educational and Professional Publishing, 1992.

Shukin, Nicole. *Animal Matter: Rendering Life in Bio-political Times.* University of Minneapolis: Minneapolis Press, 2009.

Sloterdijk, Peter. *Bubbles: Microspherology.* Translated by Wieland Hoban. Los Angeles: Semiotext(e), 2011.

Smith, Thea. "Red From Fire." *RCA Writing.* http://criticalwriting.rca.ac.uk/uncategorized/red-from-fire.

Sorokina, Elena. "Peoples' Friendship Salad and Other Culinary Expressions of Brotherhood." March 2014. http://sorokinaelena.blogspot.com/2014/03/stalin-cooking-book.html.

Sparrow, Tom. *Plastic Bodies: Rebuilding Sensation After Phenomenology.* London: Open Humanities Press, 2015.

Spector, Nancy. *All in the Present Must Be Transformed: Matthew Barney and Joseph Beuys.* New York: Guggenheim Museum Publications, 2007.

————. *Matthew Barney: The Cremaster Cycle.* New York: Guggenheim Museum Publications, 2002.

Stern, Daniel. *Forms of Vitality: Exploring Dynamic Experience in Psychology and the Arts.* Oxford: Oxford University Press, 2010.

Stein, Gertrude. *Tender Buttons.* New York: Dover Publications, 1997.

Straw, Will. "Spectacles of Waste." In *Circulation and the City: Essays on Urban Culture,* edited by Alexandra Boutros et al., 155–94.Quebec: McGill University Press, 2010.

Sutherland, Keston. *Stupefaction: A Radical Anatomy of Phantoms.* Calcutta: Seagull Books, 2011.

Swanson, Kara. "Human Milk as Technology and Technologies of Human Milk: Medical Imaginings in Early Twentieth-Century United States." *Woman's Studies Quarterly* 37, nos. 1–2 (Spring/Summer 2009): 20–37.

Syutkin, Olga, and Pavel Syutkin. *CCCP Cook Book: True Stories of Soviet Cuisine.* London: Fuel, 2015.

Tacitus. *The Histories.* Translated by W.H. Fyfe. Oxford: Oxford University Press, 1997.

Tanner, R.I., and K. Watts. *Rheology: An Historical Perspective.* London: Elsevier Science, 1998.

Taylor, Ashley P. "A Mob of Fire Ants Becomes a New Kind of Material." *Popular Mechanics,* November 26, 2013. https://www.popularmechanics.com/science/animals/a9759/a-mob-of-fire-ants-becomes-a-new-kind-of-material-16202096/.

Theweleit, Klaus. *Male Fantasies: Women, Floods, Bodies, History,* Vol. 1. Translated by Stephen Conway et al. Cambridge: Polity Press, 1987.

Timonen, Maija. *The Measure of Reality.* London: Book Works, 2015.

Trocchi, Alexander. *Cain's Book.* New York: Grove Press, 1960.

Trotter, David. *Cooking with Mud: Ideas of Mess in Nineteenth Century Art and Fiction.* Oxford: Oxford University Press, 2000.

Tsing, Anna Lowenhaupt. *The Mushroom at the End of the World: On the Possibility of Life in Capitalist Ruins.* New Jersey: Princeton University Press, 2015.

Valenze, Deborah. *Milk: A Local and Global History.* London: Yale University Press, 2011.

Velten, Hannah. *Milk: A Global History.* London: Reaktion, 2010.

Wallace, David. "Fred Moten's Radical Critique of the Present." *The New Yorker,* April 30, 2018. https://www.newyorker.com/culture/persons-of-interest/fred-motens-radical-critique-of-the-present.

Watanabe, Shin, AtsushiTero, Atsuko Takamatsu, Toshiyuki Nakagaki, "Traffic Optimization in Railroad Networks

Using an Algorithm Mimicking an Amoeba-like Organism, *Physarum* Plasmodium," *Biosystems* 105, no. 3 (2011): 225–32. DOI: 10.1016/j.biosystems.2011.05.001.

Waters, Michael. "How Clothing Made From Milk Became the Height of Fashion in Mussolini's Italy." *Atlas Obscura,* July 28, 2017. https://www.atlasobscura.com/articles/lanital-milk-dress-qmilch.

Winnicot, D.W. *Playing and Reality.* London: Routledge, 1991.

Williams, George M. *Handbook of Hindu Mythology.* Oxford: Oxford University Press, 2013.

Woodard, Ben. *Slime Dynamics: Generation, Mutation and the Creep of Life.* Winchester: Zero Books, 2012.

Zeravcic, Zorana, Vinothan N. Manoharan, and Michael P. Brenner, "Colloquium: Toward a Living Matter with Colloidal Particles." *Reviews of Modern Physics* 89, no. 3 (July–September 2017): 031001. DOI: 10.1103/RevModPhys.89.031001.

Žižek, Slavoj, *Disparities.* London: Bloomsbury Academic, 2016.

www.ingramcontent.com/pod-product-compliance
Lightning Source LLC
Chambersburg PA
CBHW071735270326
41928CB00013B/2681